How Informal Institutions Matter

How Informal Institutions Matter

Evidence from Turkish Social and Political Spheres

ZEKI SARIGIL

University of Michigan Press
Ann Arbor

For questions or permissions, please contact um.press.perms@umich.edu

Published in the United States of America by the
University of Michigan Press
Manufactured in the United States of America
Printed on acid-free paper
First published September 2023

A CIP catalog record for this book is available from the British Library.

Library of Congress Cataloging-in-Publication data has been applied for.

ISBN 978-0-472-07638-3 (hardcover : alk. paper)
ISBN 978-0-472-05638-5 (paper : alk. paper)
ISBN 978-0-472-90377-1 (open access ebook)

DOI: https://doi.org/10.3998/mpub.12334157

The University of Michigan Press's open access publishing program is made possible thanks to additional funding from the University of Michigan Office of the Provost and the generous support of contributing libraries.

To those before and after—my father MS (1948–2011) and my son DBS (2021–)

CONTENTS

List of Figures ix

List of Tables and Appendices xi

Foreword: The Importance of Informal Institutions and Norms xiii

Acknowledgments xix

1 Introduction 1

2 Conceptual and Theoretical Framework 17

3 A Symbiotic Informal Institution: Religious Marriage in Turkey 46
   Appendix 3.A. A List of Interviewees (Religious Marriage) 76
   Appendix 3.B. Factor Analysis of Religiosity 77

4 A Superseding Informal Institution: Cem Courts 78
   Appendix 4.A. A List of Interviewees (Cem Courts,
   Informal Conflict Resolution) 106

5 A Layered Informal Institution: Religious Minority Holidays
   in Turkey 107
   Appendix 5.A. A List of Interviewees (Religious
   Minority Holidays) 130

6 A Subversive Informal Institution:
   "Multilingual Municipalism" of the Kurdish Movement 131

7 Conclusions and Implications 158

Bibliography 169

Index 193

Digital materials related to this title can be found on the Fulcrum platform via the following citable URL https://doi.org/10.3998/mpub.12334157

FIGURES

3.1 Cumulative Predicted Probabilities of Marriage Comparison   66
3.2 Predicted Probabilities of Support for Mufti Marriage   72
4.1 Urban Population in Turkey (1927–2020) (% of total)   94
6.1 Electoral Popularity of Pro-Kurdish Political Parties during
     General Elections (Comparing National and Regional Levels)
     (1995–2018)   142
6.2 Turkish and Kurdish Mass Support for Some Linguistic Demands
     (2011, 2013, 2015)   152

TABLES AND APPENDICES

1.1 A Comparison of Formal and Informal Institutions 7
2.1 Helmke and Levitsky's Two-Dimensional Typology of Informal
Institutions 19
2.2 A Three-Dimensional Typology of Informal Institutions 30
3.1 A Comparison of Formal Civil Marriage and Informal Religious
Marriage in Turkey 52
3.2 The Practice of Formal Civil Marriage and Informal Religious
Marriage in Turkey (2019) 56
3.3 Descriptive Statistics of Variables 62
3.4 Multinomial Logit Models of Marriage Comparison 64
3.5 Binary Logit Models of Support for Mufti Marriage 69
4.1 A Comparison of Formal State Courts and Informal Cem Courts 83
5.1 Formal Regulation of Religious Holidays and Religious Minority
Holidays in Turkey 116
6.1 Electoral Support for the Pro-Kurdish Political Parties in
General Elections (1991–2018) 141
6.2 Electoral Popularity of Pro-Kurdish Political Parties in *Local*
(*Municipal*) Elections (1994–2019) 143
6.3 A Comparison of Formal Rules and Regulations with Informal
Multilingual Municipalism 146
7.1 A Summary of The Empirical Cases of Informal Institutions 161

Appendices

Appendix 3.A. A List of Interviewees (Religious Marriage)   76
Appendix 3.B. Factor Analysis of Religiosity   77
Appendix 4.A. A List of Interviewees (Cem Courts, Informal
    Conflict Resolution)   106
Appendix 5.A. A List of Interviewees (Religious Minority Holidays) 130

FOREWORD

The Importance of Informal Institutions and Norms

Most people, whether scholars or ordinary citizens, might consider the term "informal institutions" to be an oxymoron. Institutions are formal entities like legislatures, or the bureaucracy, or the church, and they appear identified and defined by their formality—by being written on parchment as Zeki Sarigil describes them. These institutions have internal rules and incentives to control their members, as well as to interact with their environment. Those formal structures certainly do exist, and are extremely important in our social and political lives, but they may, however, be too formal to meet many of the challenges that the society and the economy present for would-be governors.

This incomplete nature of formal institutions then creates the opening for informal patterns of behavior to emerge as institutions. Constitutions may define the ways in which legislatures function, up to a point, but beyond that point informal rules and patterns become the dominant means of shaping behavior (Lauth 2000). Conversely, the completeness of some institutions, and the detail of their rules, may also assist in the emergence of informal institutions. Doing business with some bureaucracies may be perceived as being so difficult that informal institutions—bribery or clientelism—emerge to facilitate transactions (Kaufmann, Hooghiemstra, and Feeney 2018).

Informal institutions, however, must go beyond being simple, regular patterns of behavior. Two friends who meet every Tuesday morning for coffee have not created an institution. They may, however, be functioning within an informal institution such as reciprocity, especially if they are members of a broader social network, and they agree to take turns paying for the coffee. What is important here is whether there are norms at work that structure their behavior, or is it just convenience. Phillip Selznick (1992) argued that institutionalization involved "infusing a structure with values," and in this rather simple case the regular pattern of behavior would need to be linked to some norms or values to be considered "institutional." Drawing the line between the institutional and the noninstitutional is, however, not a simple task.

For the public sector, especially in the consolidated democracies, formal institutions are expected to do most of the work of governing. Law is the primary source of norms for behavior, and those laws are enforced by agents of the public sector. However, even in the most successful governments there are some things that the formal institutions may choose not to regulate, and will permit informal institutions to control behaviors. For example, governments may stand back from major segments of the economy such as professional sports and allow self-regulation and the market to shape outcomes.

We should also recognize that some degree of informality may exist at the margins of formal institutions. Institutions not only have to control the behaviors of members of the society but they must first control the behavior of their own members. This internal control is emphasized by the normative institutionalism more than by the other varieties of institutionalism. The utilization of myths, symbols, routines, and so forth at the heart of normative institutionalism (see March and Olsen 1989) is directed primarily at the members of the institution, rather than its clients or subjects. Other forms of institutionalism, for example, rational choice versions, assume these controls will be formalized, while other versions, for example, historical institutionalism, tend largely to ignore internal control.

The internal controls of institutions may work for most members, but may also fail when those institutional members are in frequent contact with nonmembers. Street-level bureaucrats, for example, are in regular contact with citizens, and may develop their own ways of dealing with those clients that vary markedly from the formal rules. The street-level bureaucrats may need to make alliances with their clients (Bardach and Kagan 2017) in order to be effective, or they may find that formal rules constrain their capacity to respond to the individual needs and circumstances of clients. Street-level bureaucrats may also use their own values, or the values of other institutions such as religion, to make decisions, rather than rely on those promoted by the formal institution. Further, those personal values may be reinforced by those of their colleagues, leading to the creation of informal institutions at the bottom of formal institutions.[1]

Some important areas of political and social life are dominated by informal institutions. For example, although there are formal institutions such as the World Trade Organization, and some formalized network structures, much of international governance appears dominated by informal institutions. For example, a policy domain such as health may have formal institutions such as the World Health Organization, but it is also affected by the more general epistemic communities (Christensen 2021) of medicine and public health that will have fewer rules but perhaps even more influence over behaviors in the domain.

Both formal and informal institutions are mechanisms for solving collective action problems. If we begin with an assumption that individuals, and organizations, pursue self-interest, we can see that this individualistic pursuit often produces outcomes that are undesirable for the society as a whole. The "tragedy of the commons" is usually taken as the quintessential example when it produces the destruction of fishing stocks or the overuse of limited water supplies (Hardin 1968; Ostrom 1990). Other familiar examples include the "death spirals" that may occur in insurance markets with adverse selection and the risky behaviors that may occur when "moral hazard" prevails.

Much of the literature on collective action problems stresses the role of formal institutions, along with power and authority, in coping with collective action problems. Mancur Olson (1965; see also Mansbridge 2014), for example, argued that the only way to overcome problems of collective action was imposition. While formal institutions may work, they may also produce resentment from citizens and enhance distrust of government. Informal institutions can also be used to address collective action problems, especially when formal institutions lack legitimacy, or might be perceived as being too intrusive.

In summary, informal institutions and informal means of governance are important, and indeed necessary, adjuncts to the formal. The informal institutions provide means of getting institutions to work together, and for

---

1. The best example here may be of the informal norms that arise in police departments among the officers, and their mutual protection—a "blue wall"—against formal controls from above or from outside the police force (Conway and Westmarland 2021).

getting individuals within institutions to work more effectively. A world without informal institutions would be more conflict-ridden and less effective than the world that does rely at least in part on the informal.

The Contributions of This Book

Zeki Sarigil's book on informal institutions emphasizes the importance of these institutions and builds effectively on the preceding work in this field, especially that of Helmke and Levitsky (2004) and Lauth (2000). This is one of the very few extended treatments of the concept of informal institutions that exists in the social sciences, and the clear analysis of the topic adds a great deal to our collective understanding of these institutions and their role in the governance of societies.

Among several important contributions, perhaps the most important is extending the typology of informal institutions originally proposed by Gretchen Helmke and Steven Levitsky. That typology had become the standard means of understanding informal institutions, and continues to be an excellent means of approaching informality in institutions. That said, however, Zeki Sarigil argues that the typology is to some extent incomplete, and the addition of an additional dimension will provide even richer understanding of informal institutions.

The important dimension that Sarigil adds to the study of informal institutions is legitimacy—the legitimacy of the formal structures engaged in governance. The Helmke and Levitsky typology tends to assume that the formal institutions being discussed are accepted as legitimate by the actors involved. If they are not, however, the behavior of the actors involved, as well as the relationships between formal and informal actors, can be expected to be different. This fundamental difference is closely related to the logic of normative institutionalism (March and Olsen 1989), with its emphasis on the role of values and trust within institutions, and between institutions and their environment.

In addition to developing the expanded typology of informal institutions, Sarigil demonstrates how it can be used, and the insights it provides that might be missed by a more constrained typology. A good deal of theorizing in institutionalism is done in a rather abstract manner, but this book shows clearly what an institutionalist perspective can bring to empirical research. He uses each of the four new cells of his expanded typology to examine one aspect of social and political life in Turkey. This research demonstrates that not only is the expanded typology a useful theoretical addition, it is also useful for uncovering the dynamics within social and political life.

Perhaps most important in this discussion and use of the concept of informal institutions is demonstrating the utility of the concept for dealing with issues that can confound the formal institutions of government. Questions of religion and ethnicity are difficult for governments to manage through formal, legal institutions no matter how fair they may attempt to be. Informality provides a way of coping with those issues and doing so in a manner that allows greater flexibility for all parties concerned.

The use of the typology on cases from Turkey is all the more impressive because it involves analyzing difficult issues involving religion and multiculturalism. These issues are difficult to resolve in most cases, and understanding them may require substantial cultural knowledge, but the informal institutional categories used do appear to work well in these analyses. They raise questions that assist the researcher in uncovering the dynamics of these cases. The cases become not only an exhibition of the utility of this approach to informal institutions, but of institutionalism more generally.

In conclusion, the apparent oxymoron of "informal institution" is anything but internally contradictory. Many patterns of behavior that are important for determining how individuals and societies perform their tasks do not meet standards of formality usually associated with institutions. This volume by Zeki Sarigil explores and elaborates the concept of informal institutions, and shows how it can contribute to understanding a variety of political phenomena. This should be the beginning of even more research using this concept.

B. Guy Peters
University of Pittsburgh

ACKNOWLEDGMENTS

Since the start of this research project, I have received invaluable support and encouragement from many mentors, colleagues, friends, and academic organizations. First and foremost, I am very thankful to the Scientific and Technological Research Council of Turkey (Türkiye Bilimsel ve Teknolojik Araştırma Kurumu) for its financial support. Thanks to the TÜBİTAK grant (No. 118K281), I was able to conduct extensive research on symbiotic informal institutions and collect original qualitative and quantitative data. I feel indebted to B. Guy Peters, whose works on institutional theory triggered, guided, and inspired my own thinking and research on institutions. I am also thankful to him for his continuous and generous scholarly support and encouragement at each stage of my career.

I am grateful to many colleagues and friends including Yuen Yuen Ang, Eda Bektaş, Levent Duman, Berk Esen, Jeff Haynes, Soeren J. Henn, Sabina Hilaiel, Lisel Hintz, Aida Just, Ekrem Karakoç, Özge Kemahlıoğlu, Elise Massicard, Burcu Özdemir-Sarigil, Abel Polese, Aytuğ Şaşmaz, Pınar D. Sönmez, Kellee S. Tsai, and Gözde Yılmaz for their useful comments and suggestions on the initial versions of this study. I also wish to express my gratitude to the reviewers for the University of Michigan Press, who provided highly insightful and incisive comments and suggestions on book chapters.

The initial versions of this study were presented at various platforms, such as the Annual Conference of the Midwest Political Science Association, April 2019 and April 2022; the Empirical Studies in Political Analysis Workshop, January 2020; POLS TALKS seminar series of the Department of Political Science, Bilkent University, February and October 2021; and the European Consortium for Political Research General Conference, September 2021. I would like to thank all those who participated in those presentations and shared their valuable questions, comments, and suggestions, which helped me improve the book.

I also owe thanks to Tara Sylvestre for helping with editing the initial versions of the chapters. At the University of Michigan Press, I am thankful to Elizabeth Demers (editorial director) and Haley Winkle (editorial associate) for their support of this project and to Marcia D. LaBrenz (managing editor) and John Raymond (copy editor) for their assistance in preparing the final manuscript.

Finally, the endless support and encouragement of my family has been extremely helpful as I finish up the project.

CHAPTER 1

Introduction

The behavioral approach, which was the dominant paradigm in several fields of social science during the first three decades of the post–World War II period, focused on "the actual, observable beliefs and behaviors of groups and individuals" (Thelen and Steinmo 1992, 4; see also Peters 1998, 2012, 2019; Immergut 2011; Scott 2014, 8–9). With such a focus, behavioralism viewed institutions as the aggregation of individual preferences and choices. In other words, the behavioral approach treated institutions as epiphenomenal (DiMaggio and Powell 1991, 2; Lowndes 2018, 54). As Peters (2012, 1) also notes, behavioral and rational choice perspectives

> assume that individuals act autonomously as individuals, based either on sociopsychological characteristics or rational calculation of their personal *utility*. In either theory, individuals were not seriously constrained by either formal or informal institutions, but would make their own choices; in both views preferences are exogenous to the political process.

Beginning in the early 1980s, however, institutional approaches and perspectives reemerged in the social sciences, including economics, sociology, and political science. Reacting to the behavioral approach, institutional approaches rediscovered institutions and emphasized "the role of institutions and institutionalization in the understanding of human actions within an organization, social order, or society" (March and Olsen 1998, 948; see also March and Olsen 1984, 1989; DiMaggio and Powell 1991).[1] In other words, institutional perspectives have emphasized that institutional structures do matter in sociopolitical life, meaning that institutional rules and

---

1. For useful reviews of the main premises and arguments of various institutionalist approaches, see Hall and Taylor 1996; Peters 2012, 2019; Scott 2014.

regulations substantially shape individual preferences and behaviors, and thus sociopolitical processes and outcomes (see also Peters 2019).

Although formal and informal institutions play major roles in the social and political spheres, earlier institutional analyses focused on formal institutions (or parchment institutions), ignoring or underestimating the role of informal institutional factors and mechanisms. The main research question those analyses raised was how formal institutional rules and regulations shape social, political, and economic behaviors, processes, and outcomes. Metaphorically speaking, by focusing on formal institutional arrangements, which are relatively more structured and visible than informal rules and regulations, earlier institutional studies pondered just the tip of the iceberg. Otherwise stated, these studies failed to shed light on the invisible (probably larger) part of the iceberg. As Helmke and Levitsky (2004, 725–26) also observe,

> informal rules have remained at the margins of the institutionalist turn in comparative politics. Indeed, much current literature assumes that actors' incentives and expectations are shaped primarily, if not exclusively, by formal rules. Such a narrow focus can be problematic, for it risks missing much of what drives political behavior and can hinder efforts to explain important political phenomena.[2]

However, it is reassuring that subsequent institutional analyses have paid greater attention to the role of informal rules and mechanisms in sociopolitical life. The relatively recent institutional literature does acknowledge that informal rules and constraints are quite pervasive in the social and political spheres, profoundly molding social and political behaviors and processes in various settings.[3] For instance, regarding the pervasiveness of informal constraints, North (1990, 36) states that "in our daily interac-

---

2. For similar observations, see Peters 1998; Carey 2000; Ingraham, Moynihan, and Andrews 2008; MacLean 2010; Radnitz 2011; K. Tsai 2016.

3. See, for instance, Pejovich 1999; Böröcz 2000; Lauth 2000, 2004, 2015; Wang 2000; Brinks 2003; T. Eisenstadt 2003; Farrel and Heritier 2003; Stacey and Rittberger 2003; Collins 2004; Helmke and Levitsky 2004, 2006; K. Tsai 2006, 2007, 2016; Bratton 2007; Hu 2007; Pop-Eleches 2007; Ingraham, Moynihan, and Andrews 2008; C. Williamson 2009; Casson, Giusta, and Kambhampati 2010; Grzymala-Busse 2010; MacLean 2010; Painter and Peters 2010; Radnitz 2011; Azari and Smith 2012; Christiansen and Neuhold 2012; Morris and Polese 2014; Waylen 2014; Xu and Yao 2015; Aliyev 2017; Ledeneva 2018; Levitsky and Ziblatt 2018; Peters 2019; and Polese 2021.

tion with others, whether within the family, in external social relations, or in business activities, the governing structure is overwhelmingly defined by codes of conduct, norms of behavior, and conventions [i.e., informal constraints]." Levitsky and Ziblatt (2018, 100) also emphasize the abundance of informal rules in political life by stating "as in all facets of society, ranging from family life to the operation of businesses and universities, unwritten rules loom large in politics."

Many of those studies emphasize that even highly formalized institutional or organizational settings involve various informal rules and practices, exerting substantial influence on formal processes and outcomes (North 1990, 1993b; Knight 1992; Lauth 2000; Helmke and Levitsky 2004, 2006; Hu 2007; Ingraham, Moynihan, and Andrews 2008; Azari and Smith 2012; Peters 2019). For instance, North (1993b, 20) suggests that the effective working of formal institutions requires that formal rules "must be complemented by informal constraints (convictions, norms of behavior) that supplement them and reduce enforcement costs." Similarly, Ingraham, Moynihan, and Andrews (2008, 68) assert that "informal rules . . . which are indeed harder to change, are usually in existence alongside formal rules, often ingrained in the values of organizations and societies." Along the same lines, Knight (1992, 172) states, "informal rules are the foundation on which formal rules are built." Azari and Smith (2012, 36) also remark that formal institutions do not operate in a vacuum. Instead, they "coexist with a framework of unwritten or *informal* rules that structure collective expectations about how disputes will be resolved." Böröcz (2000, 352) also maintains that "much organizational life is necessarily informal, even amid clearly defined formal rules and regulations." Finally, K. Tsai (2016, 279) highlights the coexistence of formal and informal institutions by using the analogy of a Möbius strip: "It would be more theoretically progressive to regard institutions as a single two-dimensional Möbius strip with both formal and informal components. . . . Informal and formal institutions are coterminous, as seen in the two sides of the Möbius strip."

That being said, other than presenting some ad hoc generalizations and partial theoretical accounts, the existing theoretical literature on informal institutions does not really offer a comprehensive conceptual and theoretical framework of informal rules and regulations. In other words, despite increasing attention to the role of informal institutions in the social and political spheres, compared to formal institutions, informal institutions still remain an undertheorized issue in the existing institutional literature.

Moreover, it is striking that the existing theoretical institutional litera-ture neglects the role of informal institutions in Muslim-majority contexts. However, given the abundance of strong and influential informal institu-tions in Muslim-majority countries (e.g., Turkey), such settings provide researchers valuable opportunities to gain novel insights into informal institutions. Hence, conducting further conceptual, theoretical, and empir-ical research on informal institutions in different settings would enhance our knowledge and understanding of the role of informal institutions in the sociopolitical world, and thus contribute to the progress of institutional theory. As Peters (2019, 217) recommends, "Bringing informal institutions into institutional theory enriches the theory and enables institutionalists to explain a wider pattern of behavior than would be possible using only for-mal structures." Thus, this study focuses on the role of informal institutions in the social and political realms and provides in-depth analyses of several empirical cases of informal institutions as derived from the Turkish socio-political setting.

This study raises the following conceptual and theoretical research questions: Why and how do informal institutions emerge? To ask this dif-ferently, why do agents still create or resort to informal institutions despite the presence of formal institutional rules and regulations? How do informal institutions matter? What roles do they play in sociopolitical life? How can we classify informal institutions? What novel types of informal institutions can we identify and explain? How do informal institutions interact with formal institutions? How do they shape formal institutional rules, mecha-nisms, and outcomes? Finally, how do existing informal institutions change? What factors might trigger informal institutional change?

Definition of Key Terms

First, we need to define and clarify the key concepts that will be used throughout the book: institutions, formal institutions, and informal institu-tions. I am aware that there is no single definition of the notion of institu-tion. As Moe (2005, 226) observes, "there is still no agreement on what an institution is. Some scholars see institutions as rules of the game, others see them as formal organizations, others as patterned behavior, still others as 'myths' and ideational structures." My main motivation in this conceptual part, however, is not to present conceptual problems or challenges in the existing literature but to provide a working definition of the key concepts and notions, which is essential for further analysis.

To begin with the notion of *institution*, it is widely defined as a set of rules, norms, and procedures that structure and regulate social and political interactions and relations by constraining or enabling actors' behavior, or doing both (see Hall 1986; North 1990; Knight 1992; Carey 2000; Helmke and Levitsky 2004; Levitsky and Murillo 2009; Mahoney and Thelen 2010; Scott 2014; Lauth 2015; Lowndes 2018).[4] Thus, as a set of rules and regulations devised and shared by human agents, institutions provide certain incentives or disincentives (material and ideational) for individuals, and thus, they prescribe or proscribe individual behavior.

Most institutions encompass the following three elements or pillars: *regulative* (regulating human behavior), *normative* (morally encouraging or forcing human agents to act in an "appropriate" way, as defined by institutional values and norms), and *cultural-cognitive* (shared and taken-for-granted conceptions, interpretations, meanings, frames, and schemas) (see Scott 2014). The salience of these elements might, however, differ within a particular institutional order and across different institutional settings.

One should also acknowledge that the strength of institutions might vary across space and time. In other words, some institutions might be relatively more powerful and effective than others. In addition, the power of a particular institution might increase or decrease across time. In the case of a powerful institution, the existing rules and regulations would be fairly stable and enforceable (i.e., complied with in practice) and the violation of those rules and regulations would result in punishment (Levitsky and

---

4. In terms of the distinction between an institution and an organization, many studies treat institutions as "the rules of the game" and organizations as "the players of that game" (see North 1990, 3–5; 1993a, 36; and 1998, 249; see also Khalil 1995; Levi 1997; Stacey and Rittberger 2003, 860; Helmke and Levitsky 2004; Lauth 2004; Heritier 2007, 5–6; Hu 2007; Mantzavinos 2011; Lowndes 2018, 61). Unlike institutions, organizations comprise groups of individuals with some common motivations and goals (Knight 1992, 3; North 2001, 16). Thus, as agential entities, organizations are collective actors (e.g., political parties, firms, trade unions, cooperatives, social clubs, and universities). It is, however, important to indicate that most organizational settings involve certain institutionalized rules, norms, and regulations. In other words, organizations are governed by certain rules and regulations (formal and informal) (Knight 1992; Scott 2014). Ellickson (1991, 31) calls those rules and regulations "organization rules."

Murillo 2009). Thus, an effective and powerful institution mainly involves shared expectations among relevant human agents, rule-driven behavioral regularities, and the mechanisms of enforcement and sanctions.

Formal institutions refer to the formally codified or inscribed rules, procedures, and regulations that are "created, communicated, and enforced through channels widely accepted as official" (e.g., electoral systems, constitutions, laws, treaties, party statutes, regulations, and contracts) (Helmke and Levitsky 2004, 727; K. Tsai 2006, 125; Lauth 2015, 57; Voigt 2018). Formal institutions are also referred to as parchment institutions (see Carey 2000).

Informal institutions, in a highly cited definition, are "socially shared rules, usually unwritten, that are created, communicated, and enforced outside of officially sanctioned channels" (Helmke and Levitsky 2004, 727; see also Lauth 2004, 69; L. Tsai 2007, 13). Similarly, Bratton (2007, 96) treats informal institutions as "unwritten codes embedded in everyday social practice." North (1990, 40) associates informal institutions with "(1) extensions, elaborations, and modifications of formal rules, (2) socially sanctioned norms of behavior, and (3) internally enforced standards of conduct" (see also Hu 2007, 22).

Helmke and Levitsky (2004) warn that informal institutions should not be conflated with informal behavioral regularities, such as fashions, trends, or routines. Treating informal institutions as rule-bound and rooted in shared expectations about other actors' behavior, they note that "to be considered an informal institution, a behavioral regularity must respond to an established rule or guideline, the violation of which generates some kind of external sanction" (2004, 727; see also MacLean 2010; Azari and Smith 2012; Lauth 2015). Some examples of informal institutions from the social, political, and economic spheres are honor killing, blood feuds (vendetta), reciprocity, conventions, clientelism, bribery, corruption, nepotism, patrimonialism, patronage, customary law, consociationalism, diplomacy, networks (e.g., *guanxi, wasta, blat*, kinship, and *hemşehrilik*), the black market, and the informal economy.

Regarding the differences between informal and formal institutions, Stacey and Rittberger (2003, 861) state that "unlike the latter, the parties to informal institutions are not legally bound to their rules; in terms of enforcement, aggrieved parties can only rely on political sanctions that carry negligible legal force. In contrast, the rules of formal institutions are legally enforceable by a third-party judicial body . . . which possesses the authority to issue binding legal sanctions." For C. Williamson (2009, 372), the key difference between the two is that whereas formal constraints are centrally designed and enforced, informal institutions are self-enforced. Treating formal institutions as "structured" and informal institutions as "unstructured," Shepsle (2006, 28–29) suggests that unstructured institutions are "more amorphous and implicit rather than formalized." They "emerge informally and often are not actually written down as formal rules; they simply come to be known as 'the way things are done around here.'" On the distinction between formal and informal institutions, Grzymala-Busse (2006, 6) warns that

> informal institutions are more than behavioral regularities or unintentional byproducts of formal institutions. They are not simply clashing, weak, or absent formal institutions. Moreover, even without formal enforcement mechanisms, they can be imposed by informal means such as ostracism or shunning. Finally, like formal institutions, informal institutions can be either weakly or strongly influential, and effectively or ineffectively enforced. Their informality does not presuppose either their extent or their impact.

In the light of all these conceptualizations and treatments, table 1.1 provides a brief comparison of formal and informal institutions on various dimensions.

TABLE 1.1. A Comparison of Formal and Informal Institutions

Formal Codification	Coordinating Center	Source of Legitimacy	Enforcer	Enforcement Mechanisms
Formal				
Formal codification (de jure); more structured and visible	Yes	State authority, law	State agencies, public authorities, civil servants, courts	Legal, official
Informal				
No formal codification (de facto); more amorphous; less visible	In some cases	Social, communal (social acceptance and approval)	Society, community, social groups, networks	Social (e.g., naming and shaming, ostracism, condemning)

Source: Adopted from Lauth (2015, 58) with some modifications.

Methodological Approach

To answer the above conceptual and theoretical research questions, this study examines the role of informal institutions in various social and political domains of the Turkish setting. The Turkish case constitutes a quite valuable theory-building case for couple of reasons. First, informal institutions have been quite abundant and influential in the Turkish sociopolitical world. As several existing institutional analyses claim, formal institutions suffer from a limited degree of effectiveness, especially in the developing world (e.g., see O'Donnell 1994; Starn 1999; Collins 2004; Helmke and Levitsky 2004, 2006; Hydén 2006; K. Tsai 2006; Van Cott 2006; Bratton 2007; Xu and Yao 2015). For instance, Levitsky and Murillo (2009, 116) observe that "many formal institutions in Africa, Latin America, Asia, and the former Soviet Union are neither minimally stable nor regularly enforced. In other words, instead of taking root and generating shared behavioral expectations, formal rules are widely contested, routinely violated, and frequently changed." As one might expect, the weakness of formal bodies and institutions is likely to motivate agents to resort to informal rules and mechanisms (e.g., see Helmke and Levitsky 2006; Van Cott 2006; MacLean 2010; Xu and Yao 2015; Aliyev 2017). This suggests that when inscribed formal institutions remain weak, unwritten rules and regulations might hold more sway.

This observation is particularly valid for Turkey. One can find several examples from the social and political domains in the Turkish context suggesting that formal rules and regulations have been frequently circumvented, ignored, or sometimes openly violated. For instance, constitutional law scholars argue that violations of the constitution and the principle of the rule of law have been common in Turkish political culture (e.g., see Ozbudun 2015). One emblematic case is that during the First Gulf War (August 1990–February 1991), President Turgut Özal (1927–93), who was eager to get Turkey involved in the war on the side of the US-led coalition forces (without the approval of the parliament), stated "it is not a problem to violate the Constitution once" (Özen 2013, 83). Süleyman Demirel (1924–2015) made similar remarks. Responding to claims about the presence and illegal activities of the informal deep state (*derin devlet*) in Turkey, President Demirel stated (in February 2000) that "sometimes, the state might take action deviating from its routine operation and practice." Assuming that the term "routine" in his statement refers to the existing formal rules, regulations, and practices, Demirel's statement can be interpreted as a confession of the presence of informal politics at the state level.[5]

Another example, which well illustrates the strength and omnipresence of informal institutions and practices in the Turkish context is that of *favoritism* (*kayırma/torpil*). The results of the Informal Institutions in Turkey Survey (Türkiye'de Enformel Kurumlar Anketi, TEKA 2019) (see Sarigil 2019)[6] show that the vast majority of participants (90%) state that personally knowing someone who works at a state agency would facilitate or speed up one's transactions in that particular public agency. Furthermore, the vast majority of people think that employment in the public sector is not really merit-based: 82% of respondents state that in order to get a job in the public sector, one should find a *torpil* (i.e., an influential acquaintance or supporter at higher echelons in public administration or a supportive politician, usually from the ruling party). Finally, 86% of respondents declare that in order to get or win a public tender or bid, a private company should be close to the government. All these responses clearly confirm the prevalence and power of favoritism as a major informal institution in Turkish sociopolitical life.

We also see several cases in which formal rules and regulations are almost completely replaced by informal rules and practices. One striking example from the social realm is pedestrian crossings or crosswalks in Turkey. They are designated for pedestrians to cross a road safely. It is a written, formal rule that at crosswalks without traffic lights, drivers should stop and let pedestrians cross the road.[7] Thus, for the formal rules and regulations, pedestrians have the right of way at crosswalks. However, in practice, drivers do not really reduce their speed or stop at those crossings to let pedestrians cross the road. In other words, drivers generally do not follow or obey the formal traffic rule. Interestingly, knowing this de facto practice, pedestrians do not attempt to use the crossings without traffic lights, or they use those crossings when there is no traffic on the road or the speed of traffic is quite slow. This de facto practice is common knowledge, shaping the expectations of both pedestrians and drivers. Violations of that unwritten, informal rule usually result in serious traffic accidents and injuries to pedestrians. In sum, the formal rule of pedestrian crossing exists on paper. In

---

5. For a study on the informal deep state in Turkey, see Soyler 2013, 2015.

6. For more information on the TEKA 2019 dataset, see chapter 3.

7. See, for instance, Article 74 of the Law on Highway Traffic (Law No. 2918). https://www.mevzuat.gov.tr/MevzuatMetin/1.5.2918.pdf, accessed September 3, 2021.

practice, pedestrian crossings are almost entirely regulated by unwritten, informal rules and regulations. This means that informal reality substantially deviates from formal reality in this particular case.

In brief, given the weakness of formal institutional arrangements and the plethora of strong and influential informal rules and regulations (*yazılı olmayan kurallar*) in Turkish social and political spheres (e.g., patriarchy, favoritism, patronage, vote buying, clientelism, nepotism, bribery, honor killing, blood feuds, blood money, informal economy), the Turkish case offers us an excellent social and political laboratory for studying and theorizing informal institutions. Thus, from the perspective of case selection, the Turkish case constitutes a *typical case*.[8] Such exemplary cases are highly valuable because they might be quite useful in terms of generating or building novel hypotheses and theories or improving the existing theories about a particular phenomenon. Thus, as an apt case, the Turkish setting offers us several opportunities to theorize the role of informal institutions in the sociopolitical world. By focusing on such a representative case, which is rich in powerful informal institutions, we can discover novel types of informal institutions, enhance our understanding of the interplay between formal and informal institutions, and better identify the mechanisms and processes through which informal institutions shape sociopolitical behaviors and outcomes.

Another reason why the Turkish case is valuable is that, as noted above, the extant studies on informal institutions have paid greater attention to informal institutions in post-Soviet, Asian, African, and Latin American settings (e.g., see Ledeneva 1998; Brinks 2003; Helmke and Levitsky 2006; K. Tsai 2006; L. Tsai 2007; Bratton 2007; MacLean 2010; Xu and Yao 2015; Aliyev 2017). Hence, the existing theoretical and empirical institutional analyses neglect the role of informal institutions in Muslim-majority settings. As a developing country in the Global South, Turkey is a Muslim-majority country and such a context can help us gain fresh insights into the role of informal institutions in a Muslim-majority setting.

It is unfortunate that such a valuable case has been mostly ignored by institutional accounts. Existing institutional analyses of the Turkish case are centered on formal institutions and structures, such as the state, the military, political parties, the legislature, the judiciary, constitutions, electoral

---

8. For a discussion on case study methodology and different types of cases and case studies, see Eckstein 1975; George and Bennett 2005; and Gerring 2017.

rules, and the party system.[9] (Such a tendency in the literature is probably because formal institutions are relatively more visible and the data on them are relatively easier to collect or access.) In brief, paying greater attention to this particular case, which is characterized by an abundance of powerful informal rules and regulations, would not only enhance our understanding of the role of informal institutions in the Turkish sociopolitical setting but also contribute to our broader efforts of theorizing informal institutions.

This study conducts a within-case analysis by examining several cases of social and political informal institutions in the Turkish context. In other words, it probes the plausibility of the conceptual and theoretical framework by focusing on the Turkish case. As a particular type of case study, plausibility probes help researchers "demonstrate the empirical relevance of a theoretical proposition by identifying at least one relevant case" (Levy 2008, 6–7; see also Eckstein 1975). More specifically, plausibility probes allow the researcher "to sharpen a hypothesis or theory, to refine the operationalization or measurement of key variables, or to explore the suitability of a particular case as a vehicle for testing a theory before engaging in a costly and time-consuming research effort" (Levy 2008, 6). The Turkish case, which involves plenty of strong and influential informal institutions in the social and political realms, is an ideal case for probing or investigating the empirical plausibility, strength, and validity of the conceptual and theoretical points advanced in this study.

Compared to studying formal institutions, conducting research on informal institutions involves additional methodological challenges. One major difficulty is that it is a more challenging task to identify and measure informal institutions. As Helmke and Levitsky (2004, 733) note:

A major issue is identifying and measuring informal institutions. In formal institutional analysis, this task is relatively straightforward. Because formal institutions are usually written down and officially communicated and sanctioned, their identification and measurement often requires little knowledge of particular cases, which facilitates large-n comparison. Identifying informal institutions is more challenging. A country's constitution can tell us whether it has a presidential or parliamentary system of government, but it cannot tell us about the pervasiveness of clientelism or kinship networks.

9. For one notable exception, see Soyler 2013, 2015.

Similarly, Lauth (2015, 65) observes:

Although political science research has increasingly acknowledged the relevance of informal institutions, empirical comparative research still focuses predominantly on formal institutions. A major reason for this is the availability of data. Data on formal institutions is readily available, which makes even qualitative research possible. This is not always the case with informal institutions, where empirical data remains difficult to obtain. Moreover, the study of informal institutions necessitates laborious case studies that require sociological and ethnological research methods (see also North 1990; Radnitz 2011; Aliyev 2017; Ledeneva 2018; Voigt 2018).

Nevertheless, we can employ a variety of research methods and data collection techniques and still get some answers to crucial questions, such as how prevalent and influential are informal institutions in social and political life, what roles do they play, and how do they interact with formal rules and regulations in a given institutional ecosystem? As Lauth (2015, 58) states, "we find informal institutions in the beliefs and attitudes of individuals. If not found there, they do not exist." If that is the case, then, research methods and techniques such as intensive fieldwork, participant observation, in-depth interviews with relevant human agents, and survey research would be appropriate research tools to capture the *observable implications* of our theoretical propositions about the role of unwritten rules and regulations in sociopolitical life. So, to investigate and theorize informal institutions, this study utilizes original qualitative and quantitative data derived from multiple data collection techniques such as seven focus groups in various regions, around 80 in-depth interviews in many provinces, and a nationwide public opinion survey (see Sarigil 2019), with a nationally representative sample of 7,250 participants.

A Summary of the Arguments

To answer the research questions listed above, this study first offers a novel and improved typology of informal institutions. The existing two-dimensional typologies of informal institutions, which differentiate informal institutions along their interplay with formal institutions, identify four basic types of informal institutions: complementary, substitutive, accommodating, and competing (see Helmke and Levistsky 2004). These typologies, however, remain underspecified and thus partial because they underestimate or ignore the legitimacy aspect of institutions. This particular study highlights the role of actors' legitimacy concerns in the interplay between formal and informal institutions in sociopolitical life. Thus, expanding the existing typologies, this study offers a new, multidimensional typology based on the following three dimensions: (1) formal institutional legitimacy, (2) formal institutional utility, and (3) the compatibility between formal and informal institutional logics. This three-dimensional typology identifies four novel types of informal institution: (1) *symbiotic*, (2) *superseding*, (3) *layered*, and (4) *subversive*. The typology enhances our comprehension of the complex interactions between formal and informal institutions, and thus helps us distinguish between different types of informal institutions. This novel typology provides a more complete picture of the interplay between formal and informal institutions. It shows that other than complementing, substitution, accommodation, and competition, informal institutions also interact with formal institutions through symbiosis (i.e., mutual benefit or dependence between formal and informal institutions), superseding (sharing the same logic with formal institutions and completely replacing them), layering (operating in parallel to the existing formal rules and regulations), and subversion (serving as an antisystemic movement's tool of resistance or a struggle against the existing exclusionary and suppressive formal arrangements).

Regarding informal institutional emergence, informal institutions might arise as a result of either intentional design or evolutionary processes. In terms of intentional design, the following factors and dynamics increase the likelihood of informal institutions emerging: the failure or reluctance of human agents to establish a formal institution; the incomplete nature of the existing formal rules and regulations; the complexity, rigidity, or inefficiency of formal institutions; the ambiguity of the existing formal rules and regulations; the exclusionary and discriminatory nature of formal institutional arrangements; and the legitimacy deficit of formal institutions. Furthermore, informal institutions might also emerge through relatively more decentralized, unintentional, evolutionary, and spontaneous processes and practices, such as habituation. In addition, informal institutional emergence might be an unintended consequence of formal institutional change. Especially in the aftermath of sudden and dramatic changes to formal institutional rules and regulations, certain formal institutions might persist and continue their life as informal institutions under a newly established sociopolitical system.

With respect to changes in the existing informal institutions, factors such as changes in the efficiency or legitimacy of formal institutions, shifts in the surrounding sociopolitical culture, and changing power relations among institutional actors are likely to trigger informal institutional change.

To illustrate each type of informal institution as well as the conceptual and theoretical points, this study examines several empirical cases of informal institutions as derived from various issue areas in the Turkish sociopolitical context (i.e., civil law, conflict resolution, minority rights, and municipal governance) and from multiple levels (i.e., national and local). The following four cases of informal institutions in the Turkish context are analyzed: *religious marriage* (as a symbiotic informal institution); the *Cem courts* of the Alevi religious minority (as a superseding informal institution); the *holidays of religious minority groups* (i.e., Alevis and Christians) (as a layered informal institution); and *multilingual municipalism* as initiated by the Kurdish ethnopolitical movement (as a subversive informal institution). Why were these particular empirical cases selected for in-depth analysis? In my case selection process, I followed a purposive or selective sampling technique, which is a form of nonprobability sampling. Accordingly, since the ultimate purpose of empirical analyses is to illustrate or exemplify the novel types of informal institutions generated by the multidimensional typology, the main motivation of case selection was to select one typical or representative case of those types of informal institutions.

Organization of the Book

As the main theoretical chapter of the book, chapter 2 presents the conceptual and theoretical framework on the role of informal institutions in sociopolitical life. The conceptual and theoretical framework constructed in chapter 2 guides the analyses of informal institutions in the empirical chapters that follow. Chapter 2 first discusses the existing taxonomic analyses of informal institutions and their limitations. It then introduces the three-dimensional typology of informal institutions, which identifies four novel types of informal institutions, and discusses the reasons for the emergence of informal institutions in sociopolitical life. Finally, the chapter deals with informal institutional change and discusses the possible factors likely to trigger shifts in the existing informal rules and regulations.

The next four empirical chapters, which span a wide spectrum of topics and sociopolitical issues in the Turkish setting, illustrate the conceptual and theoretical framework presented in the second chapter by analyzing several empirical cases of informal institutions. Overall, these empirical chapters contribute to our comprehension of the effect of informal institutions on sociopolitical processes and outcomes. Chapter 3 explores the popular religious marriage (aka *dini nikah, imam nikahı, hoca nikahı*) in Turkey as an illustrative case of a symbiotic informal institution. This chapter exemplifies how pathbreaking formal institutional changes might pave the way for the rise of informal institutions, and how formal and informal institutions (i.e., formal secular civil marriage and informal religious marriage) might complement and empower each other by increasing each other's social approval and legitimacy. The following specific empirical questions direct the analysis of informal religious marriage in the Turkish context: Why is informal religious marriage so widespread in contemporary Turkish society? What factors motivate individuals to uphold religious marriage? How does informal religious marriage interplay with formal secular marriage? What kind of a relationship is there between formal secular marriage and informal religious marriage? Finally, what demographic, socioeconomic, and ideological factors might account for the variance in people's support for religious marriage? This chapter utilizes original and comprehensive qualitative and quantitative data derived from several focus groups, in-depth interviews, and a nationally representative public opinion survey. Utilizing survey data, the chapter also provides multivariate regression analyses of individuals' support for religious marriage.

Chapter 4 is devoted to an interesting case of superseding informal institution: Cem courts (*Cem mahkemeleri*). Cem courts have been an informal conflict resolution mechanism among the Alevi community, a heterodox Muslim religious minority in Turkey. The chapter illustrates the role of informal institutions in conflict resolution processes as well as how informal conflict resolution mechanisms might transcend formal judicial processes. It also discusses how socioeconomic changes (e.g., modernization processes) might transform the existing informal institutions. The chapter utilizes data derived from several in-depth interviews with Alevi religious leaders and civil society representatives from various provinces in Turkey.

Chapter 5 investigates a case of layered informal institution: religious minority holidays in Turkey. This chapter shows that actors might comply with formal rules and regulations due to their self-interest but they may not view them as legitimate, rightful, and just. When they fail to amend or modify the existing illegitimate formal rules, they might set up or resort to relatively more legitimate institutions. Displaying a different logic or rationale, these informal institutions are layered onto the existing formal structures and so they informally operate alongside those formal rules and regulations. The chapter focuses on four particular cases of religious holidays observed and celebrated by Muslim and Christian minority groups in Turkey: Christmas (Noel) and Easter (Paskalya) by Christian religious minorities, and Aşure and Gadir Hum by the Muslim Alevi religious minority. The chapter benefits from the data derived from in-depth interviews with religious leaders and representatives of related civil society organizations, official documents and reports, and press statements.

Chapter 6 delves into a case of subversive informal institutions, set up and promoted by the Kurdish ethnopolitical movement in Turkey: multilingual municipalism (*çok dilli belediyecilik*). This chapter illustrates how the presence of discriminatory and exclusionary formal institutions facilitates the rise of informal institutions and how antisystemic minority movements set up and promote informal institutions to challenge and contest the existing authoritarian and exclusionary formal arrangements. The empirical analyses of the chapter are based on qualitative and quantitative data, derived from public opinion surveys, some in-depth interviews with pro-Kurdish political actors and activists, data from national and regional elections, newspapers, and official documents and reports.

The concluding chapter summarizes the main arguments of the book and then provides a discussion of the broader implications of the study for institutional theory. It also discusses possible extensions of the study in future research.

CHAPTER 2

Conceptual and Theoretical Framework

This chapter offers a general conceptual and theoretical framework for a more systematic analysis of the role of informal institutions in the sociopolitical world. The conceptual and theoretical framework introduced in this chapter informs the empirical analyses of various informal institutions in the following chapters.

The existing theoretical literature on informal institutions does offer some typological analyses. However, as discussed below, those typologies, which are based on two dimensions, remain partial and limited. Hence, this study proposes a novel, three-dimensional typology of informal institutions, which draws on two major paradigms or approaches in the social sciences: rational choice and constructivist perspectives. In institutional analyses, the rational choice approach emphasizes the functional efficacy of institutions in advancing individuals' self-interests, while constructivist perspectives are relatively more concerned with the social approval and legitimacy of institutions. Thus, institutional utility and legitimacy constitute two of the dimensions of the typology. As for the third dimension, the typology takes into account the compatibility between formal and informal institutional logics. As presented below, the three-dimensional typology, which identifies new forms of the formal-informal interaction, generates four novel types of informal institutions: *symbiotic, superseding, layered,* and *subversive.*

After introducing the multidimensional typology of informal institutions, this chapter provides a detailed discussion of the emergence of informal institutions in sociopolitical life by addressing the following questions: Why and how do informal institutions emerge? Why do human agents still create or resort to informal institutions despite the presence of various formal institutional rules and regulations? What are the forces and mechanisms through which new informal institutions arise? Next, this chapter deals with the issue of informal institutional change and raises the following questions: How do the existing informal institutions change? What possible factors are likely to trigger shifts in the existing informal rules and regulations? Finally, the concluding section summarizes the main conceptual and theoretical points and propositions regarding the role of informal institutions in sociopolitical life.

The Existing Typological Accounts

Typological theorizing, which is defined as "the development of contingent generalizations about combinations or configurations of variables that constitute theoretical types" (George and Bennett 2005, 233), is regarded as a useful tool to advance our understanding of multifaceted and complex social or political phenomena. As George and Bennett (2005, 233) claim, typologies allow researchers to "address complex phenomena without oversimplifying, clarify similarities and differences among cases to facilitate comparisons, provide a comprehensive inventory of all possible kinds of cases, incorporate interaction effects, and draw attention to 'empty cells' or kinds of cases that have not occurred and perhaps cannot occur." Similarly, Doty and Glick (1994, 230) assert that typologies are more than classification systems or schemes. They suggest that typologies should be understood as the theoretical constructs or statements that "provide a parsimonious framework for describing complex organizational forms and for explaining outcomes such as organizational effectiveness." Thus, as "organized systems of types" (Collier, Laporte, and Seawright 2008, 152), typologies have not only descriptive purposes (e.g., identifying analytic types or categories of an overarching concept) but also explanatory and predictive aspects as well (e.g., specifying or predicting relationships among those types) (see also Elman 2009).

Typological theorizing is also frequently utilized in the existing theoretical analyses of informal institutions. In line with the increasing interest in informal institutions, we see an increasing number of typologies of informal institutions in relatively recent literature on institutions (e.g., see Lauth 2000; Helmke and Levitsky 2004; Grzymala-Busse 2010; Azari and Smith 2012; Voigt 2018). As those taxonomic schemes classify informal institutions, they look at informal institutions' interactions with formal rules and structures. In other words, those typologies hinge on the functional relationship between formal and informal institutions. For instance, focusing on the functions of informal institutions, Grzymala-Busse (2010) proposes that informal institutions can *replace* (substitute), *undermine* (weaken), or *support* (reinforce or strengthen) formal institutions. Similarly, Azari and Smith (2012) suggest that informal institutions *complete* (fill gaps, resolve ambiguities in formal institutions), *coordinate* (integrate the operation and output of several intersecting institutions), or *operate parallel to* (jointly structure or regulate the same behavior) their formal counterparts.

Helmke and Levitsky (2004) provide a highly cited and utilized fourfold typology of informal institutions, which is again based on informal institutions' functional relationship with formal institutions.[1] Their typology is based on two dimensions: (1) the degree to which formal and informal institutional outcomes converge, and (2) the effectiveness of the relevant formal institutions. "Convergence" refers to whether adherence to informal rules generates a similar or different outcome from the expected result of adhering to or following formal rules strictly and exclusively. "Institutional effectiveness" simply refers to the extent to which formal rules and regulations shape (constrain or enable) behavior. In the case of effective formal institutions, actors are aware that noncompliance will result in sanctions. As a result, formal rules are enforced and complied with in practice. Put differently, effective formal institutions are associated with a high degree of compliance. Utilizing those two dimensions, Helmke and Levitsky identify four types of informal institutions: *complementary, substitutive, accommodating,* and *competing* (see table 2.1).

Complementary informal institutions coexist with effective formal institutions, and they have convergent outcomes. Helmke and Levitsky (2004,

TABLE 2.1. Helmke and Levitsky's Two-Dimensional Typology of Informal Institutions

		Formal Institutions	
		Effective	Ineffective
Outcomes	Convergent	Complementary	Substitutive
	Divergent	Accommodating	Competing

---

1. Helmke and Levitsky build their typology on Lauth's (2000) classification, which identifies three types of relationships between formal and informal institutions: *complementary, substitutive,* and *conflicting.*

728) explain that "such institutions 'fill in gaps' either by addressing contingencies not dealt with in the formal rules or by facilitating the pursuit of individual goals within the formal institutional framework" (see also Lauth 2000). Such informal institutions are likely to enhance formal institutional effectiveness by offering incentives to agents to obey or follow formalized rules and regulations. Helmke and Levitsky provide certain judicial norms and customs (e.g., the "Rule of Four") that ease the work of the US Supreme Court as a typical example of complementary informal institutions. *Accommodating* informal institutions result from the coexistence of effective formal institutions and divergent outcomes. They are usually created by actors who are critical of formal rules and regulations but fail to amend them. Accommodating informal institutions are likely to encourage agents to act in ways that change the substantive effects of formal institutions; however, their goal is not to violate them directly (i.e., challenging the spirit of formal institutions but not the letter). This type of informal rules and mechanisms may also promote the stability and effectiveness of formal rules (e.g., consociationalism in the Netherlands and the *blat* system in the Soviet Union).[2]

Competing informal institutions are generated by a combination of ineffective formal rules and divergent outcomes. Such institutions are incompatible with the formal rules. Hence, when actors follow those competing informal institutions, they would ignore or violate formal rules. For Helmke and Levitsky, the most familiar examples of competing informal institutions are clientelism, patrimonialism, clan politics, and corruption. Finally, the combination of ineffective formal institutions and compatible outcomes produce *substitutive* informal institutions. Such institutions "achieve what formal institutions were designed, but failed, to achieve" (Helmke and Levitsky 2004, 729). Substitutive informal institutions are more likely to arise in sociopolitical contexts in which state structures are weak and have limited authority. One of Helmke and Levitsky's examples for this final type is rural northern Peru, where state weakness generated limited legal protection and ineffective courts during the late 1970s. In response, citizens set up informal *rondas campesinas* (self-defense patrols) for communal security and *ronda* assemblies (informal courts) for dispute resolution (see also Starn 1999; Van Cott 2006).[3]

---

2. Using the words of Ledeneva (1998, 1), the *blat* system refers to "the use of personal networks and informal contacts to obtain goods and services in short supply and to find a way around formal procedures."

3. Van Cott (2006), however, warns that although the *rondas* of Peru are substitutive

The Limitations of Two-Dimensional Typologies

One major limitation of the existing typologies of informal institutions is that they are underspecified and so partial. Although those partial typologies reveal a lot about the patterns of formal-informal institutional interactions and the role of informal institutions in sociopolitical life, they also hide a great deal. In other words, by contracting or reducing the complex property space too much, such partial typologies overlook important combinations of attributes. For instance, if we take Helmke and Levitsky's highly cited and utilized typology, as stated above, institutional effectiveness, which is the core dimension of their fourfold typology, is about institutional enforcement and compliance. Theoretically speaking, one can identify two analytically unique perspectives on why agents adhere to or follow the existing formal institutional rules and regulations: (1) rationalist and (2) normative.

For the rationalist approach, human agents, who are assumed to have fixed and given preferences or self-interests, are primarily concerned with maximizing their expected utilities. The rationalist approach further asserts that agents are instrumentally rational in the sense that utilitarian cost-benefit calculations or assessments direct their choices among available options. Applied to institutions, the rational choice perspective would claim that instrumentally rational agents consciously and voluntarily create or design institutions to maximize individual or collective utilities or benefits, or both (e.g., see Bates 1988; North 1990; Knight 1992; Weingast 1996, 2002). In other words, the rational choice perspective considers institutions as instruments used by self-interested, strategic human agents to protect and promote their interests. Institutions help protect and advance individual or collective benefits and welfare because they have key functions, such as limiting uncertainty by providing information, stabilizing expectations, reducing transaction costs, and solving various social dilemmas and collective action problems (e.g., coordination problems, the prisoner's dilemma, commitment problems, and the problem of the commons) (see Keohane 1984; O. Williamson 1985, 1993; Bates 1988; Milgrom, North, and Weingast 1990; Moe 1990, 2005; Ostrom 1990; North 1990, 1993b; Knight 1992;

---

informal institutions (filling a vacuum of policing and judicial authority), they were not intended to take the place of the state. She suggests that the main motivations behind forming *rondas* were to connect peasant communities with the state and complement formal judicial authority (see also Starn 1999).

Knight and Sened 2001; Weingast 2002; Acemoglu, Johnson, and Robinson 2005; Mantzavinos 2011; Stiglitz and Weingast 2011; Xu and Yao 2015). Therefore, a rationalist explanation of institutional compliance would assert that human agents adhere to the existing formal rules and regulations because they expect certain benefits and rewards, or they try to avoid the possible costs of noncompliance (Ostrom 1990; Knight 1992). In other words, from the rationalist perspective, institutional compliance is a matter of utilitarian cost-benefit calculus (Hall and Taylor 1996). As Peters (2012, 49) observes:

> The fundamental argument of rational choice approaches is that utility maximization can and will remain the primary motivation of individuals, but those individuals may realize that their goals can be achieved most effectively through institutional action, and find that their behavior is shaped by the institutions. Thus, in this view, individuals rationally choose to be, to some extent, constrained by their membership in institutions, whether that membership is voluntary or not.

The normative perspective, on the other hand, would draw attention to the role of agents' legitimacy concerns as the key factor in institutional compliance. March and Olsen (1989) argue that rationalist accounts are informed by the logic of consequentiality, which is based on utilitarian cost-benefit calculus. Hence, rationalist perspectives are claimed to underestimate the role of norms and values in social and political life. Instead, they claim that political life is organized by a logic of appropriateness, which sets the standards of legitimacy or rightfulness in a given social or political context. For the normative perspective, then, actors are not only *homo economicus* but also *homo sociologicus*. In other words, human behavior is guided not only by utilitarian cost-benefit calculus (i.e., exogenously defined utilitarian self-interests or expectations) but also by taken-for-granted norms, values, principles and identities (see also March and Olsen 1989; DiMaggio and Powell 1991; Ruggie 1998; Boudon 2003; Schmidt 2010). In brief, this approach claims that human agents are not only utility maximizers but also norm-followers.

If we apply this normative perspective to institutional compliance, we might claim that when human agents consider the existing formal institutional rules and regulations as legitimate (i.e., just, rightful, appropriate, and taken for granted) and so recognize their moral and normative authority, they would follow and reproduce them without necessarily engaging in a comprehensive, utilitarian cost-benefit calculus. As March and Olsen (2006, 7) assert:

> The basic logic of action is rule following—prescriptions based on a logic of appropriateness and a sense of rights and obligations derived from an identity and membership in a political community and the ethos, practices, and expectations of its institutions. *Rules are followed because they are seen as natural, rightful, expected, and legitimate.* (emphasis added)

Similarly, Mahoney (2000, 523) observes:

> In a legitimation framework, institutional reproduction is grounded in actors' subjective orientations and beliefs about what is appropriate or morally correct. Institutional reproduction occurs because actors view an institution as legitimate and thus voluntarily opt for its reproduction. Beliefs in the legitimacy of an institution may range from active moral approval to passive acquiescence in the face of the status quo. Whatever the degree of support, however, legitimation explanations assume the decision of actors to reproduce an institution derives from their self-understandings about what is the right thing to do, rather than from utilitarian rationality, system functionality, or elite power (see also DiMaggio and Powell 1991; Olsen 2009).

Thus, for the normative perspective, which treats institutions as set of interrelated rules, norms, and values that define appropriate action (March and Olsen 1989, 160), expecting utilities or avoiding a sanction (in the case of rule violation) are not the only reasons for complying with institutions. Agents might consider the existing institutions as given, natural, appropriate, and legitimate and follow them voluntarily. As Peters (2012, 30) also observes, from the normative perspective, "if an institution is effective in influencing the behavior of its members, those members will think more about whether an action conforms to the norms of the organization than about what the consequences will be for him-or herself." Similarly, Hall and Taylor (1996, 948) observe that, from the normative perspective, once individuals are socialized into particular institutional roles, they internalize the norms and values associated with those roles. Internationalization of institutional norms and values becomes the main dynamic behind institutional compliance (see also Selznick 1957, 1992; Lauth 2015; Imerman 2018). In brief, for the normative perspective, moral and normative commitment to the institution is the main source of compliance (Peters 2012, 41).

Quite strikingly, Helmke and Levitsky (2004 and 2006) do not discuss or mention any of those distinct dynamics or sources of institutional compliance and their implications for the rise of informal institutions and for formal-informal institutional interactions. Instead, they treat institutional compliance as a matter of utilitarian cost-benefit assessments: actors comply with the institutions to achieve certain personal benefits or to avoid possible sanctions. Institutional legitimacy, obviously, is not a factor in their two-dimensional typological analyses. In other words, Helmke and Levitsky do not take into account the legitimacy of formal institutional arrangements. It appears that, in their account, formal institutional legitimacy is taken as something given (i.e., assuming that institutional actors attribute a certain degree of legitimacy to the existing formal arrangements).

However, we should neither ignore formal institutional legitimacy nor take it as something given. A better analysis of the role of informal institutions in sociopolitical life requires paying greater attention to formal institutional legitimacy and questioning or problematizing it. This claim is valid for highly powerful and effective formal institutions as well. Compliance with formal institutions, which is interpreted as having a high degree of formal effectiveness by Helmke and Levitsky, may not necessarily mean that those formal arrangements are approved and viewed as appropriate, just, and legitimate by relevant institutional actors. As March and Olsen (2006, 10) also warn, institutional efficiency and effectiveness should not be conflated with institutional legitimacy "There is . . . . no perfect positive correlation between political effectiveness and normative validity. The legitimacy of structures, processes, and substantive efficiency do not necessarily coincide. There are illegitimate but technically efficient means, as well as legitimate but inefficient means." Thus, although human agents may comply with formal rules, it may not necessarily mean that they consider those rules just, rightful, appropriate, and legitimate. For instance, in authoritarian regimes, social groups might comply with formal rules and mechanisms not because of wholehearted approval or support but primarily because they fear repressive measures or actions. In other words, the possibility of coercion or a sense of impotence, or both, might force human agents to obey repressive formal institutional structures and arrangements. Similarly, if we look at colonial regimes, colonizers imposed several formal institutional arrangements upon indigenous people. Compliance with those imposed formal rules and regulations did not mean that those formal institutions enjoyed widespread social approval and legitimacy among indigenous people. As Schoon (2022) also suggests, if actors participate in a relationship involuntarily or against their will, then, this situation is antithetical to the notion of legitimacy. Thus, a high degree of compliance (i.e., a high level of formal institutional effectiveness) should not necessarily be taken as an indicator of a high degree of approval and legitimacy.

In brief, either cost-benefit calculus (i.e., expecting benefits or utilities or avoiding possible sanctions in case of rule violation) or normative concerns (i.e., legitimacy and appropriateness) might drive agents' conscious adherence to and compliance with the existing formal institutions. We should treat those factors as analytically distinct and separate but equally important drivers of institutional compliance. Paying due attention to those dimensions is useful, even necessary, not only for our understanding of formal institutional compliance but also for the analyses of agents' desire for informal institutions, the way formal and informal institutions interact, and the possible roles that informal institutions play in sociopolitical life. Thus, distinguishing and utilizing those two unique sources of institutional compliance, the following section builds a new, multidimensional typology of informal institutions.

An Alternative Typology of Informal Institutions

Constructing better typologies will advance our conceptual and theoretical understanding of the role of informal institutions in sociopolitical life. As Lauth (2015, 65) suggests, "with a few notable exceptions . . . the study of informal institutions had not yet led to the emergence of theoretical constructs. A typology of informal institutions can provide a point of departure for a new research program on informal institutions." Thus, this study offers a novel and improved typology of informal institutions, which is based on the following three dichotomous variables: *formal institutional legitimacy*, *formal institutional utility*, and the *compatibility between formal and informal institutional logics*.[4] This three-dimensional typology is heuristically

4. Following the conventional approach in typological analyses of informal institutions, this three-dimensional typology is also based on informal institutions' functional

fruitful in the sense that it improves our conceptual, theoretical, and empirical reasoning about informal institutions and their interactions with formal ones. Far from rejecting the existing typological analyses and approaches, this study seeks to broaden and extend them with this relatively more comprehensive typology.

To briefly introduce each dimension of the typology, a widely cited definition of legitimacy states that it refers to the perception or assumption that something is "desirable, proper, or appropriate within some socially constructed system of norms, values, beliefs, and definitions" (Suchman 1995, 574). Likewise, Zelditch (2001, 33) claims that "something is legitimate if it is in accord with the norms, values, beliefs, practices, and procedures accepted by a group" (see also Johnson, Dowd, and Ridgeway 2006, 57). Then, formal institutional legitimacy simply refers to the degree to which relevant human agents view the existing formal institutional rules and regulations as acceptable, credible, just, moral, fair, rightful, and appropriate (see also Scott 2014; Deephouse et al. 2017). In the case of a high degree of institutional legitimacy, actors recognize and approve the moral authority of those formal institutions, and thus they have a strong loyalty and allegiance toward formal rules and regulations. Ceteris paribus, a high level of legitimacy is likely to promote adherence to and compliance with institutional rules and regulations (see also Beetham 2011; Imerman 2018; Lenz and Viola 2017). Therefore, legitimacy is quite significant in terms of institutional performance (i.e., rule enforcement, effectiveness, and stability). Perceived illegitimacy is likely to undermine the moral or normative authority of institutions, and so lead to social or political unrest and uncertainty (see also Beetham 2011).

We should not treat formal institutional legitimacy as fixed or stationary. Rather, it might vary across time (see also Gilley 2008; Deephouse et al. 2017; Imerman 2018). For instance, changes in social beliefs, norms, and values might create a gap between formal institutional logic and social culture. An emerging discrepancy between formal institutional logic and changing social values and norms might decrease the perceived appropri-

---

relationship with formal rules and regulations. One might, however, claim that all these typological analyses attribute priority to formal rules and regulations. Yet this should not pose a major limitation because, in modern sociopolitical systems, states regulate public and private realms with complex and comprehensive codified or written rules. Thus, in modern societies, informal rules, regulations, and practices constantly interact with official rules and regulations in multifarious ways.

ateness of formal institutions, resulting in a legitimacy deficit. Using the words of Beetham (2011, 1419), "if the rules are only weakly supported by societal beliefs or are deeply contested, we can talk of a legitimacy deficit." Over time, a legitimacy deficit might result in the overthrow of formal institutional arrangements (North 1990; Pierre 1993; Lenz and Viola 2017). The rise of the antislavery movement in the US constitutes a good example of such a discrepancy between the existing formal institutional arrangements and changing cultural values. Until the mid-1800s, in many southern states in the US, the practice of slavery was legal. This formal institution was the primary cause of the American Civil War (1861–65). Toward the end of the Civil War, however, slavery was abolished by the Thirteenth Amendment to the US Constitution. As North (1990) indicates, the antislavery movement was not due to cost-benefit calculus such as shifts in relative prices. Rather, North claims, slavery was still profitable at the time of the Civil War. The antislavery movement was a result of an ideational shift in society, or the "growing abhorrence on the part of civilized human beings of one person owning another" (1990, 85; see also Kaufman and Pape 1999). Another example is the apartheid regime, a system of racial segregation implemented in South Africa. Based on white supremacy, the apartheid regime formally limited the rights and freedoms of the black majority and other ethnic groups. Regardless of its effectiveness, apartheid was viewed as illegitimate by many domestic and international circles because it violated internationally established norms against race discrimination. Thus, one major factor behind the removal of this formal institution in the mid-1990s was its legitimacy deficit (see also Gilley 2008). In brief, independent from formal institutional efficiency and effectiveness, formal institutional legitimacy emerges as an important factor in human agents' compliance with formal rules and regulations. As the typology presented below suggests, it might also be an important factor in human agents' search for informal arrangements. Limited formal institutional legitimacy can motivate or encourage human agents to resort to relatively more legitimate informal arrangements.

Formal institutional utility refers to actors' cost-benefit calculations and assessments with respect to the existing formal rules and regulations. Actors might assess or evaluate the existing formal institutions as beneficial (favorable, advantageous, benign) or nonbeneficial (disadvantageous, harmful, pernicious), depending on whether the existing formal arrangements advance their ideational and material interests (such as wealth, power, security, prestige, status, recognition, approval, self-esteem, reputation, and self-realization). If actors expect certain benefits or rewards (symbolic or material, or both) from the existing formal rules and regulations or at least if they perceive them as innocuous or harmless, they are more likely to abide by those rules.[5]

It is worth repeating the above point that we should not conflate formal institutional legitimacy and formal institutional utility. Formal institutional benefits or utility may not mean that actors view the existing formal rules and regulations as rightful, appropriate, and legitimate. For instance, during the 1980–83 military regime in Turkey, the military government effectively ended a bloody civil war between leftist and rightist groups. Furthermore, a major economic recovery was achieved during the military regime. Despite those achievements, the majority of Turkish voters did not vote for the political party that the Turkish military promoted (the Nationalist Democracy Party, Milliyetçi Demokrasi Partisi) during the 1983 general elections. The opposite is also true: a high level of formal institutional legitimacy may not come with a high level of formal institutional benefits. For instance, a government elected through fair and competitive elections might enjoy substantial democratic legitimacy, but certain policies or actions of the government might still harm certain social groups.

With respect to the third variable of the typology (the compatibility between formal and informal institutional logics), the notion of institutional logic differs from the institutional outcomes dimension that Helmke and Levitsky use. For Friedland and Alford (1991, 248), institutional logic refers to a "set of material practices and symbolic constructions—which constitutes [an institutional order's] organizing principles and which is available to organizations and individuals to elaborate." For a more detailed definition, it refers to

> the socially constructed, historical pattern of material practices, assumptions, values, beliefs, and rules by which individuals produce and reproduce their material subsistence, organize time and space, and provide meaning to their social reality. . . . Institutional logics are both material and symbolic—they provide the formal and informal rules of action, interaction, and interpretation that guide and constrain decision makers in accom-

---

5. Obviously, actors' utilitarian considerations about formal institutions might also involve the expected costs of violating them. If they think or expect that rule violation would result in some kind of sanction or punishment, resulting in a net loss for them, they would be more likely to comply with those rules.

plishing the organization's tasks and in obtaining social status, credits, penalties, and rewards in the process. . . . These rules constitute a set of assumptions and values, usually implicit, about how to interpret organizational reality, what constitutes appropriate behavior, and how to succeed. (Thornton and Ocasio 1999, 804)[6]

As these definitions and several other studies acknowledge (e.g., see Selznick 1957; Hall 1989, 1992, 1993; March and Olsen 1989, 1998; Schmidt 2008, 2010; Scott 2014; Kraatz and Block 2017), each institution (formal or informal) contains certain symbolic/ideational and material elements (e.g., values, norms, principles, beliefs, meanings, schemas, practices, resources, and goals), and such elements together form the logic of that particular institution. Institutional logic in return constitutes the spirit, rationale, and raison d'être of a given institution.

As the institutional logics perspective also emphasizes, most institutional environments (formal and informal) involve multiple logics (e.g., see Lounsbury 2007; Thornton, Ocasio, and Lounsbury 2012). In other words, there might be several formal or informal logics, or both, in a particular institutional setting, leading to institutional heterogeneity. Regarding the relations between formal and informal institutional logics in an institutional order, they might be either concordant or discordant.[7] The former involves a certain degree of overlap, agreement, or harmony between formal and informal institutional logics. For instance, formal and informal institutions might share similar values, norms, principles, missions, or goals. Discordance refers to a disagreement or inconsistency between formal and informal institutional logics. Thus, certain elements or ingredients of formal and informal institutional logics (e.g., norms, values, principles, or goals) might contradict one another. This would lead to tensions and sometimes open conflict or a clash between formal and informal institu-

---

6. The notion of "institutional logic" was introduced in the late 1980s (see Alford and Friedland 1985; Jackall 1988; Friedland and Alford 1991). Since then, it has become a core concept in the institutional analyses in various fields of the social sciences such as economics, sociology, political science, management, and organization theory. For further reading on the concept of institutional logic and the institutional logics perspective, see Thornton and Ocasio (2008); Thornton, Ocasio, and Lounsbury (2012); and Ocasio, Thornton, and Lounsbury (2017).

7. Not surprisingly, the agreement or compatibility between formal and informal institutional logics is a matter of degree. For the sake of simplicity, however, I treat it as a dichotomous variable as I build the typology.

tions. For instance, informal institutions such as clientelism, corruption, and favoritism (e.g., nepotism) would conflict with the logic and spirit of formal democratic institutions, contradicting such democratic principles as transparency, accountability, responsiveness, and equality. However, the logic of clientelism would be in concordance with formal institutions in most authoritarian political regimes (see also Lauth 2015). To give another example, after the collapse of the Ottoman Empire, the founding fathers of the Turkish Republic wanted to establish a modern (i.e., pro-Western) and secular nation-state. To achieve this objective, they abolished traditional Islamic laws and, instead, adopted several modern codes from Europe. For instance, in 1926, the young Republic adopted the Swiss Civil Code as the new Turkish Civil Code. Based on the principle of "gender equality," the new civil code was imposed on a highly traditional and patriarchal society. Naturally, this led to a contradiction or discordance between a fairly egalitarian logic of formal rules and regulations and a highly patriarchal logic of informal rules and practices within Turkish society.

Thus, utilizing those three dichotomous variables, the typology, presented in table 2.2, identifies four novel and distinct types of informal institutions: *symbiotic*, *superseding*, *layered*, and *subversive*.

Symbiotic. To begin with the cases, which involve concordance or harmony between formal and informal institutional logics, there are two new types of informal institutions: symbiotic and superseding. The combination of formal institutional benefits or utility and low or limited formal institutional legitimacy generates symbiotic informal institutions. Sometimes actors might find the existing formal rules and regulations beneficial (advancing their ideational or material interests, or both) and so voluntarily abide by formal institutional rules and regulations. However, they may still consider those formal arrangements limited or unsatisfactory in terms of

TABLE 2.2. A Three-Dimensional Typology of Informal Institutions

		I: Formal institutional *legitimacy*			
		Legitimate		Illegitimate	
		II: Formal institutional *utility*			
		Beneficial	Nonbeneficial	Beneficial	Nonbeneficial
III: Institutional logics	Concordant	Complementary	Substitutive	*Symbiotic*	*Superseding*
	Discordant	Accommodating	Competing	*Layered*	*Subversive*

appropriateness and legitimacy. Under such conditions, actors are likely to set up or resort to informal arrangements that have a symbiotic relationship with formal institutions. In the case of the symbiotic type, there is a mutually beneficial relationship between formal and informal institutions. By enhancing each other's effectiveness or legitimacy and approval, or both, formal and informal institutions reinforce each other (i.e., a relationship based on interdependence). If we illustrate this with an analogy, they represent different sides of the same coin.

For instance, if we take the case of marriage in contemporary Turkish society, there are two types of marriage: formal state marriage (aka *devlet nikahı, belediye nikahı,* or *resmi nikah*), solemnized and registered by municipalities, and informal religious marriage (*dini nikah*), conducted by men of religion. As chapter 3 details, there is a symbiotic relationship between these two types of marriage. Formal state marriage represents legal recognition and legitimacy, while informal religious marriage provides religious legitimacy to marriage. Thus, official civil marriage and informal religious marriage reinforce each other (hence a symbiotic relationship). As a result, the vast majority of couples getting married in Turkish society adhere to informal religious marriage as well. As the results of the TEKA study (see Sarigil 2019) confirm, 88% of marriages involve both formal state marriage *and* informal religious marriage.

The main difference between symbiotic and complementary informal institutions is that, in the case of the former, mutual benefit is the underlying principle in formal-informal interaction. In the latter, formal institutions benefit from informal rules and mechanisms. In other words, by empowering formalized rules and regulations (e.g., enhancing formal efficiency), complementary informal institutions serve formal ones. Symbiotic informal institutions are also different than substitutive ones. In the former, one does not replace the other. They coexist within a mutually beneficial and dependent relationship.

Superseding. This type of informal institution emerges when formal institutional benefits and formal institutional legitimacy are very low or absent. For several reasons, agents may find the existing formal institutions detrimental to their self-interests and, additionally, may consider them illegitimate. As a result, formal rules and regulations would simply remain on paper, failing to shape sociopolitical behaviors and processes. Under those conditions, agents are likely to resort to informal institutions, which would supersede or transcend formal rules and regulations. Unlike subversive informal institutions, in the case of superseding informal institutions there is a certain degree of concordance between formal and informal institutional logics. These informal institutions are also different than substitutive ones. They do not stand in lieu of formal arrangements nor do they play a subsidiary or auxiliary role. Rather, these informal institutions set aside, surpass, and completely displace formal institutions. For instance, if we take dispute resolution practices in the Ottoman Empire, Alevis, who are regarded as a heterodox Muslim minority community, used to avoid resorting to Ottoman state courts led by *kadı*, the official judges in *sanjaks* (provinces) and *kazas* (districts) who applied Islamic (*şeri*) and Ottoman customary (*örfi*) law in dispute resolution. Rather, they resolved their disputes at informal communal courts during Cem meetings (see Dressler 2006, 273; Metin 1992; van Rossum 2008; Yıldırım 2013). Thus, in the case of dispute resolution practices within the largely rural Alevi community, informal Cem courts superseded formal Ottoman courts.

Layered. The typology generated two discordant informal institutions: layered and subversive. Similar to symbiotic informal institutions, actors might comply with formal rules and regulations due to their self-interest but they may not necessarily view them as legitimate, rightful, and just. In other words, despite their adherence to formal rules, human agents might directly or indirectly question or challenge the legitimacy and moral authority of those formal institutional arrangements. These circumstances pave the way for layered informal institutions. Having a logic or rationale that differs from the existing formal arrangements, layered informal institutions informally exist and operate next to the formal rules and regulations.[8]

Layered informal institutions are especially likely to emerge in restrictive or exclusionary sociopolitical settings. Ethnic and religious minority groups, which have norms, values, traditions, and beliefs different from the dominant majority group, are likely to contest the moral authority of the existing formal rules and regulations that usually reflect the values and preferences of the majority group. Lacking the capacity and resources to displace or amend the existing exclusionary formal arrangements, they continue to abide by those formal rules but utilize layered informal institu-

---

8. In institutional studies, the concept of *layering* refers to a particular type of gradual institutional change, in which new institutions or rules are introduced on top of or alongside the existing ones (see Mahoney and Thelen 2010, 15–22). In this study, however, layering refers to a particular type of interaction between formal and informal institutions.

tions, characterized by a relatively higher degree of social approval and legitimacy within that particular group.

The key difference between a layered and a symbiotic informal institution is that, in the case of the latter, formal and informal institutional logics are in a harmonious relationship (hence a symbiotic relationship). That is not really the case with respect to layered informal institutions. Although layered informal institutions operate alongside the existing formal institutions, there is an implicit or explicit tension between them. Otherwise stated, the rationale of layered informal institutions tends to diverge, and sometimes clash, with the rationale of formal institutional arrangements. Thus, due to their different logic, layered informal institutions imply different expectations and behavioral regularities than the existing formal arrangements. Layered informal institutions are also different from subversive informal institutions. As human agents abide by layered informal rules, they also try to comply with the formal rules and regulations. In other words, although the logic of layered informal institutions diverges from the logic of the existing formal rules and regulations, actors do not employ such informal institutional structures to contest, challenge, or subvert those formal arrangements.

There are also substantial differences between layered and superseding informal institutions. First, as noted above, since layered informal institutions have institutional logics different from formal institutional logic, they are discordant ones. Second, in the case of layered informal institutions, although actors consider the existing formal institutions illegitimate, they still consider them as beneficial or at least innocuous. Either due to expecting certain benefits or avoiding possible sanctions in case of rule violation, they comply with those formal arrangements. Thus, rather than replacing formal institutions, which is the situation with superseding informal institutions, layered informal institutions coexist with formal arrangements. This, in return, leads to the rise of informal institutional layers in that particular institutional environment.

Subversive. Finally, subversive informal institutions, which emerge as a result of illegitimate and nonbeneficial formal institutions, are contentious, destructive, and sometimes insurrectionary or seditionist informal institutions with a diverging institutional logic or rationale. Some examples of subversive informal institutions are conscientious objection against conscription, and the Mafia.

Certain sociopolitical settings are more conducive for the rise of subversive informal institutions. For instance, such informal institutional arrangements might be an instrument of contentious politics, especially in authoritarian or suppressive sociopolitical systems. Suppressed, excluded, or marginalized groups in authoritarian settings are likely to resort to such informal arrangements to advance their cause and to confront, contest, and resist the existing disadvantageous, suppressive, and illegitimate formal rules and regulations. In that case, informal institutions become tools of resistance or struggle against the formal institutions of the existing sociopolitical system. One reason why opposition groups and movements in repressive political regimes are likely to prefer setting up such informal institutions is the relatively invisible, amorphous, or inconspicuous nature of informal institutions. By establishing such rebellious informal arrangements, opposition movements challenge the legal and moral authority of the existing exclusionary or suppressive formal rules and structures.

Furthermore, one might expect subversive informal institutions to emerge in weak states that are plagued with disadvantageous and illegitimate formal arrangements. Taking advantage of formal institutional weakness, agents might set up and expand such informal institutions at the expense of formal institutional rules and structures.

In the long run, subversive informal institutions might have some impact on formal institutions. Such contentious and disruptive informal institutions might trigger a change in the formal institutional arrangements. They might even further weaken the effectiveness and legitimacy of formal institutions. This process might result in formal institutional exhaustion. In that case, formal institutions would completely lose their capacity to shape human agents' behavior, and thus be replaced by subversive informal institutions.

The main difference between subversive and competing informal institutions is that, in the former, informal institutions directly challenge the legal and moral legitimacy and authority of formal institutions. That is not necessarily the case with competing institutions. Rather than questioning the legitimacy of formal institutions, competing informal institutions operate within those institutions. In other words, as is the case in nepotism, clientelism, and corruption, they are likely to be embedded in formal institutional arrangements. In a way, competing institutions have parasitic features: as they benefit from formal institutions, they also inflict damage to their hosts over time. Although competing informal institutions depend on the existence of formal institutions, because their logic contradicts the rationale of formal institutions, they are likely to undermine formal institutions over time (see also Lauth 2000, 26). However, subversive informal institutions are not really embedded in formal institutions. Isolated and distant from formal bodies and institutions, subversive informal institutions directly or indirectly contest or challenge the existing official rules and regulations.

In sum, by modifying and expanding a highly utilized two-dimensional typology of informal institutions, the three-dimensional typology presented above identifies and differentiates further forms or patterns of formal-informal interactions, and, therefore, new types of informal institutions. The three-dimensional typology of informal institutions confirms that distinguishing formal institutional utility from formal institutional legitimacy, as well as the inclusion of formal institutional legitimacy as a separate dimension in the typological analyses of informal institutions, would be highly fruitful in terms of understanding diverse forms or patterns of formal-informal interplay and of discovering novel types of informal institutions. For instance, the general assumption in the literature is that when formal institutional rules and regulations are highly beneficial and effective, agents would not need to resort to informal institutions; therefore, informal institutions would be weak (e.g., see Wang and Wang 2018). The three-dimensional typology presented above suggests that this is not necessarily the case. Even if formal institutions are highly beneficial, powerful, and effective, human agents might still resort to or set up various informal institutions. That's because a high level of informal institutional utility may not come with a high level of formal institutional legitimacy, and human agents' legitimacy needs might encourage them to resort to informal arrangements as well. This suggests that strong and influential formal and informal institutions might coexist. They might even mutually reinforce each other. In addition, when powerful and effective formal institutions have a suppressive and authoritarian nature, agents might resort to informal institutions to bypass or to contest and challenge the existing effective but exclusionary formal institutional arrangements. In brief, the three-dimensional typology presented above advances our understanding of informal institutional emergence, the nature of informal institutions, and their complex interplay with formal ones.

Utilizing the implications of the three-dimensional typology presented above and the existing theoretical and empirical analyses, the following section discusses the conditions under which informal institutions are likely to emerge.

The Rise of Informal Institutions

Having identified several novel types of informal institutions, we can move on to another important question: How do informal institutions emerge? Where do they come from? What are the reasons and mechanisms behind the rise of informal institutions in the social and political realms? Why do human agents resort to informal institutions? Regarding some of the ways through which institutions emerge, institutions might result from either intentional, purposive design or evolutionary processes (e.g., see North 1990; Goodin 1996; Knight 1992, 2001; Strang and Sine 2002; Scott 2014). These dynamics should be applicable to informal institutions as well. In other words, informal institutions might result either from deliberate, intentional, centralized, and strategic processes or from relatively more unintentional, spontaneous, decentralized, and evolutionary practices and processes.

In the case of deliberate, intentional, and strategic human design, informal institutions are traceable to the conscious and strategic efforts of certain actors. Lauth (2015) proposes that while designing informal institutions, agents might be motivated by the reduction of transaction costs, fixed expectations, order and stability, and power and interests. However, such objectives could also be achieved through formal rules and mechanisms. Then, despite the presence of a complex system of formal rules and regulations in modern sociopolitical settings, why do actors still set up informal rules and mechanisms? Because the existing formal rules and structures sometimes fail to satisfy human agents' material or ideational needs and interests, or both. In other words, certain limitations or deficiencies of the existing formal institutions might encourage human agents to resort to informal means and mechanisms.

First, human agents who fail to set up a formal institution to meet a particular need or solve a particular problem (e.g., coordination or defection problems) might prefer resorting to informal mechanisms as the second-best strategy (Milgrom, North, and Weingast 1990; North 1990; Ostrom 1990; Helmke and Levitsky 2004, 2006). For instance, Ostrom (1990) shows that to overcome certain collective action problems (such as governing the commons and preventing free-riding behavior), individuals might voluntarily develop certain rules and procedures outside of formal institutions or channels to maximize collective welfare. In other words, facing the difficulties or challenges of establishing formal rules and arrangements, human agents might prefer utilizing informal institutions, which are relatively more amorphous and obscure. The more amorphous and ambiguous nature of informal institutions might be appealing to human agents for another reason. As Peters and Pierre (2020) note, informal institutions work in the twilight or in the shadows. This nature of informal institutions allows actors to pursue goals that are not considered publicly appropriate or acceptable (e.g., clientelism, favoritism, corruption, vote buying, blood money, democratic backsliding) (Helmke and Levitsky 2004, 2006; Zgut 2022). Hence, agents might be reluctant to establish formal rules and regulations and instead prefer to utilize relatively more inconspicuous informal means and mechanisms to achieve certain objectives.

Furthermore, as several studies also suggest, formal institutions, which set general principles and parameters for action, usually remain incomplete (e.g., Farrell and Heritier 2003; Helmke and Levitsky 2004; Azari and Smith 2012; Heritier 2012). Using the words of Azari and Smith (2012, 41), "A formal institution may remain "incomplete"—its terms not fully specified— due to unresolved conflict over what the terms should be, or because it would have been prohibitively difficult to specify all contingencies at the time of its creation (here, "incomplete institutions" resemble "incomplete contracts")." Due to failure to cover all contingencies, formal rules and regulations usually involve some loopholes, and thus a gap of uncertainty (Hu 2007; Levitsky and Ziblatt 2018). Therefore, there is usually a need to develop informal rules, norms, and mechanisms to enhance the efficiency of the existing formal rules and arrangements. As Helmke and Levitsky (2006, 19) note, "actors operating within a particular formal institutional context develop norms and procedures that expedite their work or address problems not contemplated by the formal rules." Likewise, Peters (2019, 215) remarks, "what informal institutions all do, in their own ways, is to fill in the interstices left by formal institutions" (see also North 1990; Stacey and Rittberger 2003; Levitsky and Ziblatt 2018).

Moreover, the complexity, rigidity, and inefficiency of the existing formal structures and arrangements might result in the failure of formal arrangements to meet actors' utilitarian needs. Thus, certain limitations of formal institutions would also encourage agents to resort to informal means and mechanisms to achieve particular objectives. In other words, complex, rigid, or inefficient formal arrangements and rules might create incentives for agents to set up or resort to informal rules and mechanisms (Stacey and Rittberger 2003; Helmke and Levitsky 2004, 2006; Van Cott 2006; Reh

2012; Marcic 2015; Aliyev 2017; Peters 2019). As Peters (2019, 215–16) also notes, informal institutions

> attempt to overcome some of the rigidities and inefficiencies that are built into many formal structures. The dysfunctions of public bureaucracies, if often exaggerated, are well known and informal structures within these organizations and between them and the public may help to overcome those barriers to performance.

For instance, Reh (2012) suggests that agents, who face increasingly complex formal modern politics and policymaking processes and structures, devise various coping strategies to deal with the increasing complexity of formal governance structures. One of those prominent coping strategies, she suggests, is to resort to informal arrangements, which are likely to reduce transaction costs and speed up collective decision-making processes within complex and cumbersome formal institutional structures. Similarly, in his analysis of informality in socialist regimes, Aliyev (2017) observes that the chronic rigidities and inefficiencies of the socialist system led to flourishing informal rules and regulations, networks, and practices in the social, political, and economic spheres of those countries (e.g., extreme level of patronage, nepotism, corruption, the *blat* system, and the informal economy). In brief, human agents might resort to informal arrangements to enhance the efficiency of the existing formal rules and regulations or to cope with the various limitations of the existing formal arrangements (see also Heritier 2012, 342).

Regarding other formal sources of informal institutional creation, we should also take into account the degree of ambiguity of the existing formal rules and regulations. Formal institutional ambiguity increases the likelihood of the rise of informal institutions. Most institutions, even highly formalized ones, involve some degree of ambiguity (see Mahoney and Thelen 2010). This means that human actors must interpret the existing formal rules and regulations before they implement them. In other words, since some degree of ambiguity is an intrinsic feature of many institutions; institutions are subject to interpretation and reinterpretation by relevant institutional actors (see also Sheingate 2010; Hall 2010). Formal rules with a high degree of complexity and ambiguity, in particular, are subject to multiple creative interpretations. As actors interpret those rules and regulations, they also devise de facto solutions and practices attached to the existing formal structures. Through continued adoption and repetition across time, those de facto solutions and practices can evolve into informal rules and regulations, reducing formal institutional ambiguity. In brief, de jure formal ambiguity is likely to pave the way for de facto informal practices, rules, and regulations. Hence, one might postulate that a high degree of formal institutional ambiguity creates favorable conditions for the rise of informal institutions.

Informal institutions are also likely to emerge when actors face restrictive, constraining, or repressive formal institutional arrangements. The restrictive nature of formal institutional arrangements might encourage or force certain actors to set up alternative rules and regulations in the informal domain. As K. Tsai (2006, 119) observes, formal institutions "comprise a myriad of constraints and opportunities that may motivate everyday actors to devise novel operating arrangements that are not officially sanctioned. With repetition and diffusion, these informal coping strategies may take on an institutional reality of their own." One might expect such dynamics to be especially prevalent in authoritarian regimes. In such political systems, social or political movements that contest the existing suppressive formal arrangements might set up or revive various informal structures. In this case, informal rules and practices become a tool of resistance, contention, and political mobilization against the existing authoritarian formal rules and regulations. In other words, informal institutions might operate as a strategic tool of social or political opposition movements, especially in repressive authoritarian political systems.

Other than material motivations and concerns, we should also take into account agents' more symbolic or ideational concerns and needs, especially legitimacy-related incentives, in the conscious or purposive design of informal institutions. An important but ignored factor in informal institutional creation is agents' legitimacy needs. As the three-dimensional typology presented above suggests, agents might create or maintain an informal institution when the legitimacy of formal institutional arrangements remains incomplete or unsatisfactory. Sometimes the existing formal rules and regulations may not be in harmony with prevailing norms, values, and beliefs. This situation would result in a legitimacy deficit of formal arrangements, which is likely to encourage human agents to resort to informal arrangements. As the analysis of religious marriage in Turkey illustrates, in addition to formal marriage licensed by municipalities, the vast majority of couples getting married also arrange informal religious marriages, solemnized by men of religion (such as imams). Thus, the official, legal legitimacy of formal marriage is supplemented by the religious legitimacy of informal marriage performed by men of religion. This implies that the presence of highly powerful and effective formal rules and regulations may not prevent the rise or continued use of informal rules, regulations, and practices. However powerful and effective formal arrangements are, they might still be limited in terms of social approval and legitimacy. The legitimacy deficit of formal rules in return would incite human agents to resort to informal arrangements and practices.

With respect to relatively more decentralized, unintentional, evolutionary, and spontaneous processes through which informal institutions emerge, certain practices or patterns of behavior in a particular social or political domain might gradually evolve into informal institutions (Berger and Luckmann 1967; Knight 1992; Heritier 2012, 337). One key mechanism in such an evolutionary and spontaneous way of informal institutional emergence is *habituation*, which refers to "the psychological mechanism by which individuals acquire dispositions to engage in previously adopted or acquired (rule-like) behavior" (Hodgson 2006, 18). Similarly, Fleetwood (2008) suggests that through habituation, certain practices become internalized and embodied within agents and generate dispositional behavior. Thus, as a largely nondeliberative, nonstrategic, insentient, and evolutionary process, habituation helps a particular practice or action become routinized and taken for granted (see also Sarigil 2015a). As several studies also emphasize, routinization through repeated interactions is an important aspect of institutionalization (e.g., see March and Olsen 1998). As certain practices are repeated and routinized, they gradually acquire particular meanings. In other words, actors gradually infuse certain meanings and values into those routines, and thus they become institutionalized (Selznick 1957). In sum, through the mechanisms of repetition and routinization and habituation, a particular practice may gradually evolve into a rule-guided behavior. Many customs, conventions, and traditions in sociopolitical life emerge through such processes.

Finally, informal institutions might also emerge through the unintended consequences of formal institutional changes or transformations. After major socioeconomic changes or political transformations that involve substantial and sudden changes in the existing formal rules and regulations, a formal institution might continue its life as an informal institution. For instance, certain dramatic events (such as revolutions, wars, economic crises, natural disasters, and major technological developments) usually open up opportunities for human agents to initiate pathbreaking changes to the existing formal rules and regulations. During those critical moments or junctures, agents break away from the existing parchment institutions and initiate a new formal institutional path. In other words, human agents abolish or proscribe several formal institutional rules and regulations during those critical moments. However, due to the mechanisms of "taken for grantedness," internalization, and habituation, certain actors might still consider some of those traditional formal institutions morally acceptable and culturally appropriate, and thus maintain them informally under a new formal political regime. Otherwise stated, despite a complete rupture with an old regime, certain formal institutions of a previous sociopolitical system might persist and continue as informal institutions under a newly introduced formal system.

For instance, in the aftermath of the Independence War (1919–23), the founding fathers of the Turkish Republic initiated substantial reforms (imposed in a top-down fashion) to set up a modern, secular, and centralized nation-state from the remnants of the Ottoman Empire. Within this top-down and comprehensive reform process in various domains (e.g., law, administration, religion, education and science, and technology), several traditional Ottoman formal institutions were legally abolished or replaced with new formal institutions. Some of those traditional Ottoman institutions, however, persisted and continued as informal institutions during the Republican period. As the empirical chapters illustrate, religious marriage was a formal institution during the Ottoman period. A more secular formal marriage, one registered by municipalities, was introduced after the transition to the Republican regime. However, religious marriage persisted and maintained itself as an informal institution during the Republican era. In brief, discontinuous and radical formal institutional changes might pave the way for informal institutions. Certain abolished formal institutions might persist and operate as informal institutions. In other words, the legacies of old formal institutions might persist and informally shape sociopolitical processes under a new sociopolitical system. This is a more likely outcome if newly introduced formal institutions do not meet the material or ideational needs and demands of the beneficiaries of the former rules and regulations.

Informal Institutional Change

Shifts in informal rules and regulations have direct consequences for their roles in sociopolitical life and also for their interactions with formal arrangements. If so, then, how do the existing informal institutions change? What factors might trigger informal institutional change? Several studies claim that compared to formal structures, informal institutions are relatively more resistant to change (see North 1990; Knight 1992; Lauth 2000, 2015). For instance, treating informal institutions as "extensions, elaborations, and qualifications of [formal] rules," North (1990, 83) asserts that informal institutions have "tenacious survival ability because they have become part of habitual behavior." Similarly, Lauth (2015, 58) notes,

> while formal institutions can be changed solely by state authorities, the process of change within such socially-based institutions is extremely lengthy, as informal institutions are internalized by the participating actors and reproduce themselves by shaping future behavioral expectations.

The absence of rule-making authorities who can centrally amend the existing informal institutions, and the fact that informal institutions are based on "deeply rooted social practices" or "habituation," should not mean that informal institutions are immutable. Like formal rules and regulations, informal institutions change (gradually or abruptly) (see also MacLean 2010; Aliyev 2017). If so, what factors might trigger informal institutional change, and how does it take place?

First, informal institutional change might be related to the linkage between formal and informal institutions. Otherwise stated, informal institutional change might result from changes or shifts in formal structures (North 1990; Helmke and Levitsky 2004; Aliyev 2017). North (1990, 87) suggests that "a major role of informal constraints is to modify, supplement, or extend formal rules. Therefore, a change in formal rules or their enforcement will result in a disequilibrium situation. . . . A new informal equilibrium will evolve gradually after a change in the formal rules." Certain social, economic, and political developments might cause a substantial decline or increase in the efficiency or legitimacy of formal institutional rules and regulations. Decreases in the legitimacy of formal institutions, or their failure to respond to agents' interests and expectations, might encourage human agents to resort to informal means and mechanisms. As a result, agents might revive or amend the existing informal rules and practices. Increases in formal efficiency and legitimacy might also have a substantial impact on informal institutions. The empowerment of formal institutions might reduce informal institutions' appeal among human agents and undermine or weaken them over time. In brief, it would be problematic to think of informal institutions as isolated from their formal environment. As Aliyev (2017, 60) also notes, "formal rules and conventions are both influenced by and exert continuous influence on informal institutions and practices." Therefore, shifts or changes in formal structures and arrangements are likely to trigger changes in informal rules and regulations. As a case in point, Aliyev (2017) suggests that the collapse of the command economy and the economic liberalization in the postcommunist era undermined the Russian practice of *blat* and its role in obtaining certain insufficient goods and commodities.

Second, changes in the surrounding sociopolitical culture (norms, values, and traditions) might also trigger informal institutional change (Brunsson and Olsen 1993; Helmke and Levitsky 2004; Peters 2019). Because informal institutions are embedded in the broader sociopolitical culture, it is natural that they are responsive to changes or shifts in their environment. As Peters (2019, 211–12) notes, "changes in the political culture may also generate change [in informal institutions], given that informal institutions are perhaps more than formal institutions embedded in society and culture." For instance, shifts in social values and norms as a result of major socioeconomic developments (such as modernization) might undermine the legitimacy and the effectiveness of informal institutions. Such shifts are also likely to alter the nature of formal-informal interaction, leading to different types of informal institutions. As the chapter on the case of Cem courts illustrates, although modernization processes in the 1960s and 1970s weakened informal Cem courts as the key mechanism of dispute resolution within Turkey's Alevi community, urban Alevi communities have revived these informal courts since the 1990s. As a direct result of such changes, a superseding informal institution evolved into a complementary one.

Increasing discrepancy between the broader social culture and a particular informal institution encourages actors either to modify the existing informal institutions or abandon them completely. Abandoning or ignoring informal institutions might ultimately result in informal institutional decay or exhaustion.[9] For instance, in Turkish society, the "bride price" used to be a widespread practice in marriages. However, such a tradition is no longer widely practiced and has become almost obsolete.[10]

Informal institutional change might also result from relatively more endogenous dynamics and factors. As a set of rules and regulations, institutions (formal and informal) might have major distributional consequences. Institutions are likely to distribute resources, power, status, and prestige unequally among institutional actors, creating winners and losers (Stinchombe 1968; Levi 1990; Fligstein 1991; Brint and Karabel 1991; Knight 1992; Colomy 1998; Hira and Hira 2000; Mahoney 2000; Farrell and Heritier 2003; Acemoglu, Johnson, and Robinson 2005; Moe 2005; Heritier 2007; Mahoney and Thelen 2010). In other words, the existing formal and informal institutions might favor the ideational or material interests, or both, of certain actors, while disadvantaging some others' interests. This suggests that it is quite often the case that, in an institutional setting, certain actors would be more supportive of institutional change while others would prefer to maintain the institutional status quo. This implies that the existing rules and regulations are usually contested, at least by some set of actors in that particular institutional setting. As March and Olsen (2006, 14) also acknowledge, "while the concept of institution assumes some internal coherence and consistency, conflict is also endemic in institutions. . . . There are tensions, 'institutional irritants,' and antisystems, and the basic assumptions on which an institution is constituted are never fully accepted by the entire society." If so, then, when shifts in the power structure among the members of a particular informal

---

9. This implies that the dynamics of legitimacy are quite different across formal and informal institutions. As Lauth (2000, 24–25) also notes: "In contrast to formal institutions which receive their legitimacy through the state . . . informal institutions are based on auto-licensing (that is, self-enactment and subsequent self-assertion). Whilst the nature of formal institutions can be shaped and changed by actors with rule-making authority, this is not the case with informal institutions, as these develop, so to speak, indigenously. They do not possess a centre which directs and co-ordinates their actions. If their actual recognition lapses, so does their existence with it, whereas ineffectual formal institutions continue to be in demand and, in form at least, to exist." Thus, formal institutions might continue to exist, at least on paper, despite their declining legitimacy. However, when the legitimacy of informal institutions declines, they are highly likely to disappear or vanish.

10. The results of TEKA study (Sarigil 2019) confirm that the "bride price" has become a rare practice among relatively recent marriages.

institution empower pro-change agents, then the likelihood of a shift in informal rules and regulations increases (see also S. Eisenstadt 1964; Levi 1990; Knight 1992, 2001; Levitsky and Murillo 2009; Heritier 2012, 342). In other words, power shifts might open a window of opportunity for pro-change agents to alter the extant informal arrangements.

Conclusions

This chapter presents a conceptual and theoretical framework for the role of informal institutions in sociopolitical life. The theoretical framework is based on an improved, multidimensional typology of informal institutions. Given the limitations of the existing two-dimensional typologies, this chapter offers a three-dimensional typology, which generates four novel types of informal institutions: (1) *symbiotic*, (2) *superseding*, (3) *layered*, and (4) *subversive*.

Then, the chapter analyzes the conditions under which informal institutions are likely to emerge. The following factors and conditions increase the likelihood of informal institutional emergence: the failure or reluctance of human agents to establish a formal institution; the incomplete nature of the existing formal rules and regulations; the rigidity, complexity, and inefficiency of formal institutions; the ambiguity of the existing formal rules and regulations; the presence of exclusionary and discriminatory formal institutions; and the legitimacy deficit of formal institutions. Informal institutions might also emerge through relatively more unintentional, evolutionary, and decentralized processes and practices such as habituation. In addition, unintended consequences of formal institutional change might trigger informal institutional emergence. Especially in the aftermath of sudden and dramatic changes to formal institutional rules and regulations, certain formal institutional arrangements might persist and continue their lives as an informal institution.

Regarding changes in existing informal institutions, changes in the efficiency or legitimacy of formal institutions, shifts in the surrounding sociopolitical culture, and changes in power structures (i.e., the empowerment of pro-change institutional actors) are likely to trigger informal institutional change.

The following empirical chapters illustrate most, if not all, of the above conceptual and theoretical points by providing in-depth analyses of four empirical cases of informal institutions as derived from the Turkish sociopolitical context.

CHAPTER 3

A Symbiotic Informal Institution

Religious Marriage in Turkey

The current chapter examines religious marriage in Turkey (aka *dini nikah*, *imam nikahı*, or *hoca nikahı*) as an illustrative case of a symbiotic informal institution.[1] The Turkish Civil Law (Türk Medeni Kanunu) (Law No. 743)[2] recognizes and regulates only civil marriage (aka *resmi nikah, devlet nikahı*, or *belediye nikahı*). In other words, the existing formal rules and regulations do not recognize or regulate religious marriage.[3] Hence, religious marriage remains an informal institution in the Turkish social landscape. Although it is not legally recognized, and thus does not bring any legal rights or responsibilities, informal religious marriage is a highly popular practice and tradition in Turkish society, coexisting side by side with official civil marriage.

This chapter raises the following research questions: How widespread is religious marriage in contemporary Turkish society? What kind of a relationship is there between formal civil marriage and informal religious marriage?

---

1. This chapter is based on a research project entitled "The Role of Informal Institutions in Sociopolitical Life" (Enformel, Gayriresmi Kurumların Sosyo-Politik Hayattaki Rolü), which was fully funded by the Scientific and Technological Research Council of Turkey (Türkiye Bilimsel ve Teknolojik Araştırma Kurumu, TÜBİTAK) (Project No. 118K281). Assoc. Prof. Dr. Gözde Yılmaz and Dr. Eda Bektaş took part as researchers, and Pinar D. Sönmez served as the graduate student in the project. As the principal investigator, I would like to thank all of them for their contribution to this research project.

2. The Turkish Civil Law was enacted in 1926 and it was modeled on the Swiss Civil Code. In general, the Civil Law improved women's rights and freedoms, such as banning polygamy and granting women equal rights in terms of divorce, child custody, and inheritance (see also Magnarella 1973; Ilkkaracan 1998). It was replaced by a new Civil Law, enacted in November 2001 (Türk Medeni Kanunu, Kanun No. 4721).

3. The only reference to religious marriage in the Civil Law is that religious marriage is not a necessary condition for official marriage but official marriage is a precondition for religious marriage.

Which social circles resort to religious marriage? Why do people adhere to religious marriage? What factors (religious, ideological, socioeconomic, and demographic) might account for the variance in people's support for religious marriage? For instance, to what extent and how do religious (religious-secular), sectarian (Sunni-Alevi), ethnic (Turks-Kurds), and class divisions affect individuals' adherence to informal religious marriage?

This chapter first presents the main data sources utilized in the empirical analysis of religious marriage in Turkey. The subsequent section compares and contrasts informal religious marriage with formal civil marriage, presents the main motivations behind religious marriage, and identifies the symbiotic relationship between official civil marriage and unofficial religious marriage. Then the chapter provides multivariate regression analyses of individuals' support for religious marriage. Exploratory regression analyses, which are based on original survey data provided by TEKA study (see Sarigil 2019), enhance our understanding of the factors behind support for informal religious marriage in Turkish society. This section also presents a statistical analysis of individuals' support for a controversial formal institutional change, one that is likely to influence informal religious marriage in the country: the authorization of religious officials (i.e., muftis and imams) to administer formal civil marriage in October 2017. Finally, the chapter provides the broader conceptual and theoretical implications of the case of informal religious marriage in Turkey.

Data Sources

To analyze religious marriage as a popular informal institution in the Turkish context, I utilized at least three different data sources: focus groups, in-depth interviews, and a nationwide public opinion survey.

Focus groups. As a research technique, focus group simply refers to qualitative, semistructured group interviewing and group discussion and interaction on a particular topic, moderated and facilitated by the researcher. As well as getting information on a group's thoughts, views, and attitudes about a particular issue (informal religious marriage in this particular study), this research technique allows researchers to uncover the meanings, emotions, and norms behind those attitudes (see Morgan 1996; Bloor et al. 2001; Cyr 2019).

In this study, focus groups serve auxiliary purposes. As Bloor et al. (2001, 8) suggest, "more common than the use of focus groups as a standalone method is the use of focus groups as an adjunct of other methods." For instance, the researcher can use the contextual data generated by focus groups to design a survey study. Such focus groups are known as prepilot focus groups (Bloor et al. 2001, 9):

> Pre-pilot focus groups may be used as an alternative to depth interviews in the initial phase of a large survey study. Prior to the drafting and piloting of the survey instrument itself, focus groups may be used in the early days of the study for exploratory purposes, to inform the development of the later stages of the study.

Likewise, Cyr (2019, 23) notes that

> focus groups have regularly been used as a pre-test for large-N, and especially survey-based, research. With focus groups a researcher can: refine question phrasing; revise close-ended questions to include the full range of responses; and ensure that all dimensions of a particular topic are covered in the survey.

Following such a research strategy, this study also uses exploratory focus groups as a first step for further data collection. In other words, focus groups are supplementary to the survey research. To gather some initial views about individuals' adherence to religious marriage, we conducted several exploratory and presurvey focus groups. It is unfortunate that we lack any comprehensive and nationwide survey data on religious marriage in the Turkish setting. As a result, we had to design a novel survey instrument from scratch. So, given the lack of a comprehensive survey on this underresearched issue, the focus group data and insights about religious marriage helped enormously to structure the content and wording of the public opinion survey, which was conducted with a nationally representative sample.

Taking into account religious (Sunni vs. Alevi) and ethnic diversity (Turks vs. Kurds) in Turkish society, we conducted focus group studies in seven provinces (Ankara, Diyarbakır, İstanbul, İzmir, Hatay, Trabzon, and Tunceli) between March and July 2019. The focus groups were composed of five to seven individuals with diverse social, political, and economic backgrounds and took between 45 and 90 minutes.[4]

---

4. In order to recruit appropriate individuals, who are eligible for and willing to participate in the focus group research, and to find a suitable meeting place in those prov-

In-depth interviews. In addition to focus groups, we conducted several in-depth, semistructured interviews (30 in total) with academics, writers, religious officials, and theologians who have expertise in Islamic law (*fiqh*) related to family and marriage, and with lawyers who have training on and experience with Turkish Civil Law. The interviews were conducted in 12 provinces between March and July 2019.[5] The primary purpose of interviewing experts on this matter was to get a better sense of the general status of religious marriage in Islamic and secular law. We also tried to get an initial sense of people's motivations for arranging religious marriage as well as possible regional differences in the practice, and symbolic meanings, of religious marriage across various localities. The information that we gleaned from expert interviews was highly valuable and helpful in terms of finalizing the content, structure, and wording of the draft survey.

Public opinion survey. The survey data, derived from a nationwide comprehensive public opinion survey and entitled "Informal Institutions in Turkey Survey 2019" (Türkiye'de Enformel Kurumlar Anketi, TEKA 2019) (see Sarigil 2019), constitute the main data source in the analysis of religious marriage in Turkey. From the insights that we gleaned from the focus groups and expert interviews, we drafted the survey questionnaire. Then, with survey experts from a professional public opinion research company based in Istanbul, we further revised the draft survey. After finalizing the draft survey, we conducted pilot tests in Istanbul, Ankara, and Diyarbakır with 45 randomly selected participants in late September 2019. The members of the research team participated in those pilot tests. Based on the feedback from the pilots, we further revised the draft survey. Finally, on October 12–13 and 19–20, trained and experienced researchers of the research company implemented the survey through face-to-face interviews with 7,240 respondents aged 18 or older. The survey was implemented in 300 neighborhoods and villages from 50 (out of 81) provinces.[6] We used multi-

---

inces, we cooperated with a research company based in Istanbul, as well as local intermediaries such as universities and civil society organizations in those provinces.

5. Those provinces include Ankara, Diyarbakır, Gaziantep, Hatay, İstanbul, İzmir, Mardin, Rize, Sivas, Şanlıurfa, Trabzon, and Tunceli. For a list of interviews, see the appendix 3.A. The interviews relied upon voluntary informed consent.

6. The following provinces are included into the survey: İstanbul, Ankara, Çankırı, Kırıkkale, Çorum, Sakarya, Kocaeli, Bursa, İzmir, Erzincan, Elazığ, Malatya, Adıyaman, Kahramanmaraş, Şanlıurfa, Samsun, Gaziantep, Burdur, Aksaray, Sivas, Eskişehir, Zonguldak, Tekirdağ, Kırklareli, Batman, Afyon, Isparta, Manisa, Kilis, Denizli, Mardin, Van, Osmaniye, Aydın, Antalya, Nevşehir, Edirne, Adana, Giresun, Mersin, Trabzon, Hatay, Balıkesir, Kayseri, Bingöl, Diyarbakır, Konya, Erzurum, Rize, and Çanakkale.

stage, stratified cluster-sampling procedures to identify households. Then, we applied age and gender quotas to select one individual from each household.

Informal Religious Marriage in Turkey

Religious marriage simply refers to an informal marriage arrangement, which involves a man of religion (e.g., imam, sheikh, *dede*, and *mele*) and prayers. As a widespread informal practice, it coexists with formal secular civil marriage in contemporary Turkish society. The sharp division between formal secular civil marriage and informal religious marriage in the Turkish context emerged after the transition to a secular Republican regime in the early 1920s. In other words, during Ottoman times, there was no such division. Instead, *Kadıs* (aka religious judges) or their surrogates (e.g., imams) used to register marriages, based on Islamic rules and principles (Magnarella 1993; Ortayli 1994; Behar 2004).[7] As the official judges in *sanjaks* (provinces) and *kazas* (districts), *Kadıs* had training and expertise in Islamic (*sharia*) and Ottoman customary (*örfi*) law. As well as judicial duties, *Kadıs* had various administrative roles, such as city planning, supervising charitable foundations, controlling and regulating markets, and providing marriage permits (*izinname*) and registering matrimonial contracts. Thus, Islamic beliefs and principles and the religious establishment played a substantial role in the official regulation of nuptial matters in the Ottoman Empire (see also Magnarella 1973; Orucu 1987; Ortayli 1994, 2000; Tucker 1996; Apaydın 2000; Behar 2004; Martykanova 2009).[8]

After the establishment of the secular Republic in 1923, however, many conventional Islamic institutions and organizations (such as Islamic law, the Caliphate, the Ministry of Sharia, Sharia courts, and *madrasas*) were abolished and replaced by secular rules and regulations. Regarding the state regulation of matrimonial contracts, the 1926 Turkish Civil Law introduced a fully secular marriage, solemnized and registered by municipalities. In other words, the secular rules and regulations of the Republic eliminated

---

7. Marriages were recorded in *kadı* registers (*şer'iyye sicilleri*). However, it would be wrong to assume that all marriages in the Ottoman Empire were registered (Ortayli 2000).

8. Historians suggest that local traditions and customary law also played a major role in marriage in the Ottoman Empire (see, for instance, Ortayli 1994, 2000).

the role of religion and religious actors in matrimonial contracts (see also Magnarella 1973; Orucu 1987; Starr and Pool 1974; Arat 2021). As Magnarella (1973, 103) notes, "with the adoption of the Swiss Civil Code, the traditional imam marriage ritual lost its legal standing. In its place a civil ceremony became compulsory." Similarly, Orucu (1987, 225) observes that "the Civil Code secularised marriage so that only civil marriage, which is a legal contract, has legal effect; it is the only possible foundation of a legally recognised family."

However, the Republican regime imposed secular formal rules and regulations upon a largely conservative and traditional society (see also Metinsoy 2021). As one might expect, this led to a legitimacy deficit of many formal arrangements and structures. Subsequently, individuals who got married through formal secular civil marriage informally resorted to men of religion to have a separate religious marriage as well. In addition, especially in rural areas, many villagers maintained the traditional practice and continued to perform marriages without registering them with the state (see also Starr and Pool 1974; Magnarella 1993; Metinsoy 2021). In brief, religious marriage persisted as an informal institution under the secular Republican regime. As a result, a sharp formal-informal duality emerged in marriage arrangements in the aftermath of the transition to a secular Republican regime in the early 1920s (see also Erinç 2017).

Table 3.1 provides a comparison of these two forms of marriage. Although they have a similar logic and serve the same goal (family formation, marriage), there are still some substantial differences in terms of expectations, behavioral regularities, source of legitimacy, and enforcement mechanisms. In formal civil marriage, the expectation is to base marriage on a formal contract, to be arranged and licensed by authorized public agencies (i.e., municipalities, village heads, or foreign missions) as defined in formal law.[9] In religious marriage, however, the main expectation is that marriage arrangements should involve men of religion and prayers. These expectations lead to different behavioral regularities: to apply to legally authorized public officials (e.g., municipalities) for marriage in the former, and to resort to men of religion (e.g., imams, sheikhs, dedes, or *meles*) in the

---

9. In case of formal civil marriage, marrying couples should apply to legally authorized public officials (i.e., municipalities in cities, village heads in villages, and foreign missions abroad). Other than submitting some documents such as a petition, identification papers, health certificate, and photos, the couples should also arrange at least two competent adults to become witness to the formal matrimonial contract.

TABLE 3.1. A Comparison of Formal Civil Marriage and Informal Religious Marriage in Turkey

Type of institution	Institutional logic	Shared expectations	Behavioral regularities	Sources of legitimacy	Enforcement mechanisms
Civil marriage *(resmi nikah, devlet nikahı, belediye nikahı)*					
Formal, officially recognized and regulated (de jure)	Family formation	Marriage should be based on a formal contract, to be arranged and licensed by public agencies	Applying legally authorized public officials (i.e., municipalities, village heads, foreign missions)	State agencies, codified laws and norms	Official, legal sanctions by formal courts
Religious marriage *(dini nikah, imam nikahı, hoca nikahı)*					
Informal, no official recognition and regulation (de facto)	Family formation	Marriage should involve men of religion and prayers	Applying men of religion (e.g., imams, sheikhs, *dedes, meles*)	Religious and social beliefs, myths, traditions, and norms	Communal and social, such as naming and shaming, social exclusion

latter. With respect to the source of legitimacy, in the case of formal civil marriage, codified laws and regulations constitute the source of legitimacy, while the legitimacy of religious marriage originates from religious beliefs and social traditions and norms. Regarding enforcement mechanisms, formal civil marriage is enforced by official, legal sanctions, while the enforcement mechanisms of religious marriage are primarily communal and social, such as naming and shaming and social exclusion.

Religious marriage is usually conducted in either the bride's or the groom's house. In the case of Sunni citizens, imams and *meles*[10] usually conduct religious marriage, while Alevi citizens mostly resort to dedes for their religious marriages. Regarding the timing of religious marriage, people have it either much earlier than, during, or after their formal civil marriage. The official policy of the Presidency of Religious Affairs (Diyanet İşleri Başkanlığı, hereafter Diyanet), however, is that religious

---

10. In Turkey, imams are state employees who are authorized with providing religious services at the mosques. On the other hand, *mele* is the Kurdish name for mullah. Although they do not have any official status, *meles are accepted and respected as religious leaders and scholars in Kurdish-majority provinces.

marriage *should* be conducted either during or after the formal state marriage. Many imams and muftis that I interviewed stated that before they administer religious marriage, they ask for an official document proving that the applicants are officially married. Interviewees indicated that religious marriage without formal civil marriage can be abused and result in disadvantageous consequences, especially for women. Having said that, there are many people who prefer to have an informal religious marriage during their engagement (i.e., much before a formal civil marriage). Several interviewees and focus group participants indicated that couples prefer to have a religious marriage during or right after their engagement so that they can meet more comfortably throughout their engagement. Conservative circles, in particular, believe that dating without marriage is sinful or an act of adultery. Thus, informal religious marriage is utilized to morally and religiously justify partners' dating during their engagement. Indeed, quite strikingly, more than half of survey respondents (52%) declared that religious marriage should be conducted during engagement (i.e., much before formal civil marriage).

The Popularity and Rationale of Religious Marriage

How popular and important is religious marriage in Turkish society? Why do individuals resort to informal religious marriage? What are the main motivations for arranging a religious marriage? The results of the TEKA (2019) suggest that religious marriage is quite widespread in Turkish society. For instance, 88% of marriages involve both formal civil marriage and informal religious marriage.[11] Regarding single individuals, 83% declared that if they get married through a formal civil marriage, they would also arrange an informal religious marriage. Finally, 70% of respondents stated that they would like to have their children arrange a religious marriage as well. All these results clearly indicate that religious marriage is a popular informal institution within Turkish society.

---

11. The data provided by the Turkish Statistical Institute (Türkiye İstatistik Kurumu, TÜİK) also confirm the omnipresence of religious marriage in Turkish society. For instance, by 2006, 86% of married couples had both official and religious marriages. Those who were only officially married constitute around 10%. Similarly, regarding marriages that took place in 2011, 94% of couples had both official and religious marriages. Only 3.3% preferred only official marriage in that year. The data are available online at http://www.tuik.gov.tr

The popularity of religious marriage is puzzling because for many Islamic jurists and theologians "the presence of a man of religion is not necessary for the marriage to be valid and binding and does not constitute a seal of legitimacy" (Behar 2004, 540). Along the same line, many of the Diyanet officials I interviewed stated that formal civil marriage, regulated in the Turkish Civil Law, already fulfills the basic requirements of Islamic marriage. In other words, many religious experts emphasized that official civil marriage does not really contradict the principles of Islamic marriage. From a rationalist point of view, then, it becomes redundant and inefficient to have a separate informal religious marriage in addition to a formal civil marriage. Despite this, survey results confirm that religious marriage is omnipresent in Turkish society. Why is that so? What factors motivate individuals to resort to informal religious marriage?

We see several motivations and reasons for individuals' adherence to, and practice of, religious marriage. First, religious marriage adds religious legitimacy to official, secular state marriage. Focus groups and interviews indicate that many marrying couples resort to informal religious marriage to sanctify or bless (*kutsamak*) their formal civil marriages. Several men of religion, who also conduct religious marriages, emphasized that people think that formal civil marriage conducted and registered by municipalities is not enough. They highlighted that many people want a man of religion to play some role in their marriage, cite certain verses from the Quran (e.g., *Nisa Surah*, verses 2 and 3; *Rum Surah*, verse 21; *Nur Surah*, verse 32; and *Al-Fatihah Surah*) and the hadiths, and pray for the marrying couple.[12] Indeed, the main differences between secular civil marriage and informal religious marriage are the presence of a man of religion and prayer. Thus, people who utilize informal religious marriage consider formal civil marriage a civic contract and, therefore, insufficient or incomplete in terms of moral and religious justifications and legitimacy. Certain circles even consider having only formal civil marriage to be illicit and *haram* (banned by Islamic law). Otherwise stated, it is believed that formal civil marriage becomes *halal* (in accordance with Islam) and morally acceptable only after a religious marriage (which is viewed as a religious covenant). Survey results also confirm that the main motivation behind religious marriage is individuals' religious beliefs. For instance, 86% of those who arranged or

---

12. Other than citing certain verses from the Quran and hadiths, imams also cite the Diyanet's official marriage prayer (*nikah duası*).

intended to arrange religious marriage declared that they adhered to religious marriage because it is a requirement of their religious beliefs.

Compliance with family tradition constitutes the second most popular reason couples abide with this informal practice. Some of the men of religion that I interviewed as well as several participants from the focus group studies indicated that many people conduct religious marriage because their parents want that arrangement, and they do not want to offend their parents.[13] According to the results of TEKA 2019 study , around 12% of respondents declared that they conducted a religious marriage because their parents wanted them to have it. Thus, certain circles adhere to religious marriage as a family tradition. One might suggest that such traditions in society are rooted in religious beliefs. Hence, for the vast majority of people, religious beliefs and orientations constitute the main motivation behind their support for, and practice of, informal religious marriage (in addition to formal civil marriage).

The Symbiosis

With respect to the nature of the relationship between formal civil marriage and informal religious marriage, it seems that there is a mutually beneficial (i.e., symbiotic) relationship between them. Formal civil marriage, which involves the official registration of the marriage, defines and secures the legal rights and responsibilities of marrying couples. As a result, it provides the marriage with legal recognition, protection, and legitimacy. For instance, in the case of informal religious marriage without any official registration, if a husband divorces his wife, his wife cannot demand any alimony or any share from the property acquired during marriage. Official state marriage provides such rights and guarantees to marrying individuals, especially to women (see also Arat 2021). On the other hand, the insights from focus groups and interviews suggest that informal religious marriage provides the marriage with moral and religious justifications and legitimacy. Thus, while formal civil marriage ensures more material guarantees, informal religious marriage provides relatively more spiritual assurance. In brief, formal civil marriage and informal religious marriage empower each other (hence a symbiotic relationship).

One observable implication of a symbiotic relationship between formal

---

13. Interview with dede Ali Ekber Yurt.

TABLE 3.2. The Practice of Formal Civil Marriage and Informal Religious Marriage in Turkey (2019)

		Informal Religious Marriage	
		Yes	No
Formal Civil Marriage	Yes	Dual marriage (88.3 %)	Only formal civil marriage (8.4 %)
	No	Only informal religious marriage (3.3 %)	No marriage (single)

civil marriage and informal religious marriage is that the number of families with dual marriage would be higher than the number of those with only formal civil marriage or only informal religious marriage. As table 3.2 indicates, that is indeed the case. While 8.4% of married respondents had only formal civil marriage and 3.3% had only informal religious marriage, 88.3% of respondents declared that they had both marriages.

Another empirical evidence for the symbiotic relationship between these two types of marriage is that, when asked how they would rank them in terms of importance, 23% of respondents said that formal civil marriage is more important and 10% said that religious marriage is more important. The majority (67%), however, thought that both are significant. Similarly, 86% of participants stated that it is inappropriate to get married through only informal religious marriage. Furthermore, 72% of survey respondents declared that it would be insufficient and inappropriate to get married through only formal civil marriage. As a result, the majority of Turkish society prefers to have both of them. All of this confirms that these two types of marriage seem to constitute the two main pillars of the family. To use another analogy, they represent different sides of the same coin. Therefore, there is a symbiotic relationship between formal civil marriage and informal religious marriage in the Turkish social landscape.

Other Possible Motivations for Religious Marriage

The findings of focus groups and interviews from several localities across Turkey indicate that there are some other, though marginal, motivations behind religious marriage. For instance, although relatively less common, certain circles utilize religious marriage for material benefits. As a case in point, the focus groups and interviews show that certain widows who would like to remarry resort to informal religious marriage so as to continue benefitting from their widow's pension. If they were to get married through formal civil marriage, then they would no longer be entitled to their widow's pension. As a result, the couples arrange an informal religious marriage. In other words, religious marriage is also instrumentalized to maintain or attain certain material benefits.

Another reason for resorting to informal religious marriage is to bypass certain formal restrictions and constraints. Focus groups and interviews indicate that religious marriage is also instrumentalized for polygyny. The existing Turkish Civil Law allows only monogamy. Thus, some males marry more than one woman through religious marriage to avoid the legal proscription of polygamy (see also Vergin 1985; Ilkkaracan 1998). This means that, although few, certain men have one official wife as well as multiple informal wives thanks to religious marriage.

Religious marriage is also utilized to bypass another formal restriction: the minimum legal age for formal marriage. According to Turkish Civil Law, the legal age of marriage is 18. However, there are some exceptions to this formal rule. First, a 17-year-old person is allowed to get married with the consent of his or her parents or legal guardian. Second, a 16-year-old person may be granted permission to get married by a court decision and with the consent of his or her parents or legal guardian. Given these formal rules and restrictions, certain individuals under 16 resort to informal religious marriage to get married. Although the exact number of underage marriages is unknown, the results of TEKA 2019 study indicate that 5% of married participants had their first marriage when they were under 16. Furthermore, birth certificates indicate that there are many child mothers: we can assume that many, if not most, of these individuals got married through informal religious marriage.[14]

Does the symbiotic relationship between formal civil marriage and informal religious marriage hold in the case of these relatively more marginal motivations? We should acknowledge that symbiosis would not be valid for such marginal cases simply because such cases do not involve for-

---

14. See, for instance, "Antalya Kepez Devlet Hastanesi'nde son iki yılda 274 çocuk doğum yapmış" [In the last two years, 274 children have given birth at Antalya Kepez State Hospital], *T24*, August 27, 2019, https://t24.com.tr/haber/antalya-kepez-devlet-hastanesi-nde-son-iki-yilda-274-cocuk-dogum-yapmis,836625, accessed November 11, 2021.

mal civil marriage. Hence, we cannot talk about a symbiotic relationship between formal civil marriage and informal religious marriage in such situations. Instead, such cases represent the instrumentalization of a particular informal institution (i.e., religious marriage) to bypass certain formal rules or constraints. These cases suggest that in any institutional environment (formal or informal) there might be certain actors resorting to the existing rules and regulations with different intentions. Having said that, such cases remain marginal and infrequent in Turkish society.[15] As shown above, the most common intention behind religious marriage is to sanctify formal civil marriage: the majority of people resort to informal religious marriage (close to 90%) because they find formal civil marriage limited in terms of religious legitimacy. As a result, it is still valid and appropriate to treat religious marriage in Turkey as an illustrative case of symbiotic informal institution.

Multivariate Analyses

To have a better sense of the factors behind informal religious marriage in Turkish society, I conducted multivariate analyses. Thus, utilizing TEKA 2019 data, I conducted some exploratory multiple regression analyses of societal support for informal religious marriage.

Hypotheses

Regarding the key variables of interest, as is widely acknowledged, religious (secular vs. religious), sectarian (Alevi vs. Sunni), ethnic (Turks vs. Kurds), ideological (left vs. right), and socioeconomic divisions and cleavages are the main fault lines of Turkish sociopolitical life. Thus, in this chapter, I investigate the possible impact of religious, sectarian, ethnic, ideological, and socioeconomic variables and factors on individuals' adherence to the informal institution of religious marriage.

---

15. For instance, support for polygamy remains low in Turkish society. The results of TEKA 2019 study indicate that 7.2% of respondents support the legalization of polygamy. If we compare male and female support, only 3.4% of women approve the codification of polygamy, while 11% of men advocate it. In addition, as age decreases, support for polygamy also decreases, indicating that younger generations lend lower support to the formalization of polygamy.

Religiosity. Regarding religiosity, as claimed above, informal religious marriage, which involves men of religion and prayers, appears to complete the legal legitimacy of formal civil marriage by adding religious legitimacy to marriage. If that is the case, then, one might expect religious individuals to be more likely to embrace, support, and practice informal religious marriage. This reasoning yields the following hypothesis:

H_1: Religious individuals are more likely than nonreligious individuals to adhere to informal religious marriage.

Sectarian identity. Sectarian differences might also matter in terms of attitudes toward religious marriage. First, one might expect individuals with stronger secular orientations to be less likely to adhere to religious marriage. In the Turkish context, compared to Sunni citizens, Alevi citizens are regarded as having stronger secular values and tendencies (e.g., Shankland 2003; Carkoglu 2005). Second, due to their persecution and marginalization under the Ottoman administration, Alevi circles strongly welcomed the replacement of the Ottoman Empire with the secular Republican regime in the early 1920s. As a result, Alevis in general have stronger adherence to and veneration for secular Republican institutions such as the Civil Law. This should lead to relatively stronger support for formal civil marriage but weak support for informal religious marriage within the Alevi religious minority. Given all these conditions, another hypothesis to test is the following:

H_2: Compared to Alevi citizens, Sunni citizens are more likely to adhere to informal religious marriage.

Ethnic identity. With respect to the impact of ethnicity, Kurds are claimed to be more religious and traditional (see also Sarigil 2018a). If that is the case, one might expect stronger support for religious marriage within the Kurdish ethnic minority. Another mechanism through which ethnicity might matter is that, compared to Turks, Kurds have been more peripheral in the Turkish sociopolitical landscape (see also van Bruinessen 2000; Bayir 2013; Oran 2021). As detailed in chapter 6, the Turkish state had highly discriminatory and suppressive attitudes and policies toward Kurdish ethnic identity until the early 2000s. Not surprisingly, such a state attitude led to skeptical and negative attitudes among Kurds toward the central state.

For instance, the existing empirical analyses show that, compared to Turks, Kurds are more likely to have lower levels of trust in central state agencies (e.g., see Karakoc 2013; Sarigil 2015b). One might expect these two conditions (i.e., relatively stronger religiosity among Kurds and their peripheral and marginal status) to generate relatively higher level of support for informal religious marriage than formal civil marriage among Kurds. Thus, I test the following hypothesis regarding the impact of ethnicity:

H_3: Compared to Turks, Kurds are more likely to support informal religious marriage.

Ideology. We should also take into account the possible role of ideological factors in religious marriage's appeal to individuals. Left-oriented individuals are likely to have stronger secular values and orientations, and thus are less likely to adhere to religious traditions and institutions (formal and informal). This reasoning leads to the following hypothetical expectation:

H_4: Compared to left-oriented individuals, right-oriented individuals are more likely to adhere to religious marriage.

Socioeconomic status. One might also expect individuals' socioeconomic status to shape their attitudes and orientations toward religious marriage. Similarly, one might postulate that individuals with better socioeconomic status (i.e., with better education and income levels) are likely to develop stronger secular attitudes, and thus are less likely to resort to religious traditions, practices, and institutions. This line of thinking yields the following hypothesis:

H_5: Individuals with better socioeconomic status are less likely to adhere to religious marriage.

Variables and Measurement

Dependent variable. Individuals' adherence to religious marriage as an informal institution constitutes the dependent variable in the multivariate analyses below. In order to measure the dependent variable, I utilize the survey item, which asks the participants to compare the types of marriage (i.e., formal civil marriage and informal religious marriage) in terms of importance. The majority of respondents (67%) declared that both marriages were important, 23% stated that formal civil marriage was more important, and 10% expressed that informal religious marriage was more important. Thus, the dependent variable "*marriage comparison*" is a trichotomous variable that codes '1' for "civil marriage more important," '2' for "religious marriage more important," and '3' for "equal importance."

Independent variables. Regarding the measurement of *religiosity*, considering various dimensions of religiosity (such as belief, practice, and attitude), we incorporated multiple religion-related items into the survey questionnaire. Because almost all participants expressed their belief in Allah and an afterlife, we excluded these belief-related items. To check whether it is possible to reduce the remaining variables to a small set, I conducted factor analyses, which generated one factor (see appendix 3.B). Adding those religion-related items, I constructed a religiosity index. The religiosity index is an ordinal variable, which ranges from 0 to 8. High values mark stronger religiosity.

To identify participants' *sectarian origin*, I utilized respondents' self-identification with respect to religious sect. Thus, I included into the models a "*Sunni*" variable, which codes '1' for "being Sunni" and '0' for "other." Similarly, in measuring respondents' ethnic origin, I rely on self-identification. Accordingly, the *Kurdish* variable is a binary variable, which codes '1' if the respondent self-identifies as Kurdish and '0' otherwise.

To grasp individuals' *ideological orientations*, I employ responses to a survey item that asks participants how they would position themselves on the left-right ideological spectrum. This variable ranges from 1 (far left) to 5 (far right).

Finally, in order to quantify socioeconomic status, I use education and income levels as proxies. The *education* variable is an ordinal variable, ranging from '1' for "illiterate" to '7' for "graduate degree." Regarding income levels, I use monthly total *household income*. I recoded this continuous variable into a categorical variable. Thus, the income variable is also an ordinal variable that codes '1' for the lowest income group and '11' for the highest income group.

Control variables. In multivariate analyses, I control for the possible impact of age, gender, marriage experience, and regional factors (i.e., rural-urban distinction and residing in the eastern and southeastern regions). The *female* variable is a binary variable that codes '0' for male and '1' for female. The *marriage experience* variable is also a binary variable, coded as

TABLE 3.3. Descriptive Statistics of Variables

Variables	N	Min	Max	Mean	Std. Dev.
Dependent					
Marriage comparison	7,209	1	3	2.44	0.839
Independent					
Religiosity index	6,962	0	8	4.65	2.216
Sunni	7,135	0	1	0.92	0.270
Kurdish	7,158	0	1	0.12	0.330
Ideology	6,938	1	5	3.18	0.871
Education	7,240	1	7	4.27	1.381
Income group (household)	6,755	1	11	3.63	1.849
Control					
Age	7,240	18	94	40.17	14.405
Female	7,240	0	1	0.50	0.500
Marriage experience	7,240	0	1	0.74	0.439
Rural-urban	7,240	1	4	3.12	1.026
Region (east and southeast)	7,240	0	1	0.14	0.348

'0' for "no experience at all" and '1' for "some experience" (such as being married, divorced, or widowed). The *rural-urban* variable is measured on an ordinal scale, which ranges from '1' for village to '4' for metropolitan areas. The *region* variable is a binary variable that codes '1' for residing in the eastern and southeastern regions and '0' for residing in the rest of the country. Table 3.3 presents the descriptive statistics of all the variables.

Results

Because the dependent variable has three nominal categories that are difficult to order (aka discrete choices), I used multinomial logit in estimating the models.[16] Expecting a strong correlation among predictor variables (i.e., religiosity, Sunni sectarian identity, Kurdish ethnic identity, ideology, and education), I conducted some multicollinearity tests (e.g., cross-tabular analyses and variance inflation factor tests). The tests confirmed the presence of some degree of multicollinearity among predictor variables. Thus, I decided to run a separate multinomial logit model for each variable of

16. On logistic regression models, see Long 1997; Hosmer, Lemeshow, and Sturdivant 2013.

interest. For comparison purposes, I also report the results of the full model (Model 1f), which includes all the variables of interest and the control variables. The results are presented in table 3.4. The response "civil marriage is more important" constitutes the baseline or reference category in the multinomial logit models.

The results of multivariate analyses confirm almost all of the hypothetical expectations presented above. Regarding the impact of religiosity, increases in religiosity increase the likelihood of attributing equal or more importance to religious marriage relative to the referent group (i.e., considering formal civil marriage as more important). This relationship holds across various model specifications, including the full model. These results clearly indicate that religiously conservative people are more likely to favor informal religious marriage. This finding is in line with the religious legitimacy argument presented above and provides further empirical support for the symbiotic relationship between formal civil marriage and informal religious marriage.

Similarly, moving from a non-Sunni to a Sunni respondent increases the likelihood of attributing equal or more importance to religious marriage (with regard to favoring only civil marriage). This is probably because compared to Sunni citizens, Alevis, who constitute the second largest religious community after the Sunni majority in Turkey, have relatively stronger secular orientations and they are less likely to uphold informal religious marriage. Furthermore, this finding also confirms that Alevi citizens have stronger veneration for "secular" Republican institutions, including official civil marriage.

In terms of ethnicity, moving from a non-Kurdish individual to a Kurdish individual increases the likelihood of attributing more importance to religious marriage, but it does not have any statistically significant impact on the likelihood of attributing equal value to those marriages. The reason for Kurds attributing greater importance to informal religious marriage is probably because, on average, the Kurdish ethnic minority appears to be more religious and traditional than the Turkish majority (this difference in average religiosity across Turks and Kurds is statistically significant). Another possible reason for such a pattern (i.e., relatively weaker Kurdish support for official civil marriage) is that, as the members of a relatively disadvantaged and peripheral ethnic minority, Kurds seem to be relatively more distant from formal state institutions and organizations.

Ideological orientations count as well: compared to a left-oriented indi-

TABLE 3.4. Multinomial Logit Models of Marriage Comparison

Dependent variable: Which type of marriage is more important?

	Model 1a		Model 1b		Model 1c		Model 1d		Model 1e		Model 1f	
	2: Religious marriage	3: Both marriages	2: Religious marriage	3: Both marriages	2: Religious marriage	3: Both marriages	2: Religious marriage	3: Both marriages	2: Religious marriage	3: Both marriages	2: Religious marriage	3: Both marriages
Religiosity	0.509*** (0.025)	0.403*** (0.016)									0.367*** (0.028)	0.291*** (0.019)
Sunni			1.094*** (0.155)	1.868*** (0.101)							0.250 (0.184)	1.112*** (0.117)
Kurdish					0.843*** (0.141)	0.172 (0.110)					0.523*** (0.159)	−0.076 (0.127)
Ideology							0.766*** (0.056)	0.651*** (0.037)			0.374*** (0.064)	0.258*** (0.044)
Education									−0.644*** (0.044)	−0.401*** (0.030)	−0.377*** (0.048)	−0.223*** (0.034)
Income									0.023 (0.026)	−0.064*** (0.017)	0.051 (0.028)	−0.025 (0.019)
Age	0.001 (0.004)	−0.008** (0.003)	0.004 (0.004)	−0.005 (0.003)	0.003 (0.004)	−0.007* (0.003)	0.001 (0.004)	−0.009** (0.003)	−0.017*** (0.004)	−0.019*** (0.003)	−0.008 (0.005)	−0.013*** (0.003)
Female	−0.150 (0.096)	0.051 (0.064)	−0.136 (0.092)	0.097 (0.061)	−0.142 (0.091)	0.075 (0.059)	−0.126 (0.094)	0.046 (0.061)	−0.336*** (0.097)	−0.022 (0.062)	−0.229* (0.104)	0.053 (0.069)
Marriage experience	0.043 (0.133)	0.583*** (0.087)	0.372** (0.125)	0.798*** (0.083)	0.405*** (0.125)	0.856*** (0.080)	0.272* (0.128)	0.746*** (0.083)	0.007 (0.133)	0.612*** (0.084)	−0.248 (0.143)	0.439*** (0.094)
Rural-urban	−0.159*** (0.047)	−0.139*** (0.033)	−0.204*** (0.045)	−0.167*** (0.031)	−0.278*** (0.045)	−0.232*** (0.031)	−0.201*** (0.046)	−0.163*** (0.032)	−0.184*** (0.046)	−0.151*** (0.032)	−0.119* (0.050)	−0.064 (0.035)
Region (east/southeast)	0.996*** (0.147)	0.727*** (0.120)	1.305*** (0.140)	0.951*** (0.114)	1.005*** (0.151)	0.946*** (0.118)	1.479*** (0.143)	1.122*** (0.115)	1.194*** (0.149)	0.914*** (0.120)	0.826*** (0.168)	0.805*** (0.134)
Constant	−2.605*** (0.232)	−0.312* (0.156)	−1.610*** (0.249)	−0.576*** (0.170)	−0.482* (0.198)	1.344*** (0.134)	−2.879*** (0.273)	−0.729*** (0.179)	3.174*** (0.323)	3.795*** (0.220)	−1.513*** (0.435)	−0.562 (0.299)
N	6,943		7,112		7,137		6,917		6,732		6,287	
AIC	10,457.400		11,227.260		11,608.330		10,958.560		10,755.960		9,315.399	

Note: Reference category: "1: Civil marriage is more important." * p < 0.05; ** p < 0.01; *** p < 0.001. Standard errors are in parentheses.

vidual, a right-oriented individual is more likely to attribute equal or greater importance to religious marriage. In other words, a left-oriented individual is more likely to consider formal civil marriage as much more important and valuable than religious marriage. Likewise, individuals with a higher level of education are more likely to attribute greater significance to formal civil marriage. Otherwise stated, better-educated individuals appear to be more likely to prefer formal civil marriage over informal religious marriage.

Moving to the control variables, age does not have a consistent impact on marriage preferences. Regarding gender, it appears that gender differences do not matter in terms of preferences across those two types of marriage. In terms of formal marriage experience, individuals with such experience are more likely to attribute equal or greater importance to religious marriage. This might be due to the socializing impact of marriage, which usually involves the practice of religious marriage as well.

The results indicate that regional differences also matter. Individuals living in urban centers are more likely to attribute greater value to formal civil marriage than those who live in rural areas. We see the same tendency among those who live in the western parts of the country. In other words, the likelihood of preferring civil marriage over religious marriage is higher among those who reside in western regions.

To have a better sense of the substantive impact of the variables of interest on individuals' adherence to religious marriage, I calculated the predicted probabilities of preferences for marriage types. As presented in figure 3.1, moving from the lowest to the highest level of religiosity reduces the probability of attributing greater importance to formal civil marriage (category 1) by 55%, but increases the probability of favoring informal religious marriage (category 2) by 13% and both types (category 3) by 43%. Similarly, compared to non-Sunni circles, the probability of attributing greater importance to formal state marriage is 38% lower among Sunnis. Being Sunni increases the probability of attributing equal importance to these two forms of marriage by 38%. In terms of ethnic differences, Kurds are less likely to attribute greater importance to formal civil marriage (4% less) but more likely to prefer religious marriage (8% more). Likewise, moving from a leftist to a rightist ideological position reduces the probability of preferring state marriage by 45%, and it increases the likelihood of attributing equal and greater importance to religious marriage by 36% and 9%, respectively. Finally, increases in education level increase the probability of favoring civil marriage by 40%, but

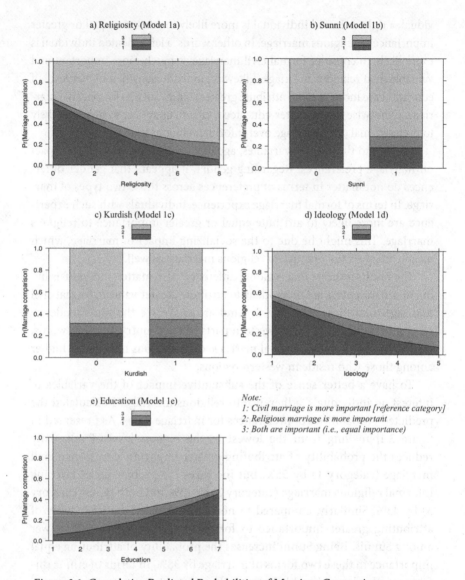

a) Religiosity (Model 1a)

b) Sunni (Model 1b)

c) Kurdish (Model 1c)

d) Ideology (Model 1d)

e) Education (Model 1e)

Note:
1: Civil marriage is more important [reference category]
2: Religious marriage is more important
3: Both are important (i.e., equal importance)

Figure 3.1. Cumulative Predicted Probabilities of Marriage Comparison

reduce the probability of attributing equal and higher importance to religious marriage by 20% and 19%, respectively.

"Religionizing" Formal Civil Marriage

In October 2017, the government initiated an interesting "formal institutional change," one that is likely to influence informal religious marriage in the country. The parliament, controlled by the conservative Justice and Development Party (Adalet ve Kalkınma Partisi, AKP) government, passed an amendment to the Civil Registry Services Law (Law No. 5490) (Nüfüs Hizmetleri Kanunu).[17] This change enables the Ministry of Interior Affairs to authorize the offices of mufti in provinces and districts to solemnize and register formal civil marriage. In other words, muftis, who are men of religion employed by the state to deal with religious matters and services in provinces and districts, can also administer official state marriage (instead of only the municipalities). Thus, individuals can now apply to either the municipalities or the office of the mufti for a formal civil marriage.

After this formal institutional change, muftis and imams started to play formal and informal roles in regard to marriage. Informally, they continue to conduct religious marriage; formally, they administer official civil marriage. This suggests that the formal institutional reform that took place in 2017 merged formal civil marriage and informal religious marriage at the office of the mufti.

How would this formal arrangement affect informal religious marriage in the country? First, this formal change, which *authorizes religious public employees (i.e., muftis and imams) to conduct and register official civil marriage*, should be interpreted as the Islamization of secular civil marriage (see also Gözler 2020). In other words, a religious component was added to formal civil marriage. As stated above, the vast majority of couples who get married through formal civil marriage also arrange religious marriage, primarily because it adds religious legitimacy to the legal legitimacy of official state marriage. This new formal arrangement, which religionizes civil marriage, might encourage marrying couples to apply to the office of the mufti for formal civil marriage and discourage them from applying for a separate

---

17. The law is available at https://www.mevzuat.gov.tr/MevzuatMetin/1.5.5490.pdf, accessed November 11, 2021.

informal religious marriage. From the perspective of "efficiency," one might expect marrying couples to apply to the office of the mufti for marriage because they could have a formal civil marriage and an informal religious marriage at the same time, at the same public agency. In other words, it would be much more convenient and efficient to apply to the offices of the mufti rather than to the municipalities for formal civil marriage. If that is the case, can we conclude that this formal arrangement (i.e., the authorization of religious officials to administer formal civil marriage) would undermine informal religious marriage in the country? We cannot because *the reform of mufti marriage involves the religionization of formal civil marriage rather than the codification of religious marriage.* Thus, since religious marriage is not legally recognized or regulated yet, it still operates as an informal institution. The main change regarding religious marriage is that state imams (i.e., formal actors) will now conduct informal religious marriage at an official state agency (i.e., the office of the mufti) as well.

Furthermore, such reasoning seems to be invalid for several social circles. Many groups seem to prefer to apply to municipalities (rather than the office of the mufti) for formal civil marriage and arrange a separate religious marriage. For instance, when we look at the practice of religious marriage among Alevi citizens, they are likely to apply to Alevi religious leaders, known as dedes, rather than imams or muftis. Hence, the involvement of imams or muftis in formal civil marriage may not reduce the appeal of religious marriage among Alevi citizens. Also, regarding civil marriage, Alevis (who are known as relatively more secular) are more likely to prefer civil marriage administered by municipalities than by the office of the mufti. One might expect similar attitudes among less religious, left-oriented, and better-educated individuals; these circles are likely to have a strong secular outlook and be more critical of the religionization (i.e., Islamization) of formal civil marriage.

Indeed, the results of TEKA 2019 study suggest that Turkish society appears to be divided on this formal institutional change (i.e., authorizing the office of the mufti in formal civil marriage). Fifty-eight percent of participants support such a change, while 42% of respondents oppose it. Even more interestingly, almost three-quarters of the single respondents declare that, rather than apply to muftis, they would still apply to municipalities for civil marriage. Quite strikingly, the vast majority (more than three-quarters) of those single respondents who would like to apply to municipalities for civil marriage declare that they would still arrange a separate informal religious marriage.

TABLE 3.5. Binary Logit Models of Support for Mufti Marriage

Models:	*Dependent variable: Support for mufti marriage*					
	2a	2b	2c	2d	2e	2f
Religiosity	0.364***					0.293***
	(0.013)					(0.015)
Sunni		1.084***				0.453***
		(0.095)				(0.113)
Kurdish			0.282***			0.043
			(0.082)			(0.094)
Ideology				0.546***		0.224***
				(0.031)		(0.036)
Education					-0.321***	-0.174***
					(0.024)	(0.027)
Income					-0.022	0.014
					(0.015)	(0.017)
Age	-0.004	-0.0004	-0.001	-0.002	-0.012***	-0.008***
	(0.002)	(0.002)	(0.002)	(0.002)	(0.002)	(0.003)
Female	-0.226***	-0.138**	-0.142**	-0.158**	-0.275***	-0.269***
	(0.054)	(0.050)	(0.049)	(0.051)	(0.053)	(0.058)
Marriage experience	0.163*	0.393***	0.414***	0.305***	0.220**	0.009
	(0.074)	(0.069)	(0.068)	(0.071)	(0.073)	(0.080)
Rural-urban	-0.207***	-0.236***	-0.269***	-0.218***	-0.215***	-0.180***
	(0.026)	(0.025)	(0.025)	(0.026)	(0.026)	(0.028)
Region (east and southeast)	-0.123	0.176**	0.108	0.272***	0.034	-0.156
	(0.077)	(0.072)	(0.078)	(0.074)	(0.077)	(0.087)
Constant	-0.518***	-0.134	0.957***	-0.813***	2.953***	-0.386
	(0.128)	(0.144)	(0.110)	(0.149)	(0.181)	(0.251)
N	6,902	7,065	7,088	6,880	6,695	6,264
Log Likelihood	-4,157.826	-4,628.577	-4,706.280	-4,415.021	-4,346.212	-3,720.351
AIC	8,329.652	9,271.153	9,426.559	8,844.042	8,708.423	7,464.703

Note: * $p < 0.05$; ** $p < 0.01$; *** $p < 0.001$. Standard errors are in parentheses.

To have a better sense of which social circles support the "religionization of civil marriage" and why, I conducted multivariate analyses of support for such a formal institutional change. Table 3.5 presents the results of the logistic regression analysis of support for civil marriage at the office of the mufti. Because the dependent variable is a binary variable ('0' for "no support," '1' for "support"), I used binary logit as an estimation technique. Due to multicollinearity among the variables of interest, I estimated a separate model for each predictor. I also report the results of the full model (Model 2f), which includes all the predictors and control variables.

The results indicate that, as one might expect, religious individuals are more likely to support imams' involvement in formal civil marriage. This relationship holds across various model specifications, including the full model. Similarly, compared to Alevi citizens, Sunni citizens are more supportive of mufti marriage. This difference might be due to two factors. First, as noted above, Alevis are likely to have stronger secular orientations, and thus they are relatively more critical of the religionization of secular civil marriage through the involvement of religious officials in matrimonial contracts. Second, the Diyanet follows Sunni-Hanefi teachings and rejects the formal recognition of Alevi practices and beliefs. As a direct result of such an exclusionary understanding and attitudes, certain Alevi circles strongly distrust of the Diyanet. Therefore, one would expect these circles to be critical of the involvement of Diyanet officials in formal state marriage. Moreover, because the Diyanet does not recognize Alevi teachings, practices, and beliefs, religious marriage arrangements in the aftermath of civil marriage at the office of the mufti would be based on Sunni teachings, understandings, and practices. This would not be desirable in many Alevi circles. This appears to be another factor that reduces Alevi support for civil marriage at the office of the mufti.

Ethnic differences matter as well: compared to the Turkish majority, the Kurdish minority appears to be more supportive of civil marriage at the office of the mufti. The Kurdish variable becomes insignificant in the full model due to its strong correlation with other predictors (such as religiosity and education variables). The relatively stronger Kurdish support for mufti marriage is probably because Kurds are relatively more religious. A higher level of religiosity among Kurds seems to boost support for the religionization of formal state marriage. Regarding the impact of ideological differences, right-oriented individuals are more supportive of the involvement of the Diyanet in civil marriage. Again, this is probably due to relatively stronger secular orientations among left-oriented individuals. Education level matters as well: better educated individuals are less likely to approve the religionization of civil marriage. This might be due to the relatively stronger secular attitudes and orientations among individuals with higher levels of education. An individual's income, however, seems to be irrelevant in terms of whether they support civil marriage administered by religious officials.

Regarding control variables, interestingly, women are less likely than men to support mufti marriage. It might be worthwhile to think about the relatively weak support among women for the religionization of civil marriage. On the other hand, individuals with experience in marriage are more supportive of such a formal institutional change. Regional factors matter as well: compared to individuals living in rural areas, individuals living in urban settings are less likely to support mufti marriage (however, living in the east and southeast does not have consistent impact on whether individuals support authorizing religious officials in civil marriage).

I calculated the predicted probabilities of support for mufti marriage as well, presented in figure 3.2. Moving from the lowest to highest level of religiosity increases the probability of support for mufti marriage by 62%. In terms of the impact of sectarian differences, being Sunni enhances the probability of support for mufti marriage by 26%. Similarly, the probability of support for mufti marriage is 7% higher among Kurds. With respect to ideological orientations, moving from the left of the ideological spectrum to the right increases support for mufti marriage by 49%. Education, on the other hand, reduces support for mufti marriage: moving from the lowest to the highest level of education shrinks the probability of approving mufti marriage by 43%.

What are the implications of these findings? The findings imply that even if it were more convenient to have civil and religious marriages at the same public agency (i.e., the office of the mufti) at the same time, several circles (the less religious, Alevi, left-oriented, and better educated) are less likely to approve of the involvement of religious officials in formal civil marriage. For these circles, a major concern with this new formal arrangement is that the religionization of civil marriage is incompatible with the principle of secularism, and thus these circles consider the arrangement inappropriate and illegitimate. Hence these circles would continue to apply to municipalities for formal civil marriage and then arrange a separate informal religious marriage. This suggests that in analyzing individuals' assessments of the existing institutional rules and regulations (formal or informal), we should pay due attention to their material and ideational preferences and concerns. A high degree of institutional efficiency and efficacy may not result in their automatic approval because actors might still consider those rules and regulations unjust and illegitimate. The opposite is also possible: actors might adhere to "inefficient" but still "legitimate" institutional arrangements.

We should emphasize that most of the circles who are critical of the religionization of civil marriage are not against religious marriage itself. It is quite striking that the great majority (more than three-quarters) of single respondents, who prefer civil marriage to be officiated by municipalities rather than by the office of the mufti, declared that if they were to get mar-

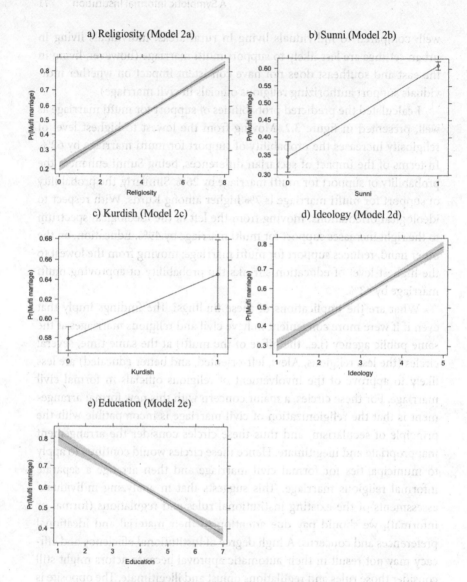

Figure 3.2. Predicted Probabilities of Support for Mufti Marriage

ried through formal civil marriage, they would arrange a separate informal religious marriage as well. This finding confirms that those who oppose the Diyanet's involvement in formal matrimonial contracts are against the religionization of secular civil marriage rather than against religious marriage itself. This interesting finding has a major implication in terms of the role of religion in sociopolitical life. Individuals who embrace, protect, and promote the secular nature of the state might still uphold religious traditions and practices in their private lives. In other words, individuals might develop diverse attitudes toward religion across the private and public realms. Hence, further research on individuals' differing attitudes toward the role of Islam across social and political domains would be highly rewarding in terms of having a better understanding of the nature of social and political Islam.

Conclusions and Implications

This chapter analyzed religious marriage in Turkey as a representative case of symbiotic informal institution. This particular case has several implications for our theoretical understanding of the role of informal institutions and of their interplay with formal rules and regulations in sociopolitical life. First, the case of religious marriage in Turkey implies that major shifts and transformations in formal rules and regulations are likely to trigger the rise of informal institutions. Especially after abrupt formal systemic changes, certain formal rules and regulations of the previous regime may persist and continue as informal institutions under a newly introduced sociopolitical system. In other words, in the aftermath of pathbreaking, dramatic formal systemic changes, agents might move certain formal rules and practices into the informal domain and maintain them informally. This suggests that formal pathbreaking change might pave the way for the rise of informal paths. This would be even more likely if newly introduced formal rules and regulations have an exclusionary or restrictive nature, and thus fail to meet actors' ideational or material needs, or both. Thus, political developments at the macro level might trigger the rise of informal practices, rules, and regulations at the micro level. As MacLean (2010, 22) suggests, informal institutions do not emerge ahistorically and apolitically. Rather, formal state decisions and actions at the macro level might shape the origin and subsequent evolution of informal institutions at the micro level.

Second, regarding formal-informal institutional interactions in socio-political settings in developing countries, Helmke and Levitsky (2006, 279) observe that

> in contrast to the literature on informal institutions in the United States and western Europe, much of which focuses on informal norms that complement formal institutions, research on the developing world focuses largely on those that *subvert* formal institutions. Several factors seem to account for this pattern. One is that many formal institutions in the developing world are imported from the West, rather than indigenously created.

The in-depth analysis of religious marriage in Turkey, however, suggests that informal institutions may not necessarily undermine or challenge formal institutions in developing countries. Rather, formal and informal institutions might empower one another in those countries as well. In other words, in addition to competitive or conflictual relations, there might be mutually beneficial (i.e., symbiotic) and harmonious interactions between formal and informal institutions in the developing world.

Third, Helmke and Levitsky (2004, 734) rightly note that "the issue of how informal institutions sustain or reinforce—as opposed to undermine or distort—formal ones has not been well researched." The case of religious marriage in Turkey advances our understanding of how informal institutions might reinforce or sustain existing formal institutions. This particular case suggests that one of the mechanisms through which informal institutions might reinforce formal institutions is *legitimation*. Although religious marriage is not officially recognized, it is a quite common informal practice in Turkish society. From a purely utilitarian perspective, it is inefficient to conduct another marriage in addition to a formal civil marriage. If so, then why is it so popular among marrying couples? It is because religious marriage complements the legal legitimacy of formal civil marriage with religious and traditional legitimacy. This suggests that as well as enhancing formal institutional efficiency and effectiveness, informal institutions might also increase the social approval and legitimacy of formal arrangements.

This point further implies that even if the existing formal institutions are highly efficient and effective, agents might still resort to informal institutions. In other words, even if agents benefit from the existing formal institutional rules and regulations and adhere to those formal arrangements, they may still resort to informal arrangements because the existing formal structures may fail to meet their ideational or symbolic needs. In other words, the limited legitimacy of formal arrangements is likely to urge human agents to utilize informal means and mechanisms.

This suggests that effective formal institutions might coexist with strong and influential informal rules and regulations. Many studies assume that informal institutions are more likely to emerge when formal arrangements are ineffective and weak. Formal institutional weakness and ineffectiveness does increase the likelihood of informal institutional emergence (see also Hyden 1983, 2006; Tripp 1997; Bratton 2007). However, it would be wrong to assume that informal institutions emerge only when formal rules and regulations remain weak. Although formal institutional weakness is likely to facilitate the rise of informal institutions, the presence of effective and powerful formal institutions would not necessarily prevent the rise of strong informal institutions. All this leads to the conclusion that in an institutional environment, formal and informal rules and regulations might be equally weak or equally strong. When both formal and informal institutions are weak in a given sociopolitical setting, it means that the level of institutionalization remains low and so human agency plays a substantial role. This, in turn, would increase uncertainty in that particular setting. When both of them are effective and strong, the outcome would depend on the compatibility between formal and informal institutional logics. If they are discordant, then, a tug-of-war between formal and informal institutions is the likely outcome. If formal and informal institutional logics are concordant, then, the outcome would be the overdetermination of actors' behaviors in that particular institutional environment.

Finally, this particular case has some implications for the assumption of a zero-sum, oppositional relationship between secular and religious arrangements and practices in Muslim-majority countries. In almost all analyses and conceptualizations, the secular-religious relationship in Muslim settings is assumed to be conflictual and antagonistic. Indeed, the existing literature identifies and treats the secular-religious division and polarization as one of the fault lines of Turkish sociopolitical life (e.g., see Göle 1997; Navaro-Yashin 2002; Cizre 2008; Yavuz 2009; Kalaycıoğlu 2012). This particular case, however, indicates that secular and religious arrangements and practices do not always compete or conflict; rather, they might complement and empower each other. At least, the symbiotic relationship between formal secular civil marriage and informal religious marriage in the Turkish setting indicates that we should take into account the possibility of a harmonious and mutually beneficial relationship between secular and religious arrangements and practices as well.

Appendix 3.A. A List of Interviewees (Religious Marriage)

No.	Name and Surname	Job/Position	Date	Location
1	Pınar Çağlayan Aksoy	Assoc. Prof., Bilkent University	March 12, 2019	Ankara
2	Ramazan Coşkun	İzmir Deputy Mufti, İzmir İl Müftülüğü	March 21, 2019	İzmir
3	Gülnihal Eken	Preacher (Vaiz), İzmir İl Müftülüğü	March 21, 2019	İzmir
4	Mesut Harmancı	Bornova District Mufti, Bornova İlçe Müftülüğü	March 22, 2019	İzmir
5	İsa Gürler	Karşıyaka District Mufti, Karşıyaka İlçe Müftülüğü	March 22, 2019	İzmir
6	Pınar Altınok Ormancı	Assoc. Prof., Bilkent University	March 28, 2019	Ankara
7	Fatih Yıldız	Deputy Religious Expert, Din Hizmetleri Genel Müdürlüğü, T. C. Diyanet İşleri Başkanlığı	May 10, 2019	Ankara
8	Halis Kuru	Imam, Divriği Kültür Merkez Cami	June 1, 2019	Sivas
9	Ramazan Kumru	Imam, Divriği Kültür Merkez Cami	June 1, 2019	Sivas
10	Fatih Doğan	Graduate Student at the School of Islamic Law	June 2, 2019	Sivas
11	Zeycan Saltuk Koçuk	Ana	June 4, 2019	Tunceli
12	Zeynel Batar	Dede	June 4, 2019	Tunceli
13	Nesimi Öz	Dede, Tunceli Cemevi (Cem House)	June 4, 2019	Tunceli
14	Ali Ekber Yurt	Dede	June 5, 2019	Tunceli
15	İbrahim Halil Baysan	Imam, Tunceli Paşa Camisi	June 6, 2019	Tunceli
16	Ömer Evsen	Chairperson of Diyanet-Sen (Memur-Sen)	June 7, 2019	Diyarbakır
17	Zahit Çiftkuran	Mele (mullah)	June 8, 2019	Diyarbakır
18	Şevket Dilmaç	Yenişehir District Mufti, Yenişehir İlçe Müftülüğü	June 10, 2019	Diyarbakır
19	Tayyip Elçi	Mele (mullah); Chairperson of the Foundation for Madrasa Scholars (Medrese Alimleri Vakfı , MEDAV)	June 10, 2019	Diyarbakır
20	Mahsun Taşçı	Kızıltepe District Mufti, Kızıltepe İlçe Müftülüğü	June 14, 2019	Mardin
21	Adem Dobur	Eyyübiye District Mufti, Eyyübiye İlçe Müftülüğü	June 17, 2019	Şanlıurfa
22	Ahmet Çelik	Gaziantep Province Mufti, Gaziantep İl Müftülüğü	June 17, 2019	Gaziantep
23	Hamdi Kavillioğlu	Hatay Province Mufti, Hatay İl Müftülüğü	June 18, 2019	Hatay
24	Ali Yeral	Chairperson of the Foundation for Ahl al-bayt Culture and Solidarity (Ehlibeyt Kültür ve Dayanışma Vakfı, EHDAV)	June 19, 2019	Hatay

25	Aydın Yığman	Beyoğlu District Mufti, Beyoğlu İlçe Müftülüğü	July 8, 2019	İstanbul
26	Mehmet Muslu	Beşiktaş District Mufti, Beşiktaş İlçe Müftülüğü	July 8, 2019	İstanbul
27	Vehap Kapıcıoğlu	Fatih District Mufti, Fatih İlçe Müftülüğü	July 9, 2019	İstanbul
28	Ali Genç	Arsin District Mufti, Arsin İlçe Müftülüğü	July 22, 2019	Trabzon
29	Hasan Ayyıldız	Expert of Religious Services, Rize İl Müftülüğü	July 23, 2019	Rize
30	Akif Köse	Preacher (Vaiz), Rize İl Müftülüğü	July 23, 2019	Rize

Appendix 3.B. Factor Analysis of Religiosity

Variables	Factor loadings Factor 1: Attitude/practice
Opposition to financial interest	0.517
Daily prayer (five times)	0.663
Fasting during Ramadan	0.660
Headscarves for primary students	0.753
Headscarves for public employees[a]	0.693
Priority of religion	0.776
Friday as official holiday	0.596
Gender-segregated schools	0.670
SS loadings	3.595
Proportion var.	44.9
Reliability analysis	$\alpha = 74.4$

Note: "Polycor" package in R is used to conduct factor analysis.

a In Turkey, female students and public employees had been banned from wearing headscarves at schools and public buildings. The long-standing ban was removed in 2013. Thus, in contemporary Turkey, use of the headscarf by students and public employees has been a common practice and many social circles appear to have accepted this situation. Thus, one might claim that this item (i.e., support for female public employees' wearing headscarf) is no longer a good indicator of religiosity. However, with or without this item, the religiosity index generates similar patterns.

CHAPTER 4

A Superseding Informal Institution

Cem Courts

This chapter illustrates the notion of "superseding informal institution" by focusing on the role of informal institutions in dispute resolution processes and practices. Otherwise stated, informal conflict resolution practices and processes are utilized to demonstrate how superseding informal institutions might operate in sociopolitical life. As several studies also acknowledge, informal factors and mechanisms (e.g., rules, norms, practices, networks) also play substantial roles in dispute resolution processes in various sociopolitical settings (e.g., see Starr 1978; Ellickson 1986, 1991; Starn 1999; Wang 2000; Hensler 2003; Xu 2005; Van Cott 2006; MacLean 2010; Wall, Beriker, and Wu 2010; Ang and Jia 2014). This observation, regarding the role of unwritten rules of conduct in dispute resolution processes, should be even more valid for the developing world, where formal institutions tend to suffer from a limited degree of efficiency and effectiveness. The case of the Cem courts (*Cem Mahkemeleri*) of Turkey's Alevi community confirms that informal dispute resolution mechanisms and practices might supersede or transcend formal judicial processes.

Examining informal conflict resolution processes and practices, this chapter broaches the following questions: What roles do informal institutions play in conflict resolution processes? Why do human agents resort to informal mechanisms of conflict resolution instead of litigation? How do informal conflict resolution mechanisms interact with formal arrangements? What would the broader implications of such an analysis be for the role of informal institutions in sociopolitical life? To answer these questions, this chapter investigates informal community mediation and analyzes an interesting case of informal dispute resolution in the Turkish context: the informal Cem courts.

The following section briefly introduces the Alevi community in Turkey. Then, the chapter presents informal Cem courts and analyzes the role of these courts in conflict resolution processes during the Ottoman and Republican eras. The final section summarizes the results of the empirical analyses and reflects upon the broader theoretical implications.

The Alevi Community in Turkey

Known as a heterodox Muslim community, Alevis constitute the second largest religious group after Sunni Muslims in Turkey.[1] Alevi belief is considered a syncretistic integration of various beliefs such as Central Asian Turkish shamanistic beliefs, Islam, and local rituals and religious convictions in Anatolia (Shankland 2003; Massicard 2013, 2014; Dressler 2015; Issa 2017). For this reason, in the dominant Sunni Muslim understanding, Alevis are treated as a heretical or deviant community (Massicard 2014; Issa 2017; Lord 2017b; R. Yıldırım 2018). Due to their social, economic, and political marginalization, Alevis have been reluctant to reveal their identities; this makes it difficult to know exactly how many Alevis live in Turkey. However, the size of the Alevi community is estimated to be between 15% and 25% of the population (e.g., see Erman and Göker 2000; Shankland 2003; Erdemir 2005; Poyraz 2005; Şahin 2005; Massicard 2014; Karakaya-Stump 2018; Gedik, Birkalan-Gedik, and Madera 2020; Lord 2018, 2020; Oran 2021). Alevism crosses ethnic boundaries; although the vast majority of Alevis are ethnic and linguistic Turks (around 70%), there are also Kurdish/Zaza (around 25%) and Arab Alevis living in Turkey. Turkish Alevis generally dwell in provinces located in central and eastern Anatolia. Kurdish/Zaza Alevis live in eastern Anatolian provinces such as the Malatya, Tunceli, Elazığ, and Bingöl Provinces. Arab Alevis are concentrated in the Hatay, Adana, and Mersin Provinces. Known as Nusayris, Arab Alevis trace their heritage to the Alawites of Syria (Stewart 2007; Massicard 2013; Oran 2021). Due to migration, a substantial number of Alevis also reside in major cities such as Istanbul, Ankara, and Izmir. We also see Alevi presence in several European coun-

---

1. The word Alevi means either "descendant of Ali" or "follower of Ali" (Çarkoğlu and Elçi 2018). Ali ibn Abi Talib (599–661) was the first imam and cousin, son-in-law, and companion of prophet Muhammad. Alevis consider Ali as the rightful and immediate successor to Muhammad. He ruled as the fourth caliph from 656 to 661.

tries such as Germany, England, the Netherlands, France, Austria, Switzerland, Belgium, and Sweden.[2]

According to the Treaty of Lausanne (July 1923), which is viewed as one of the founding documents of the Turkish Republic, the Turkish state recognizes only non-Muslim groups (i.e., Greeks, Armenians, and Jews) as official religious minorities.[3] This was due to the legacy of the Ottoman *millet system*. The notion of millet in the Ottoman Empire referred to religious communities. The Ottoman sociopolitical structure was composed of two main millets: the Muslim millet (*millet-i Islamiyye* or *millet-i Muslime*), as the dominant and ruling one (*millet-i hakime*) and the non-Muslim millet, as the dominated and ruled one (*millet-i mahkume*) (Oran 2021; see also İçduygu and Soner 2006; İçduygu, Toktas, and Soner 2008; Bayar 2014; Lord 2018). Thus, within the Ottoman millet system, non-Muslim groups were treated as religious minorities.

Such a sociopolitical tradition prevailed during the secular Republican period. Thus, similar to the Ottoman practices, the secular Turkish Republic embraced and promoted the majority religion (i.e., the Sunni version of Islam) and excluded Alevis from the list of officially recognized religious minorities. As Lord (2020, 6) notes:

> Despite the republic's ostensible secularity, the Ottoman legacies of the state incorporation of Islamic institutions, the emergence of religion as an ethnic marker and demographic Muslimization of the lands, resulted in the institutionalization of a Sunni Muslim majoritarian logic of operation of the state. . . . Nation-state building took the form of the construction and privileging of a Sunni Muslim Turkish majority as the basis of the nation and owners of the state with favored access to its resources (see also Shankland 2003; Bayir 2013; Massicard 2014; Lord 2017b and 2018; Oran 2021).

In brief, the Sunni-Muslim-Turkish identity has constituted the national and state identities in secular Republican Turkey (see also Çetinsaya 1999;

---

2. In the 1960s and 1970s, Alevi migration to Europe was primarily motivated by economic factors. Thus, in this first wave of migration, many Alevis migrated to Europe as guest workers. In the post-1980 period, however, we see mainly politically motivated Alevi migration to Europe. Hence, in this period, many Alevi asylum-seekers and political refugees have migrated to European countries. It is estimated that there are approximately two million Alevi migrants in several European countries (e.g., see Gedik, Birkalan-Gedik, and Madera 2020).

3. The full version of the treaty is available at https://wwi.lib.byu.edu/index.php/Treaty_of_Lausanne, accessed June 25, 2021.

Lord 2017b, 2018). Within such a framework, Alevi belief has been treated as a heterodox interpretation of Islam, departing from the mainstream Sunni Islam. As Hurd (2014, 417) observes:

> The Diyanet, as well as the Turkish Ministry of Education, which directly oversees religious education policy, both treat Alevism as a heterodox or "mystic" interpretation of Sunni Islam that departs from the mainstream. This precludes Alevi claims for legal privileges granted by the state to Sunni institutions and practices, while also denying to Alevis the privileges granted to officially recognized religious minorities, including Christians and Jews. Neither fish nor fowl, the Alevi exist in a kind of legal limbo.

Similarly, Dressler (2015, 448) notes that

> through the concept of heterodoxy Alevism was integrated into the abode of Islam, even if positioned at its edge. This was sufficient to situate the Alevis within the nation. It prevented them from becoming a "minority"—in the political discourse of Turkey a term that is reserved for the non-Muslims, who are as minorities understood to be outside of the national body.

As a result, avoiding officially recognizing Alevi belief as a distinct religious identity, the Turkish state has ignored or rejected Alevis' various religious and cultural demands such as official recognition of the Alevi faith and culture; equal opportunities in religious services and public employment; removal of compulsory courses on religion at public schools; and official acceptance of cemevis (Cem houses) as places of worship (ibadethane) (more discussion on cemevis later in the chapter).[4]

---

4. This study is primarily concerned with the role of nonstate, informal Cem courts in conflict resolution processes within the Alevi community. For more discussions on the Alevi community, various aspects of Alevi beliefs and teachings, and the evolution of Alevis' relations with the Turkish state, one might consult the following studies: Olsson, Özdalga and Raudvere 1998; Vorhoff 1998; Erman and Göker 2000; Sökefeld 2002; Shankland 2003; White and Jongerden 2003; Poyraz 2005; Şahin 2005; Erdemir 2007; Stewart 2007; Dressler 2008; van Rossum 2008; Özyurek 2009; Erol 2010; Tambar 2010; Soner and Şule 2011; Köse 2013; Massicard 2013, 2014; Şirin 2013; Issa 2017; Lord 2018; R. Yıldırım 2018; Aslan 2021.

Cem Courts

After providing some background information on the Alevi community in Turkey, we can now focus on the role of informal institutions in dispute resolution processes and practices within the Alevi community. To better illustrate the role of informal institutions in conflict resolution processes, it would be useful to start with comparing traditional Cem courts with state courts. Table 4.1 provides a summary of the comparison of these two types of courts. Although they share the same institutional logic and objective (i.e., peaceful conflict resolution and justice), there are substantial differences between the two institutions. To begin with, the third party (i.e., after the claimant and defendant) in formal state courts is a specialized, professional individual: a judge sanctioned by the central state. The judge is a public official, sanctioned and appointed by the government on the basis of a law degree and his or her experiences and achievements in the field of law. Authorized and paid by the state, a judge holds the legal responsibility and authority to hear cases in a court of law and decide upon them. The authority or legitimacy of state court derives from official law, passed by the legislature. Judges, who are assumed to be impartial and independent from the litigants, simply interpret and apply the relevant formal law (civil or common) to settle cases of dispute or conflict. The enforcement mechanisms of state courts are official and legal. Because judges' decisions are binding, a litigant who does not comply with court decisions faces formal, legal sanctions (e.g., a fine or imprisonment).

In the case of informal Cem courts, however, the third party is a community and religious leader who might personally know the disputants. This leader might act either as a mediator (i.e., facilitator) who provides assistance to the disputants in resolving their differences or as an arbitrator who decides on the case and imposes a mutually acceptable solution or agreement. The legitimacy of these courts originates from communal beliefs, traditions, and norms rather than from formal, official law (Turkish law does not really recognize such communal courts). Their rulings or decisions are enforced through informal communal and social mechanisms, such as naming and shaming (or social ostracism).[5]

---

5. According to DeMeritt (2012, 598), naming and shaming refers to "punishment by publicity designed to inflict 'reputational damage on moral grounds'" (see also Pejovich 1999, 166).

TABLE 4.1. A Comparison of Formal State Courts and Informal Cem Courts

Type of institution	Institutional logic	Shared expectations	Behavioral regularities	Source of legitimacy	Enforcement mechanisms
State courts					
Formal; officially recognized and regulated (de jure)	Peaceful conflict resolution, justice	Professional judges at formal courts (i.e., public officials acting as adjudicator) to resolve conflicts by applying the law to the cases of dispute	Applying formal state courts for conflict resolution	State; codified laws and norms	Official, legal sanctions
Cem courts					
Informal; no official recognition or regulation (de facto)	Peaceful conflict resolution, justice	Community/ religious leaders (acting as mediator or arbitrator) to resolve conflicts	Bringing disputes to the Cem congregation	Community beliefs, myths, traditions, and norms	Communal, social sanctions, such as naming and shaming, social exclusion

Because the role of formal judicial bodies in conflict resolution pro-cesses are well known (e.g., see Aubert 1967), this chapter focuses on the relatively less-known Cem courts. Empirical analyses of Cem courts are based on secondary literature about the Alevi community and original field data, derived from ethnographic research that I conducted in several prov-inces in Turkey. The field research involved semistructured, face-to-face, in-depth interviews with several *dedes* (i.e., Alevi religious leaders and scholars) and researchers (see appendix 4.A for a list of interviewees).[6]

Historically, dispute resolution through informal means and mecha-nisms was a common practice within the Alevi community in Turkey (see

---

6. To access the viewpoints of Alevi circles with different ethnic backgrounds, I con-ducted interviews in several provinces including Ankara, Çorum, Diyarbakır, Hatay, Kırıkkale, Nevşehir, Sivas, and Tunceli in 2013 and 2014. I used snowball sampling to identify useful informants. The informants greeted me with enthusiasm and, without any hesitation, agreed to talk to me. The interviews took place mostly at dedes' homes and lasted from 30 minutes to almost two hours. The interviews relied upon voluntary informed consent.

also Shankland 2003; A. Yıldırım 2013; R. Yıldırım 2018).[7] Shankland (2003, 95) notes that "*Alevilik*, in contrast to [Sunni understanding,] is court and religion rolled into one: a regulatory, mediating and reconciliatory function is present in almost every part of its doctrine and practice." Cem courts, the main conflict resolution channel within the Alevi community, can be understood as a kind of "communal forum" (van Rossum 2008) or "a community justice institution" (Hensler 2003; A. Yıldırım 2013; R. Yıldırım 2018) for settling disputes among members of the community. These informal courts are summoned at a Cem ceremony (*Ayin-i Cem*), the main Alevi ritual. A Cem is a religious gathering, a ritual prayer, and a congregational ceremony, attended by men, women, and children.[8] It involves the court, religious poems, songs (*deyiş, nefes*), dance (*semah*), prayers, and sometimes a communal meal (*lokma*) at the end (Shankland 2003; Balkız 2007; Hanoğlu 2017).[9]

The Cem ceremony is presided over by *dedes*, traditional religious scholars and leaders within the Alevi community.[10] Only certain individuals can become dede. A distinguished descent (*soy*) is an important requirement of *dedelik*, the office of the dede. Dedes are thought to descend from sacred lineages. They claim hereditary lineage to the relatives of Ali ibn Abi Talib (the cousin, companion, and son-in-law of the Prophet Muhammad). Hence, an Alevi dede is also known as a *seyyid* or *evlad-ı resul*, names that indicate descent from prophet Muhammad.[11] Dedes occupy an important place within an Alevi community. An individual who respects, honors, and

---

7. For a discussion of similar alternative dispute resolution practices in some other social settings, see Hensler 2003.

8. *Cem* ceremonies take different forms across Turkish and Arabic Alevis in Turkey. For instance, in the Arabic Alevi tradition, women and children do not participate in the *Cem* congregation.

9. The temporal frequency of the Cem congregation varies substantially depending on the context. For instance, in rural settings, Cems are sometimes held only twice or three times in a year. However, in urban neighborhoods, Cems are organized with a higher frequency (sometimes held every week).

10. *Dede* literally means "elder male" or "grandfather." Thus, most Alevi religious leaders and scholars are male. However, there are a few female religious leaders, known as *Ana* (mother).

11. The dede lineages are known as *ocak*, which literally means "hearth" and refers to a holy lineage, traced to prophet Muhammad as follows: Ali, the cousin of prophet Muhammad, was one of the first believers in Islam. He also married Fatima, the daughter of prophet Muhammad. It is believed that dedes descend from the lineage of the sons of Ali and Fatima (Dressler 2006, 272; R. Yıldırım 2018). Such an understanding suggests that the title of dede passes from one generation to another by patrilineage.

follows *dede* is known as a *talip* (follower, dependent, or student) (Shankland 2003; Şahin 2005; Stewart 2007; R. Yıldırım 2018). For *talips*, dedes are not only religious leaders but also teachers and judges. As Shankland (1998, 24) observes, "The *dedes* are rightly regarded as one of the keys to Alevi society: they are at once its focus, its teachers, temporal judges and links to their religious heritage" (see also Balkız 2007; Karakaya 2018; R. Yıldırım 2018). Hence, as spiritual and community leaders, dede represent ritual and social authority within the Alevi community. In other words, *dedelik* involves not only religious but also social leadership roles and functions (see also Sökefeld 2002; Shankland 2003; Dressler 2006, 272, and 2008, 295; Eş 2013; A. Yıldırım 2013; Karakaya 2018).

During *Cem* meetings, held either in the house of the dede or of a community member,[12] the *dede* observes and directs the rituals. Many dedes play the *bağlama* or *saz* (stringed musical instruments) and sing Alevi songs (also known as *nefes* or *deyiş*) during the Cem (see van Rossum 2008).[13] As indicated above, beyond religious functions, the Cem has major social functions, such as resolving disputes among members of the community (i.e., *talips*).[14] In other words, the Cem congregation also operates as an informal court. This function is so important that the Cem does not even start without first resolving the existing grievances or disputes among community members (Massicard 2013; A. Yıldırım 2013).[15] Therefore, it would be fair to conclude that the Cem constitutes the main mechanism of justice and social control within the Alevi community (see also R. Yıldırım 2018). All these suggest that, at the Cem, the dede not only acts as the leader of the congregation but also as a mediator and judge (Dressler 2006; Balkız 2007; Karakaya 2018).[16]

---

12. In rural settings, there were no particular buildings for Cem congregations. In cities, however, Alevis have built cemevis for this purpose (more discussion on this later in the chapter).

13. As the dede plays the *bağlama* (an eight-stringed instrument) and sings *nefes* or *deyiş*, participants perform *semah*, a ritual dance (considered a prayer).

14. All Cem ceremonies might have judicial functions. However, the one held specifically for judicial purposes is known as *görgü* or *görüm* (see Bozkurt 1998, 104; Shankland 2013; Stewart 2007, 53; A. Yıldırım 2013; R. Yıldırım 2018). It takes place annually, usually in the autumn. All the members of the community are tried in this particular type of Cem.

15. This point was emphasized by all of the interviewees.

16. Dedes might act as mediators or arbitrators at other times as well. Community members might directly approach the dede and ask for help with resolving disputes before or after the Cem congregation.

Based on the interviews with dedes in several provinces in Turkey, as well as through the analysis of secondary literature on the Alevi community, we can briefly describe the mediation and arbitration processes in a Cem. At the beginning of the Cem, the dede asks the congregation if there are any disputes or conflicts among members of the community. If a participant brings a problem forward and makes a claim against another (which might involve a wide range of issues, such as a debt, a quarrel, or a problem between husband and wife), the Cem congregation turns into a semireligious, informal court and the dede acts as an "arbitrator" to settle the dispute (a third party might also inform the dede about the presence of a dispute or conflict between or among members of the community). Then, as an informal dispute resolver, the dede asks the claimant and the defendant to step forward and come to the *dar* or *meydan* (i.e., the space or square in front of the dede). The *dar* is considered to be the sacred space or territory of Hak (Allah)-Muhammed-Ali, where Cem participants are supposed to speak only the truth (van Rossum 2008).[17] During the judicial hearing, the dede also allows participants in the audience to share their thoughts about the case. After hearing both the claimant and the defendant and consulting and deliberating with the community members present at the Cem, the dede verbally shares his thoughts and ruling. The claimant and the defendant are expected to accept the dede's ruling and reconcile their differences. At the very least, they are expected to promise to solve their problems as administered or advised by the dede. If they do not accept the ruling or fail to find an amicable and peaceful settlement at that moment, they are required to leave the Cem.[18]

During the Cem, disputes are resolved verbally and extralegally by the dede. Instead of applying formal state law, the dede basically follows community beliefs, norms, values, traditions (*erkan*), and common sense to settle the claimants' differences.[19] The hearing takes place in front of com-

---

17. This stage of the judicial hearing is also known as the *dara çekmek, dara çekilmek,* or *dara durmak* (A. Yıldırım 2013; author's interview with Hüseyin Gazi Metin).

18. According to Alevi beliefs, only community members who are at peace with one another are allowed to participate in the *Cem* congregation (Sökefeld 2002; Shankland 2003; Massicard 2013; A. Yıldırım 2013).

19. Turkey's Alevis do not have any established, formalized, or shared doctrine or liturgy. As Shankland (2003, 1) observes, the Alevi belief "has developed in rural Anatolia through hereditary holy figures [dedes], who transmitted esoteric religious thought through music, poetry and collective rituals" (see also Metin 1992; A. Yıldırım 2013). Thus, the Alevi belief system has been largely based on oral traditions (Çamuroğlu 1998; Vorhoff 1998).

munity members, which enables the dede to consult or deliberate with them. This format means that community members act like a jury and that the dede's advice, judgments, and rulings reflect the will of the community. In other words, the dede also utilizes social or communal pressure to encourage or force the disputants to reconcile their differences (Metin 1992; A. Yıldırım 2013; R. Yıldırım 2018).

Regarding enforcement mechanisms, because community members care about their moral standing and status within the community, they usually follow the rulings of the *Cem* court. Disputants who do not comply with the rulings or settlements imposed by the religious leader at Cem courts face social sanctions, such as being shamed within the community.[20] Deviance may also bring religious disgrace or opprobrium to that person because noncompliance is regarded as disrespect for the Alevi path (*Alevi yolu, erkanı*) and community (see also Metin 1992, 329; Shankland 2003; A. Yıldırım 2013, 57). For instance, the dede might declare that those who violate community norms (e.g., adultery, theft, and homicide) are fallen (*düşkün*), one of the most severe punishments (R. Yıldırım 2018). In that case, the fallen would be isolated from the community: they are banned from participating in religious ceremonies, not spoken to, or not allowed to work with others on daily tasks (i.e., a form of social ostracism). The community might even expel the fallen from the village or neighborhood for several years.[21]

The existing literature does provide several cases of informal dispute resolution by dedes and draws attention to the prevalence of dispute resolution through Cem courts among Alevis.[22] For instance, one *dede* maintained that "Alevis have rarely resorted to the state court. The Alevi community has had its own judicial system. Acting as a judge, dede has resolved disputes among Alevis" (quoted in A. Yıldırım 1991, 17). Similarly, another dede remarked that "up until today, the Alevi community has never taken its cases to the court! [For instance] . . . I have reconciled a man who had shot someone, and we never saw a court!" (quoted in van Rossum 2008, 10). The dedes that I interviewed also shared their own experiences as media-

---

20. Negative gossip, for instance, constitutes one major shaming mechanism (see also Ellickson 1986, 677).

21. Some other punishments include verbal warnings, shaming, community service, and economic restitution and fines. For further examples of cases of dispute and verdicts, see Metin 1992; A. Yıldırım 2013; R. Yıldırım 2018.

22. For further discussion and details about *Cem* courts, see Metin 1992; Shankland 2003; van Rossum 2008; A. Yıldırım 2013; R. Yıldırım 2018.

tors or arbitrators and narrated numerous cases of dispute resolution (recent cases as well as ones conducted a few decades ago). Their narratives show that trivial cases (e.g., about quarrels, business transactions, or family issues) as well as major disputes (e.g., blood feuds) are brought to the Cem congregation or directly to dedes.

We see similar informal institutional mechanisms of dispute resolution in other Alevi communities in Turkey, such as with Arab Alevis (who reside mostly in the Hatay region). Sheikhs among Arab Alevis play a third-party role of mediator or arbitrator, or both, and resolve various cases of disputes among community members.[23] Sheikh Ali Yeral, an Arab Alevi religious leader residing in Hatay, stated to the author that "Alevi people in this region rarely go to the police or to court. Quite a number of cases of disputes involving various issues such as financial and marital disputes are brought to the sheikh."

The above analyses confirm that informal justice mechanisms have been highly institutionalized within the Alevi community. We should, however, acknowledge that dispute settlement through informal means and mechanisms is not limited to Alevis. Informal dispute resolution practices and processes have also been present in several other communities in the Turkish context. For instance, Starr's (1978) legal ethnographic research in a rural local community in the Aegean region shows that villagers might utilize several informal procedures and mechanisms to settle their various disputes. In addition, the author's fieldwork among Kurdish *meles* in the southeast suggests that community mediation is a common practice among Sunni-Shafi Kurds as well (see also Wall, Beriker, and Wu 2010). *Meles* are Kurdish religious leaders and scholars who are highly respected within the Kurdish community. As informal, nonstate imams, most *meles* have received "unofficial" religious education and training at *madrasas*.[24] Similar to dedes, *meles* have religious and social roles within their communities. Acting as mediators or arbitrators, or both, they also settle disputes, including serious issues between tribes (such as honor crimes and blood feuds).[25]

---

23. Alevi religious leaders are known as dede among Turkish Alevis and as *sheikh* among Arab Alevis.

24. Madrasas were officially banned in May 1924 as part of the secularization reforms in the newly established secular Republic. However, many of them continued to operate informally and secretly, especially in the Kurdish southeast.

25. For further discussion on Islamic dispute resolution methods and processes, see Köse and Beriker 2012. We see similar informal courts in other national settings, such

Why Nonstate, Informal Courts?

These types of informal community justice raise some key questions. First, why do community members turn to informal means and mechanisms of conflict resolution (e.g., *Cem* courts) instead of resorting to formal court proceedings? Why do informal legal institutions emerge? There are couple of reasons for human agents to resort to informal means and mechanisms of conflict resolution. First, especially during the Ottoman era, formal state authorities and institutions were absent or weak, especially in remote rural areas (see also Bayir 2013; Massicard 2013; R. Yıldırım 2018). Hence, informal institutions (e.g., local customs, traditions, and codes, enforced outside of officially sanctioned channels) played substantial roles in rural social life. In other words, in remote rural areas, local communities developed self-governance structures and mechanisms.[26] In those autonomous local communities and tribes, informal institutions dominated almost all spheres of local life.

Second, and more important, as van Rossum (2008) notes, Alevis brought their disputes to the Cem because they distrusted formal state institutions (including judicial bodies). Van Rossum argues that, due to this skepticism, they preferred the "Alevi way" (i.e., Cem courts) to resolve their disputes. Indeed, it is the case that due to suppression and persecution under Ottoman rule (see Güneş-Ayata 1992; Metin 1992; Vorhoff 1998; Stewart 2007; Eş 2013; Üşenmez and Duman 2015; Hanoğlu 2017; Karagöz 2017; Çarkoğlu and Elçi 2018; Karakaya 2018; Karakaya-Stump 2018; Gedik, Birkalan-Gedik, and Madera 2020), Alevis used to live in isolated rural areas in the Anatolian mountains. In other words, they remained socially, politically, economically, and judicially marginal and peripheral for centuries under the Ottoman administration, which officially embraced the Hanefi school of Sunni Islamic jurisprudence (Sökefeld 2002; Poyraz 2005; Massicard 2013; Dressler 2015; Göner 2017; Karakaya 2018; R. Yıldırım 2018; Lord 2018, 2020; Oran 2021). As a result, instead of turning to Ottoman formal courts led by *kadı*—the official judges in provinces (*sanjaks*) and districts (*kazas*) who applied Islamic (*şeri*) and Ottoman customary (*örfi*) law—Alevis resolved their disputes at the informal communal

---

as *ronda* justice assemblies in rural Peru and the *juntas vecinales* in urban Bolivia (see Starn 1999; Van Cott 2006).

26. Self-governance systems and structures have been powerful in Chinese and Latin American rural life as well (see Hu 2007; Van Cott 2006).

courts during Cem meetings (see also Metin 1992; Dressler 2006, 273; Korkmaz 2008 van Rossum 2008; Massicard 2013; A. Yıldırım 2013; Karakaya 2018; R. Yıldırım 2018). As Massicard (2013, 16) notes:

> The marginal situation of the Kızılbaş [Alevi groups] has resulted in various institutions being set up to guarantee the survival of the group and its autonomy vis-à-vis the outside world. First among these are rules controlling the frontiers of the group: the inheritance of group membership, rites of passage such as ritual initiation, the dependence of the disciple on the master, endogamy, and the prohibition of divorce. Other institutions exist to ensure mutual support, such as those consecrating the "fraternisation" of two families such as kirvelik or musahiplik. These are accompanied by an autonomous judicial system in which a tribunal headed by religious dignitaries examines and settles all conflicts prior to the cem. The sanctions can range from the death penalty to monetary fines, and include corporal punishments. One of the severest sanctions, düşkünlük—exclusion from the group for a period of varying length—amounts to excommunication.

Several interviewees also emphasized that during Ottoman times, Alevis used to apply to dedes to settle their disputes. Those who resorted to kadı would be declared as düşkün (fallen).[27] Thus, marginalized by and rejecting the central authority, Alevis created their own informal, communal judicial system during the Ottoman period. They resolved their conflicts outside of official state courts through intracommunity settlement mechanisms, facilitated by religious leaders (i.e., dedes).

Interestingly, these practices and traditions were maintained after Turkey's transition to a secular Republic in the early 1920s. It is widely acknowledged that the secular nature of the newly established Republic was appealing to Alevis. As Shankland (2003, 156) notes, "[Secular Kemalism] offered them relief from persecution, whether real or supposed, a Republic within which they were promised full rights irrespective of their sect. . . . Some dedes even say that they love him [M. Kemal Atatürk, founding father of the Turkish Republic] as much as they love Mehdi, the twelfth, vanished imam, who is supposed to return one day to rule." Thus, Alevis embraced the secular Republic and provided substantial support for the Kemalist seculariza-

---

27. Author's interviews with dedes Hüseyin Gazi Metin, Dertli Divani, Haşim Demirhan, Cemal Mutler, Nurettin Aksoy, and Nesimi Öz.

tion and modernization reforms in the 1920s and 1930s (see also Metin 1992; Vorhoff 1998; Shankland 2003; Erdemir 2005; Poyraz 2005; Köse 2013; Bardakci et al. 2017; Karakaya-Stump 2018; Akgönül 2019).[28] However, despite increasing support of the central authority during the Republican period, informal Cem courts persisted. Why?

First, as noted above, state persecution and suppression of the Alevi religious minority did decline after the transition from the Ottoman Empire to the secular Republic in the early 1920s. However, similar to the Ottoman Empire, the Sunni Islamic identity colored the official understandings of state and national identities under the secular Republican regime (see also van Rossum 2008; Toktas and Aras 2009; Tasch 2010; Soner and Toktaş 2011; Massicard 2013; Üşenmez and Duman 2015; Bardakci et al. 2017; Beylunioğlu 2017; Issa 2017; Lord 2017a, 2017b, 2018; Karakaya 2018; Akgönül 2019; Gedik, Birkalan-Gedik, and Madera 2020; Oran 2021). For instance, in 1924, the secular Republican state established the Directorate of Religious Affairs (Diyanet İşleri Başkanlığı, or Diyanet) and authorized it to provide religious services, coordinate religious affairs, and manage places of worship (i.e., mosques). As the highest public religious authority in the country, the Diyanet embraced and promoted the Sunni interpretation of Islam (see also Gözaydın 2014; Massicard 2013; Hurd 2014; Göner 2017; Lord 2017b, 2018). Hence, it is fair to claim that, as the majority identity, Sunni Islamic identity has constituted the sociopolitical center during the Republican period as well (see also Shankland 2003; Bayir 2013; Wuthrich 2013; Bardakci et al. 2017; Çarkoğlu and Elçi 2018; Lord 2018). Widely known as a syncretistic and heterodox religious group (e.g., see Shankland 2003; Dressler 2015), Alevi identity naturally deviates from the normative center, wrought by Sunni Islamic teachings, understandings, and practices. As a result, Alevis have been subject to othering by the Republican state and the Sunni Muslim majority (see Shankland 2003; Bayir 2013; Üşenmez and Duman 2015; Bardakci et al. 2017; Çelik, Bilali, and Iqbal 2017; Issa 2017; Lord 2017a, 2017b, 2018; Karakaya 2018; Sarigil 2018b; Akgönül 2019; Gedik, Birkalan-Gedik, and Madera 2020). Consequently, prejudicial and exclusionary state and societal attitudes toward Alevi identity and groups persisted during the Republican period. As Karakaya-Stump (2018, 55–56) observes:

---

28. We see the persistence of such political orientations among Alevis in contemporary Turkey. For instance, empirical research shows that Alevis are more likely to vote for secular, left-oriented political parties (see Çarkoğlu 2005).

Despite their staunch support for Mustafa Kemal Atatürk's secularizing reforms, popular prejudice and institutionalized discrimination against them did not cease under the Republic, which, although formally secular, continued to promote Sunni-Hanafi Islam as normative through the well-funded Directorate of Religious Affairs. With limited exceptions depending on who was in power, Alevis have been excluded from tables of high authority. And especially since the 1970s, they have been treated as potential threats due to their close affiliation with leftist political currents that has given them a permanent place on the state's watch list. In the highly polarized atmosphere of the 1970s, hundreds of Alevis have been victims of mob violence perpetuated by right-wing militants, often with the tacit consent of the security forces.

Thus, Alevis' marginal and peripheral status endured within the Republican sociopolitical system (see also Soner and Toktaş 2011; Bayir 2013; Dressler 2015; Bardakci et al. 2017; Karagöz 2017; Karakaya 2018). Alevis' uneasy relations with the Turkish state and the privileged Sunni Muslim majority appear to have prolonged their general distance from the central state authorities and from the Sunni majority during the Republican era. The skeptical and cautious attitudes toward formal state agencies in return sustained the appeal of traditional informal means and mechanisms of dispute resolution within the largely rural Alevi minority during the initial decades of the Republic (see also R. Yıldırım 2018).

In addition to their distrust of state agencies and authorities, Alevis maintained informal *Cem* courts during the early Republic for some other reasons such as time and money. Litigation and trial in state courts are not without costs (Aubert 1967). Settling disputes through formal and legal proceedings not only requires money (e.g., lawyer fees, litigation expenses, travel expenses) but also time (i.e., due to the inefficiency of litigation in formal state courts in the Turkish setting) (see also Starr 1978; Wall, Beriker, and Wu 2010). Given limited financial resources in the rural lifestyle, the expensive and lengthy nature of lawsuits has discouraged many Alevis from taking legal action in state courts. Ellickson (1986, 686) observes the presence of similar dynamics in dispute resolution practices among rural landowners in Shasta County, California: "Because it is costly to carry out legal research and to engage in legal proceedings, a rational actor often has good reason to apply informal norms, not law, to evaluate the propriety of human behavior."

In sum, due to distrust of state institutions as well as the relatively more costly and inefficient nature of litigation, informal institutional means and mechanisms dominated dispute resolution practices within the rural Alevi community during the Ottoman and early Republican eras. In other words, we see both ideational (e.g., trust and legitimacy concerns about formal institutional rules and regulations) and material considerations (e.g., the inefficiency of formal arrangements) behind the appeal of informal Cem courts within the Alevi religious minority.[29]

Still an Option?

Another key question arises: To what extent do informal dispute resolution practices at the *Cem* persist within the Alevi community in contemporary Turkey? Several studies acknowledge that modernization processes (e.g., secularization, urbanization, and socioeconomic progress) have posed serious challenges to Alevi traditions and institutions (see Seufert 1997; Erman and Göker 2000; Dressler 2006; Stewart 2007; Massicard 2013; A, Yıldırım 2017; R. Yıldırım 2018; Lord 2020). For instance, Seufert (1997, 173) states that

> with the opening up of the closed parochial communities and the migration of their members to the big cities, the orally mediated and simple folk-beliefs of the Alevi are confronted by an outside world which cannot be integrated into their traditional religious parameters (see also Dressler 2006, 270).

The impact of urbanization on Alevi traditions and practices deserves particular attention. During the early Republican period, the vast majority of Turkish society lived in rural areas. As figure 4.1 indicates, until the 1950s, only one-fourth of the population lived in urban areas. Since then, however, there has been a steady increase in the urban population.[30] Alevis and Kurds, most of whom used to live in remote, rural areas in Anatolia, have constituted the major groups within this human flow into urban centers (especially into metropolitan cities such as Istanbul, Izmir, and Ankara)

---

29. Van Cott (2006) suggests that similar factors (i.e., legitimacy and efficiency concerns) played a similar role in the survival of indigenous legal systems in several Latin American countries.

30. This transition was partly because of agricultural mechanization and burgeoning industrialization in Turkey in the 1950s and 1960s.

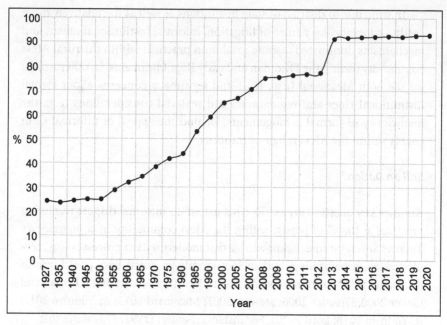

Figure 4.1. Urban Population in Turkey (1927–2020) (% of total)

(see also Güneş-Ayata 1992; Metin 1992; Bozkurt 1998; Çamuroğlu 1998; Sökefeld 2002; Poyraz 2005; Şahin 2005; Stewart 2007; Eş 2013; Massicard 2013; Karagöz 2017; Şentürk 2017; A. Yıldırım 2017; R. Yıldırım 2018; Oran 2021). As a result of this mass migration, Alevis, who used to be predominantly rural, became predominantly urban by the 1990s (Shankland 2003).

Urbanization has had a detrimental impact on the Cem, and has undermined its judicial functions. As Stewart (2007, 53) also notes, "as Alevis migrate to urban areas, living under the authority of state institutions, the *Görüm* [the Cem organized only for judicial purposes] faces a challenge to its legal primacy in Alevi culture." The transition to urban life reduced the effectiveness of informal institutional mechanisms of dispute resolution among Alevis in several ways. First, urbanization limited the effectiveness of nonstate courts by transforming traditional community structures, such as the *dedelik*, which has been one of the key social and religious institutions within the Alevi community. As Stewart (2007, 54) notes,

with the rise of [the] Alevi social network in major Turkish cities, several

Alevi journals began to emerge, laying a foundation for later political mobilization. Not surprisingly for an orally-transmitted religion, migration to the cities inevitably imposed new, urban forms of expression on *Alevilik*. When urban [Alevi] associations emerged that would supersede ancestral ties, the rigid hierarchy between *dede* and *talip* started to unravel.

Similarly, Dressler (2006, 270) observes that

in the course of the 20th century, however, the traditional community structures dissolved through secularization and urbanization. The rapid change contributed to a decline of the *dede*'s authority . . .

and that

the economically motivated exodus to the urban centers since the 1950s . . . often cut the regular personal interaction between *dedes* and their followers called *talibs* [sic], "students," and thus undermined the social fabric of traditional Alevism. (Dressler 2008, 285)[31]

My interviews with Alevi religious leaders also confirm that the influence of dedes within the Alevi community has declined with the migration to urban centers. All the dedes interviewed lamented the negative impact of urbanization on Alevi traditions and institutions. One dede, for instance, stated that "when Alevis migrated to cities, they had to leave their *dedes* and beliefs and traditions behind. As a result, the relations between *dedes* and *talips* were broken."[32] Thus, urbanization undermined the traditional authority of dedes and curbed their mediating functions. This, in return, reduced the appeal and effectiveness of *Cem* courts in the modern urban context.

Another mechanism through which urbanization undermined the role of informal *Cem* courts is related to the difficulties with ruling and enforcement in urban settings. Compared to the rural context, the urban context is less favorable for community mediation and arbitration, simply because of relatively higher informational costs. In small, rural communi-

---

31. See also Bozkurt 1998; Sökefeld 2002; Shankland 2003; Şahin 2005; Balkız 2007; Eş 2013.

32. Author's interview with dede Adiguzel Erbas. Many dedes interviewed by R. Yıldırım (2018) share the same observation.

ties, the dede is likely to know almost all members of the community. The dede is even expected to know all of his *talips* in person and develop personal relationships with them. Thus, in a rural setting, the *dede* has much better access to the information needed for resolving disputes. In the urban context, however, it is relatively more difficult to collect or access necessary information to make a sound and fair judgment or rulings, simply because the "*dede* does not necessarily know the [Cem] participants, which usually make up a random mix of Alevis from all sorts of different backgrounds" (Dressler 2006, 276; see also Metin 1992, 376; Bozkurt 1998; Eş 2013; Massicard 2013).

Regarding enforcement, the main tools of Cem courts have been social measures such as naming and shaming. Such mechanisms should be much more effective in small, rural communities. Why? The notion of "the shadow of the future" helps us answer this question. The existing studies show that this concept, which refers to the likelihood of interacting again in the future, facilitates cooperative behavior. It is argued that when the future casts a large enough shadow onto the present, cooperation based on reciprocity becomes more likely (see Axelrod 1984; Bo 2005). Using experimental evidence, Bo (2005, 1603) concludes that actors "cooperate more the greater the probability of future interaction [and] cooperate more in infinitely repeated games than in finitely repeated ones." Therefore, it is suggested that one way of promoting cooperation is to make interactions more durable and frequent (i.e., to enlarge or lengthen the shadow of the future) (Axelrod 1984). Compared to urban settings, rural settings are characterized by more durable and frequent interactions. For Axelrod (1984, 130), this is one reason why "cooperation emerges more readily in small towns than in large cities" (see also Knight 1992, 173–81). Thus, rural settings, with their relatively longer shadows of the future, provide more suitable environments for the emergence of cooperation based on reciprocity. This situation, in return, facilitates the enforcement of agreements or sanctions imposed by *Cem* courts.

Related to this notion, because people in small, rural communities are more likely to know one another, they care more about their individual or familial reputations and standings within the community (see also Ellickson 1986). Thus, the longer shadow of the future and stronger concern for reputation in small rural communities are key factors that facilitate the effective use of nonlegal, informal methods of dispute resolution. Compared to rural settings, urban settings have thus been less favorable for informal Cem courts. As Knight (1992, 181) also notes, "as the size of a community increases, the stability of informal rules is threatened by incentives for noncompliance."

We should also take into account the destructive impact of the leftist movement on Alevi community structures. It is well known that Turkish politics in the 1960s and 1970s was characterized by the rise of ideology politics (see Karpat 1973; Çarkoğlu 1998; Ozbudun 2000; Wuthrich 2015). Increasing ideological polarization and violence between the socialist left and the nationalist, conservative right led to major political turmoil in Turkey's urban settings at this time. The vast majority of Alevis migrating to cities in that period took sides with the socialist left (see also Güneş-Ayata 1992; Çamuroğlu 1998; Vorhoff 1998; Erman and Göker 2000; Shankland 2003; Şahin 2005; Dressler 2008, 285; Massicard 2013; Göner 2017; Karagöz 2017; Şentürk 2017; A. Yıldırım 2017; Çarkoğlu and Elçi 2018; Lord 2020). However, socialist leftist ideology, rooted in secularism and Marxism, has been critical of the status and role of traditional religious institutions and actors within society (e.g., dedes).[33] Thus, Alevis' involvement in the leftist political movement further decreased the prestige and status of dedes among urban Alevis. This factor, in return, reduced the appeal of Cem courts as the main mechanism of dispute settlement. Dressler notes that "with the younger Alevi generations turning to leftist ideologies in the 1960s and 70s, the *dedes*' authority was further damaged" (Dressler 2006, 274; see also Bozkurt 1998; Sökefeld 2002; Göner 2017; Şentürk 2017; A. Yıldırım 2017; R. Yıldırım 2018).

In sum, until the 1950s and 1960s, informal institutional means and mechanisms dominated dispute resolution practices within Turkey's Alevi community. Within the rural lifestyle, these informal mechanisms were much more effective and appealing than formal institutional mechanisms. In addition, due to the legacy of state suppression and persecution, particularly in Ottoman times, Alevis distrusted formal state institutions, which further limited the legitimacy of formal state courts among Alevis. Viewing formal courts as illegitimate and inefficient, members of the rural Alevi community resorted to informal Cem courts for conflict resolution. As a result, during the Ottoman and early Republican eras, Cem courts operated

---

33. Certain circles within leftist Alevi youth in the 1970s labeled dedes as "feudal exploiters" and "ignorant old men" (see Vorhoff 1998, 244; Massicard 2013, 30; also author's interviews with Ali Yaman and Veliyettin Ulusoy).

as superseding informal institutions. However, modernization processes, particularly urbanization and secularization, decreased the effectiveness of informal institutional means and mechanisms as they enhanced the use of litigation in formal state courts to resolve disputes. In other words, modernization processes led to informal institutional decay and so *Cem* courts fell into oblivion. A. Yıldırım (2017, 99) summarizes the destructive impact of modernization processes (especially urbanization) on Alevi traditions and institutions as follows:

> Another factor disrupting the traditional socio-religious order was interaction with the state apparatus. The intrusion of state agents as mediators and regulators in social, judicial, economic, and even religious (in a preventive sense) fields virtually relegated the principal institutions like the *dede*, *görgü, musahiplik* etc. . . . the order of the nation-sate disqualified Alevi institutions as social regulators and simply disbanded social control mechanisms. Likewise, *dedes* lost their central position as they left the authority of mediating disputes to the figures sanctioned by central government.

From Oblivion to Revival

Given the destructive impact of modernization processes on Alevi traditions and institutions, are informal Cem courts obsolete? Not really. In the post-1990 period, we see the rise of "identity politics" in the Turkish polity. The end of the Cold War and the collapse of the Communist bloc in the early 1990s reduced the role of ideological struggles in sociopolitical life in Turkey and paved the way for the rise of the Islamic and Kurdish movements. The replacement of class politics with surging identity politics also involved the reawakening or revival of the Alevi identity in Turkish sociopolitical landscape, also known as the "Alevi Renaissance" (see Kehl-Bodrogi, Heinkele, and Beaujean 1997; Olsson, Özdalga, and Raudvere 1998; Vorhoff 1998; Erman and Göker 2000; Sökefeld 2002; Shankland 2003; Erdemir 2005; Poyraz 2005; Şahin 2005; Dressler 2006; Dressler 2008, 939–40; Eş 2013; Massicard 2013; A. Yıldırım 2017; R. Yıldırım 2018; Karakaya-Stump 2018). As Dressler (2008, 286–287) observes,

> with religion having become a major point of reference for political identity formations, many Alevis, formerly aligned with the now largely dysfunctional left, began to assert Alevi identity within a universalistic human

rights discourse and secularist rhetoric of religious freedom and self-determination. Alevis now turned to their half-forgotten traditions, which they increasingly formulated in explicitly religious terms, thus to a certain extent appropriating the language of post-1980 Turkish identity politics. They began to forcefully confront Turkish society with their demands for recognition of Alevism as an identity significantly different from mainstream Sunni Islam. As a consequence, since the late 1980s, not only Turkey but also countries with significant numbers of Turkish migrants such as Germany witnessed reformulations of Alevism as a distinct worldview, way of life, cultural practice and religion.

In this era, the burgeoning urban, educated Alevi elite initiated several Alevi foundations, trusts, associations, federations, cultural festivals, publications, TV channels, radio stations, internet sites, and cemevis (Çamuroğlu 1998; Vorhoff 1998; Shankland 2003; Şahin 2005; Soner and Toktaş 2011; R. Yıldırım 2017, 2018; Çarkoğlu and Elçi 2018).[34] The Alevi revival since the early 1990s has also involved efforts to rediscover Alevi roots and traditions. As Erdemir (2005, 941) observes, increasing numbers of Alevis tried to "learn, claim, protect and preserve their traditions (*gelenekler*) and path (*yol*)" (see also Çamuroğlu 1998). As a result, Alevi traditions and institutions, such as Cem ceremonies, have flourished in urban settings in recent decades (Sökefeld 2002; Shankland 2003; Dressler 2006, 288; author's interview with Ali Yaman).[35]

In this period of Alevi revival, dedes have regained their prestige to a substantial degree. In the modern, urban context, however, dedes have been incorporated by Alevi associations, organizations, and foundations.[36] Integrated into civil society organizations in urban settings, dedes have also become more visible in Turkish print, visual, and cyber media.[37]

---

34. *Cemevi* literally means "house of gathering." Although they are places of worship for Turkey's Alevis, the Turkish state does not recognize them as religious sites (Eş 2013; Oran 2021).

35. Similar developments have been observed within the Alevi diaspora in Western Europe in the post-1980 period (see Sökefeld 2002).

36. Sökefeld (2002) defines such a transformation as a shift from "*dede*-centered Alevism" to "associational Alevism" (see also Massicard 2013).

37. Some dede are critical of their increasing numbers. Dede Adiguzel Erbas, for instance, lamented that "unfortunately, with the Alevi revival, we have seen an increasing number of dedes. Many Alevi individuals trace their roots to a holy lineage and claim to be a dede. The dede population has mushroomed in the last decades." Similarly,

As Dressler notes, "with the Alevi revival, the *dedes* gained new respect and were assigned an important function in reconnecting Alevism with its traditions" (Dressler 2008, 295; see also Vorhoff 1998). We see several initiatives of private courses or training programs by Alevi organizations in urban centers (e.g., Ankara, Istanbul, and Germany) to teach dedes how to better respond to the demands of the modern, urban Alevi community (Bozkurt 1998).[38]

The Alevi revival has also reinvigorated dedes' judicial functions within urban Alevi communities. In the last two decades, several cemevis have been built in Alevi neighborhoods in urban centers (Shankland 2003; Massicard 2013). According to Turkey's Ministry of Internal Affairs, as of January 2013, there were 937 cemevis among 50 provinces (out of 81).[39] The International Religious Freedom Report (2020) states that, by 2020, there were 2,500 to 3,000 cemevis in the country.[40] The vast majority of these cemevis have been built since the early 1990s (see Eş 2013), consistent with Cem congregations being organized with increasing frequency in urban settings (Sökefeld 2002; Erdemir 2005; Şahin 2005; Massicard 2013).[41] *Cemevis*, which are not formally recognized by the state as places of worship, operate as informal community centers and have religious, social, and cultural functions within urban Alevi neighborhoods (Sökefeld 2002; Shankland 2003; Balkız 2007; Massicard 2013; Hanoğlu 2017).[42] They are

---

Veliyettin Ulusoy, who is an important religious authority within the Alevi community, stated to the author that "unfortunately, we have a problem of dede inflation."

38. Also, author's interviews with Ali Balkız, Ali Yaman, Dertli Divani, and Veliyettin Ulusoy.

39. See "*Türkiye'de 82 bin 693 camiye karşılık 937 cemevi var*" (In Turkey, there are only 937 cemevis against 82,693 mosques). *T24*, March 15, 2013, https://t24.com.tr/haber/turkiyede-82-bin-693-camiye-karsilik-937-cem-evi-var,225770, accessed June 21, 2021.

40. The report is prepared by the US Department of the State: https://www.state.gov/wp-content/uploads/2021/05/240282-TURKEY-2020-INTERNATIONAL-RELI-GIOUS-FREEDOM-REPORT.pdf, accessed June 21, 2021.

41. Alevi migrants in Europe also established several cemevis in the urban centers of hosting countries. There are certain differences between the traditional, rural Cem and the modern, urban Cem. For a discussion of those differences, see Shankland 2003; Eş 2013; and Massicard 2013.

42. In Turkey, only mosques, churches, and synagogues are officially recognized as places of worship (*ibadethane*). Although the Turkish state does not recognize cemevis as places of worship, municipal councils in certain provinces such as Adana, Ankara, Antalya, Aydın, Eskişehir, Hatay, İstanbul, İzmir, Malatya, Mersin, Muğla, and Tunceli have recognized cemevis as places of worship and exempted those religious sites from

venues for religious activities such as Cem ceremonies, feasts, and funerals, as well as for various cultural and social activities such as conferences, lectures, and special courses for community members (e.g., music, dance, theater, painting, and sports) (Balkız 2007, 40–42; Eş 2013; Massicard 2013). We also see that, beginning in the 1990s, more cemevis were built in villages (R. Yıldırım 2018). As acknowledged above, the Cem congregation is not held without a dede and it only begins once any disputes among community members have been resolved. Hence, the above-noted developments suggest that as religious leaders of Alevi communities, dedes have resumed their traditional roles in settling disputes. As A. Yıldırım (2017, 110) notes, "By the 2000s, cemevis and cem ceremonies became more and more conspicuous venues for Alevi revivalism in cities; cemevis have been replacing Alevi associations as loci of urban Alevism. By the same token, the influence of the dedes, as 'hubs' of Alevi knowledge and community leaders, has steadily increased." Several interviewees also indicated that with the increasing number of cemevis built in cities, urban Alevis are again taking their various cases of disputes to Cem courts or directly to a dede.[43]

But what about the challenges of community mediation in urban settings (i.e., the difficulties with ruling and enforcement)? As indicated above, the Alevi migration to cities since the 1950s and 1960s has gradually led to the formation of Alevi communities in urban areas (see Güneş-Ayata 1992). More importantly, civil society organizations have built cemevis in several of these Alevi neighborhoods in the last decades. Eş (2013, 41) underscores that, in the urban context, Alevism has been "reinstitutionalized through cemevis." Urban cemevis, which function as informal community centers and organizations in Alevi neighborhoods, provide an environment for more durable and frequent interactions among community members. This, in return, lengthens the shadow of the future and moderates the information costs. It also contributes to enforcement by abating the difficulties of monitoring compliance. Thus, operating as community centers in urban areas, cemevis moderate the problems of information and cooperation and contribute to community mediation within the urban Alevi community.

In brief, the Alevi revival and the increasing number of cemevis in urban centers since the early 1990s have facilitated dedes' renewed roles as

certain utility costs.
43. As indicated by interviewees Cemal Mutluer, Huseyin Gazi Metin, Nurettin Aksoy, Sultan Ana, and Veliyettin Ulusoy.

mediators and arbitrators in conflict resolution within urban Alevi communities. Thus, in recent decades, the traditional, rural, and informal mechanisms of dispute resolution have reappeared in new forms in the modern, urban context. Through cemevis, informal Cem courts were transferred to urban settings in the post-1990 period and refashioned. However, compared to the Ottoman and early Republican eras, contemporary Cem courts in urban settings operate in parallel to the formal institutional means and mechanisms of dispute resolution, which are based on secular law. In other words, in the contemporary era, Cem courts function as a complementary informal institution rather than as a superseding one.

Conclusions and Implications

Historically, community mediation and arbitration have been highly institutionalized within Turkey's Alevi community through informal Cem courts, which convened at Cem congregations. In other words, Cem courts have been an important informal justice system within the Alevi religious minority. Modernization processes (e.g., urbanization and secularization), however, challenged traditional Alevi practices and institutions and weakened community mediation among Alevis. As Sökefeld (2002, 165) observes, "Alevism experienced a collective amnesia particularly between the years 1950 and 1990." However, the Alevi Renaissance, or the Alevi Revival, in the post-1990 period has revitalized Alevi traditions and institutions, including informal institutional means and mechanisms of conflict resolution. To put it in institutional terms, the deinstitutionalization process due to modernization (e.g., migration to urban centers) was replaced with reinstitutionalization when civil society organizations built increasing number of cemevis in cities in the post-1990 period.

One might postulate that decreases in the efficiency and legitimacy of formal state courts are likely to empower informal means and mechanisms of dispute resolution within the Alevi community. There have been heated political controversies and debates over the judiciary in Turkey in the last two decades. The existing scholarly studies of the Turkish judiciary suggest that, until 2010, the main problem was the judicialization of politics (aka *juristocracy, judicial tutelage, judicial activism*), which refers to the expansion of the power and influence of the courts and judges at the expense of politicians or administrators (see Belge 2006; Shambayati and Kirdis 2009;

Tezcur 2009). However, since 2010, the judiciary has suffered from another problem: the politicization of the judiciary (i.e., the increasing control and influence of the government over the judiciary). It is argued that increasing executive control over the judiciary has undermined judicial independence and impartiality in the country (see Ozbudun 2015 and 2016). For instance, according to the World Economic Forum's international ranking of judicial independence, Turkey was ranked 50th (out of 125 countries) in 2007, but 103rd (out of 137 countries) in 2018.[44] It is also observed that there are several internal problems in the judiciary, such as prolonged court cases and contradictory rulings on similar court files. As one would expect, all these judicial problems have undermined or weakened public trust in the judiciary. For instance, according to a nationwide survey conducted in late 2013 and early 2014, only 26.5% of respondents expressed confidence in the judiciary.[45] Decreases in public support of and trust in formal mechanisms of dispute resolution are likely to encourage individuals to resort to informal means and mechanisms of conflict resolution (such as community mediation). This reasoning is also very much valid for informal *Cem* courts.

The case of informal Cem courts has several theoretical implications for the role of informal institutions in sociopolitical life. First, this particular case confirms that other than formal state law, informal community law might play significant roles in dispute resolution processes. Thus, the case of Cem courts becomes relevant to research on the notion of "legal pluralism," which simply refers to the existence of more than one legal order or system in a particular social field. Legal pluralism assumes that, beyond the formal state law, there might be several other forms of law in a given social domain. Using the words of Griffiths (1986, 38), "Legal pluralism is an attribute of a social field and not of 'law' or of a 'legal system.' . . . It is when in a social field more than one source of 'law,'

---

44. Full reports are available at http://reports.weforum.org/global-competitiveness-report-2018/, accessed June 28, 2021.

45. See *"Khas 2013 Türkiye Sosyal ve Siyasal Eğilimler Araştırması"* (Khas 2013 research on social and political orientations in Turkey), May 2, 2014, https://www.khas.edu.tr/khas-2013-turkiye-sosyal-siyasal-egilimler-arastirmasi-sonuclari-aciklandi/, accessed June 28, 2021. Other public opinion surveys also identify a low level of trust in the judiciary in Turkey. See for instance, *"Yargı Bağımsızlığı ve Yargıya Güven Araştırması Raporu"* (A research report on judicial independence and confidence in the judiciary), the Social Democracy Foundation (([Sosyal Demokrasi Vakfı, SODEV), June 14, 2019, http://sodev.org.tr/sodev-yargi-bagimsizligi-ve-yargiya-guven-arastirmasi-raporu-aciklandi/, accessed June 28, 2021.

more than one 'legal order,' is observable, that the social order of that field can be said to exhibit legal pluralism."[46] From this perspective, as an interesting case of informal dispute resolution mechanism within the Alevi religious minority in Turkey, *Cem* courts constitute a typical case of legal pluralism (see also van Rossum 2008).

A further implication is that excluded, marginalized, and peripheral groups, in particular, are likely to view the existing formal arrangements as illegitimate and detrimental to their interests. As disadvantaged groups with limited resources, they are usually unable to alter those undesirable formal rules and regulations. Under such circumstances, these groups are likely to resort to informal means and mechanisms to solve particular collective problems or to meet certain group needs, and thus will design multifarious, complex informal institutions. These relatively more legitimate and efficient informal arrangements might operate quite effectively, superseding the existing formal rules and regulations.

Moreover, as the case of Cem courts indicates, shifts in demographic, political, and economic structures and conditions might undermine the strength and influence of informal institutions, resulting in informal institutional decay or exhaustion. However, the same case also suggests that depleted or exhausted informal institutions might be rediscovered and go on to have an informal institutional revival. Such changes would, of course, alter the interplay between formal and informal institutions and consequently the type of informal institutions. As detailed above, modernization processes (e.g., urbanization, secularization) weakened Cem courts and so they lost their status as a superseding informal institution. In the post-1990 era, however, these courts have been revived among Alevi communities in urban settings; but, in this era, they have been operating as complementary informal institutions. The revival of informal Cem courts as a mechanism of dispute resolution within urban Alevi communities in the last decades was not a result of a major decline in the strength of formal state courts. Thus, this particular case also corroborates that the existence of strong and effective formal institutions is not an obstruction to the emergence or revival of informal institutional arrangements. Actors might simply view informal arrangements as more legitimate and appropriate than their formal counterparts and turn to those informal means and mechanisms.

46. For more on the concept of legal pluralism, see, for instance, Griffiths 1986; Merry 1988; and Tamanaha 2021.

This case study of Cem courts also suggests that even if modern, secular, and formal law does not recognize traditional religious institutions, such informal institutions might coexist with formal ones, playing a substantial role in sociopolitical processes (see also Erdemir 2005; Köse and Beriker 2012; Eş 2013). This view implies that "modern" institutions do not necessarily replace "traditional" institutions; rather, traditional, informal institutions might reappear in new forms or shapes in modern times and settings and operate in parallel to modern formal structures (see also Vorhoff 1998; Van Cott 2006; Radnitz 2011).

Additionally, religion and religious institutions are often considered to justify and fuel conflict and violence. The case of *Cem* courts, however, suggests that rather than being part of the problem, religious actors and institutions might operate as part of the solution and play a positive role in conflict resolution processes (e.g., preventing the escalation of conflict and peacefully managing and resolving disputes among community members) (see also Ury 1999; Moix 2006).

Appendix 4.A. A List of Interviewees (Cem Courts, Informal Conflict Resolution)

No.	Name and Surname	Job/Position	Date	Location
1	Züheyla Gülen (aka Zöhre Ana)	*Ana*	January 3, 2014	Ankara
2	Mehmet Ali Alpay	Dede	January 4, 2014	Ankara
3	Murteza Şirin	Dede	January 4, 2014	Ankara
4	Cemal Mutluer	Dede	July 4, 2014	Ankara
5	Veli Aykut (aka Dertli Divani)	Dede	July 23, 2014	Ankara
6	Adıgüzel Erbaş	Dede	July 12, 2014	Çorum
7	Nurettin Aksoy	Dede	July 12, 2014	Çorum
8	Sultan Kümbet (aka Sultan Ana)	*Ana*	July 12, 2014	Çorum
9	Ali Yeral	Sheikh, Ahl al-Bayt Culture and Solidarity Foundation (EHDAV)	October 14, 2013	Hatay
10	Hasan Yeral	Sheikh	October 14, 2013	Hatay
11	Hasan Eskiocak	Sheikh	October 15, 2013	Hatay (Harbiye)
12	Nasreddin Eskiocak	Sheikh	October 15, 2013	Hatay (Harbiye)
13	Haşim Demirhan	Dede	July 18, 2014	Kırıkkale (Hasandede)
14	Veliyettin Ulusoy	Head (*Postnişin*) of the Convent of Hacı Bektaş Veli	July 18, 2014	Nevşehir
15	Derviş Aslandoğan	Dede	June 8, 2014	Sivas (Divriği, Höbek)
16	Hüseyin Gazi Metin	Dede	June 10, 2014	Sivas (Divriği, Şahin)
17	Zeycan Koçuk	*Ana*	August 4, 2013	Tunceli (Ovacık)
18	Zeynel Batar	Dede	August 4, 2013	Tunceli (Ovacık)
19	Ahmet Yurt	Dede	August 5, 2013	Tunceli (Hozat)
20	Ali Ekber Yurt	Dede, Tunceli Cem House	August 5, 2013	Tunceli
21	Nesimi Öz	Dede, Tunceli Cem House	June 4, 2019	Tunceli
22	Zahit Çiftkuran	*Mele* (mullah); Chairperson of the Association for the Solidarity of Imams (DIAYDER)	January 28, 2014	Diyarbakır
23	Abdullah Hadi Koç	*Mele*, DIAYDER	January 28, 2014	Diyarbakır
24	Tayyip Elçi	*Mele*, Foundation for Madrasa Scholars (Medrese Alimleri Vakfı, MEDAV)	June 10, 2019	Diyarbakır
25	Ali Yaman	Assoc. Prof., Abant Izzet Baysal University	May 10, 2014	Diyarbakır
26	Ali Yıldırım	Activist, Lawyer	January 22, 2014	Ankara
27	Ali Balkız	Activist, Former Chair of Pir Sultan Abdal Association	July 7, 2014	Ankara

CHAPTER 5

A Layered Informal Institution

Religious Minority Holidays in Turkey

This chapter explicates the notion of a layered informal institution, focusing on the key features of this type of informal institution and how it operates in sociopolitical life. As presented in the theoretical chapter, because layered informal institutions have a logic or rationale that diverges from the logic of the existing formal institutions, there may be tensions or frictions between layered informal institutions and the existing formal arrangements. However, these types of informal institutions do not operate in contentious or destructive ways. Rather, they operate informally in parallel to extant formal arrangements. Religious minority holidays in the Turkish context constitute an illustrative example of layered informal institutions.

In line with the conceptual discussion presented in the introduction, this chapter treats religious holidays as a case of an institution. Holidays are defined as "days on which custom or the law dictates a suspension of general business activity in order to commemorate or celebrate a particular event" (Etzioni 2004, 6). Thus, based on certain beliefs, norms, values, and practices, holidays have regulative, normative, and cultural-cognitive aspects. As an institution, holidays present certain incentives or disincentives (ideational or material, or both) for individuals, and thus they mold individual behavior.

In many national settings, while certain religious or national holidays are officially recognized and celebrated, many others, especially the ones celebrated and observed by ethnic and religious minority groups, operate in an informal domain. Thus, the case of minority holidays (religious or national) provides us with a good opportunity to gain novel insights into the role of informal institutions in sociopolitical life and into the way they interact with formal counterparts. The existing literature offers several studies that analyze the role of officially recognized public holidays (national or religious) in Turkish sociopolitical life (e.g., see Öztürkmen 2001; Roy 2006; Zencirci 2012; Acikalin and Kilic 2017; Solomonovich 2021). However, we do not have much scholarly analysis on minority holidays, which operate in an informal domain of the Turkish sociopolitical landscape.[1] Thus, this chapter advances our understanding of religious minority holidays in a Muslim-majority setting and of the notion of a layered informal institution.

Regarding data sources, the chapter benefits from 21 in-depth interviews with religious leaders and representatives of civil society organizations of religious minority groups (i.e., Muslim minorities such as Alevis and non-Muslim minorities such as Christians), official documents and reports, press statements, and newspapers. The interviews were conducted in Diyarbakir, Hatay, İstanbul, İzmir, Mardin, and Tunceli Provinces during the period of March–July 2019 (for a list of interviews, see appendix 5.A).

To better contextualize the case of religious minority holidays in the Turkish context, the following section provides some background information on the status of religious minority groups in the Turkish sociopolitical setting and the evolving state attitude toward those groups. The next section explains how the Turkish state officially regulates religious holidays. After presenting the formal rules and regulations of religious holidays, the chapter describes the main holidays informally observed by religious minority groups (Muslim and Christian) in Turkey. This section also discusses state attitudes and policy toward those minority holidays. The concluding section discusses the broad implications of the case of religious minority holidays in the Turkish context.

Religious Minorities in Turkey

To begin with, because Sunni Islam constitutes the religious majority in the Turkish context, any other religious group, such as non-Muslim communities (i.e., Greeks, Armenians, and Jews), and Muslim groups, such as Alevi communities, constitute religious minorities in the Turkish context. However, as presented in chapter 4, the Turkish Republic adopted a very narrow

---

1. For some exceptions, see Cinar 2001; Yanik 2006; Hintz and Quatrini 2021.

official definition of minority. The Turkish political elites rejected any notion of minority that was based on ethnic or linguistic differences. Instead, state officials embraced a definition of minority based on religious affiliation and recognized only certain non-Muslim religious groups (Greeks, Armenians, and Jews) as official minorities. The state granted these groups some minority rights and freedoms, such as the right to establish and manage foundations, charity organizations, religious and educational institutions, and linguistic rights, such as publishing, broadcasting, speaking, and educating in their mother tongue (see also İçduygu and Soner 2006; Ucarlar 2009; Oran 2011, 2021; Kaya 2013; Kizilkan-Kisacik 2013; Bayar 2014). Interestingly, the section of the Lausanne Treaty (July 1923) assigned to the protection of minorities (Articles 37–45), does not refer to any specific minority group. Therefore, the term "non-Muslims" used in that section should encompass all non-Muslim religious communities, including Assyrians, Chaldeans, Catholics, and Protestants (see also Grigoriadis 2012; Akgönül 2019; Oran 2021). However, Turkish political elites limited the notion of minority to Armenians, Greeks, and Jews and excluded other non-Muslim religious groups, non-Turkish Muslim ethnic groups (e.g., Kurds, Laz, and Arabs), and non-Sunni Muslim religious groups (e.g., Alevis) from the official definition of minority. Thus, in the official Turkish understanding, the notion of minority is limited to certain non-Muslim religious groups living in the country (see also Toktaş 2006; Yıldız 2007; Toktas and Aras 2009; Bayar 2014; Bardakci et al. 2017; Oran 2021). As a result of this state attitude and policy, the Turkish sociopolitical landscape involves both formal/legal (i.e., non-Muslims) and unofficial/unrecognized (e.g., Alevis and Kurds) minority groups. Because chapter 4 provides introductory information about the Alevi community in Turkey, the following section focuses on non-Muslim religious minorities in the country. This section also briefly presents the Turkish state's attitudes and policies toward these religious groups during the Republican period.

Non-Muslim Religious Minorities

The Ottoman Empire had a highly heterogeneous social structure that included multiple religious, ethnic, and linguistic groups and communities. Non-Muslims constituted around 19–20% of the Ottoman population before World War I (1914–18) (see Shaw 1978; Karpat 1985; Içduygu, Toktas, and Soner 2008). However, due to the deportation and emigration of non-Muslim groups and the inflow of Muslim population from former Ottoman lands (e.g., the Balkans and the Caucasus) to Eastern Thrace and Anatolia in the following years, the non-Muslim population declined substantially (Içduygu, Toktas, and Soner 2008; Oran 2021). Thus, when the empire collapsed at the end of the World War I, non-Muslims constituted around 15% of the total population. The Turkish War of Independence (1919–22) followed the dissolution of the empire; the Turkish Republic was established in the aftermath of this independence war. Due to further emigration during and population exchanges in the aftermath of the independence war, the non-Muslim population declined to 2.5% (Içduygu, Toktas, and Soner 2008; Lord 2018). In the following decades, we see further emigration of non-Muslim groups from Turkey. As a result, in contemporary Turkey, non-Muslims amount to only 0.1% of the total population (Lord 2018; Oran 2021).

The major non-Muslim religious groups are Armenians, Jews, and Greeks.[2] There are around 70,000 Armenians in the country and almost all of them live in Istanbul. Outside Istanbul, there is also a small Armenian community in Hatay Province. The vast majority of Armenians are Orthodox Christians (Oran 2021). In terms of the Jewish community, there were around 82,000 Jews during the initial years of the Turkish Republic. However, due to emigration (especially to Israel after its establishment in 1948) their population has declined substantially.[3] Currently, there are around 20,000 Jews in the country and most of them live in the İstanbul, İzmir, and Hatay Provinces (Oran 2021). Regarding Greeks, during and after the Turkish Independence War (1919–22), around one and half million Greeks left Anatolia to settle in Greece (Grigoriadis 2021). In addition, as required by the 1923–27 Population Exchange Agreement between Turkey and Greece, close to 200,000 Greek Orthodox people were forced to move to Greece.[4] In the following decades, due to the discriminatory and repressive sociopolitical environment and declining relations between Turkey and Greece, an

---

2. There are also several smaller non-Muslim religious communities in Turkey, such as Arab Orthodox Christians, Syriacs (Süryani), Bahaists, Yezidis (Ezidis), Protestants, Jehovah's Witnesses, and Levantines (see Oran 2021).

3. During the period from 1948 to 1951, around 40% of Turkish Jews migrated to Israel (Içduygu, Toktas, and Soner 2008, 374).

4. This population exchange between Turkey and Greece was based on religious affiliation. Accordingly, native Orthodox Christian peoples of Turkey, including many Christian Turks, were sent to Greece. In return, Turkey received both Turkish and Greek-speaking Muslims.

increasing number of Greeks left the country (Içduygu, Toktas, and Soner 2008; Oran 2021). Currently, there are around 2,500 Greeks living in Turkey, and they are concentrated in the İstanbul, İzmir, Çanakkale (Gökçeada and Bozcaada), and Hatay Provinces. The majority of Greeks are Orthodox Christians, and their religious leader is the Greek Orthodox Patriarchate, located in Istanbul.

State Attitudes toward Non-Muslim Minorities

In general, the Turkish state attitude toward non-Muslim groups has been shaped by the security-oriented approach (see also Toktas and Aras 2009; Soner 2010; Bardakci et al. 2017; Oran 2021).[5] Although the Turkish state officially recognized some non-Muslim groups as religious minorities and granted them certain religious, cultural, and educational rights, the state has had a skeptical attitude toward non-Muslim communities and their demands. Viewed as "others," "aliens," "local foreigners," "untrustworthy," "ungrateful," "the agents of foreign powers," and "potential threat for national unity and security," their loyalty and reliability were questioned (see Grigoriadis 2012, 2021; Bayir 2013; Bottoni 2013; Bayar 2014; Bardakci et al. 2017; Beylunioğlu 2017; Bouquet 2017; Lord 2018; Akgönül 2019; Oran 2021). As Içduygu, Toktas, and Soner (2008, 359) also observe,

> in the Turkish context, since Islam has been a constitutive element of the Turkish identity and nation, and being Turkish has often been equated with being Muslim . . . the nation-building process has fostered a kind of homogenization which, in practice, pointed to the demographic Islamization of the population. Non-Muslim minorities, despite their formal citizenship status, were not accepted as natural members of the Turkish nation but have remained as "others" in the Turkish-Muslim nation.

---

5. Certain historical factors appear to have led to the securitization of non-Muslim groups by the Turkish state. For instance, it is a historical fact that the autonomy enjoyed by the Ottoman Empire's religious minorities was exploited by the Great Powers. The Great Powers tried to justify their intervention into the empire's internal affairs by claiming that it was their duty to protect non-Muslim religious communities residing in Ottoman territories (see also Bottoni 2013). Furthermore, nationalist movements and revolts by many Christian groups (e.g., Greeks, Bulgarians, and Serbs) against the Ottoman rule during the 19th century accelerated Ottoman decline and disintegration. Such historical factors appear to have boosted the skeptical attitude toward non-Muslim groups in Turkish sociopolitical life.

As a result of the securitization of minorities and minority rights, the Turkish state did not hesitate to adopt restrictive and discriminatory policies and measures against these religious minorities. Some specific examples would be useful to better illustrate the Turkish state's exclusionary and discriminatory attitudes toward non-Muslim communities. For instance, as part of Turkification policies, the state supported a campaign called "Citizen! Speak Turkish" that was initiated by the students of Istanbul University in the late 1920s. This campaign was aimed at discouraging the use of languages other than Turkish in public realms (Aslan 2007; İçduygu, Toktas, and Soner 2008). Such an initiative was against the Treaty of Lausanne, which had recognized and secured the linguistic rights of non-Muslim minorities. In line with the 1924 Constitution, the Law on Civil Servants (1926) (Law No. 788) defined "being a Turk" (rather than "being a Turkish citizen") as the primary requirement for being able to serve as a civil servant. Thus, this law excluded non-Muslim citizens from the public sector (İçduygu and Soner 2006; Oran 2021). The Law on Capital Tax (Varlık Vergisi) (Law No. 4305), introduced during World War II (November 1942), constitutes another illustrative example of discriminatory attitudes and measures toward non-Muslims. In force for two years, this law was motivated by the intention to provide necessary resources for wartime spending and to prevent profiteering during the Second World War. However, the law was implemented in a highly discriminatory way: non-Muslim citizens were forced to pay much higher taxes (at least two times higher) than Muslims. To pay the tax, many non-Muslim citizens had to sell off their private properties.[6] Hence, it is claimed that, with this unequal and excessive tax, a substantial amount of capital was transferred from non-Muslim minorities to the Muslim majority (İçduygu, Toktas, and Soner 2008; Grigoriadis 2012, 2021; Bayir 2013; Oran 2021). Another interesting initiative that confirms the state's skeptical attitude toward minority groups is that, in 1962, the Turkish state established the Sub-Commission on Minorities. The commission, which included members from the National Security Council, the Office of the Chief of Staff, and the National Intelligence Organization, was authorized to monitor the activities of minority groups in the country (see also Bardakci et al. 2017).[7]

---

6. Those who failed to pay the tax were sent to labor camps in various places, such as Sivrihisar (Eskişehir), Yozgat, and Aşkale (Erzurum) (İçduygu and Soner 2006; Toktas and Aras 2009; Grigoriadis 2012; Bayir 2013; Oran 2021).

7. As part of Europeanization reforms, this commission was removed in 2004.

The state also took measures to limit the property rights of non-Muslim foundations. For instance, in 1974 the Court of Cassation ruled that corporate bodies of foreigners (referring to non-Muslim Turkish citizens' foundations) could not acquire immovable property. Then, the Turkish government decided to recognize only the list of real estate declared by non-Muslim foundations in 1936.[8] In other words, the properties of non-Muslim foundations were limited to what they had declared in 1936, and thus the properties acquired by these foundations between 1936 and 1974 were considered unlawful. As a result, they were either confiscated by the state or returned to the inheritors of those who had donated them (Grigoriadis 2008, 2021; Içduygu, Toktas, and Soner 2008; Toktas and Aras 2009; Soner 2010; Oran 2021).

As well as being subject to such restrictive and discriminatory state policies and measures, non-Muslim groups have been targeted occasionally by physical attacks by mobs or crowds. For instance, in July 1934 mobs incited by nationalist and racist propaganda verbally and physically attacked Jews living in various provinces of the Thrace (Içduygu, Toktas, and Soner 2008; Bayir 2013). After this incident, many Jews migrated to the Middle East, Europe, and the US. A further example of physical attacks are the events of September 6–7, 1955. Instigated by the Cyprus crisis between Turkey and Greece, crowds attacked Greeks and their properties, religious sites, and businesses in Istanbul.[9] More than a dozen people were killed during the September 6–7 events. Some Jews and Armenians were also targeted by the mob. In the aftermath of this pogrom against the Greek community in Istanbul, a substantial number of Greeks emigrated to Greece. When the Cyprus conflict escalated in the 1960s and 1970s, more Greeks had to move to Greece. In 1964, using citizenship regulations as an excuse, the Turkish government obliged more than 10,000 Greeks to leave Turkey for Greece (see Içduygu, Toktas, and Soner 2008; Grigoriadis 2012; Bardakci et al. 2017; Akgönül 2019).

Violence against non-Muslims has also involved attacks against clergymen, journalists, and writers. For instance, in 2006 a Catholic priest, Andrea Santoro, was murdered in Trabzon Province; in July 2006, Pierre Brunissen, the priest of the Italian Catholic Church in Samsun Province, was attacked

---

8. The 1935 Law on Foundations had required non-Muslim foundations to submit a list of their immovable properties (*beyanname*).

9. The attacks were triggered by rumors that M. Kemal Ataturk's house of birth in Salonica had been bombed (Bayir 2013; Oran 2021).

and wounded; in January 2007, Hrant Dink (the founder and editor-in-chief of *Agos*),[10] a journalist and writer of Armenian origin, was assassinated in Istanbul; in April 2007, Protestant missionaries in Malatya were killed; in December 2007, Adriano Francini, the priest of the Saint Antoine Church in İzmir, was attacked and wounded; and in June 2010 a Catholic priest, Luigi Padovese, was killed in the Iskenderun district of Hatay Province.

We should also acknowledge that, primarily due to EU accession conditions and requirements[11] and certain rulings of the European Court of Human Rights against Turkey, the Turkish governments took some steps in the 2000s to improve the rights and freedoms of non-Muslim communities (İçduygu and Soner 2006; Toktaş 2006; Yıldız 2007; Grigoriadis 2008, 2012, 2021; Toktas and Aras 2009; Soner 2010; Kaya 2013; Yılmaz 2016; Bardakci et al. 2017; Beylunioğlu 2017; Akgönül 2019; Kılınç 2019; Aslan 2021; Oran 2021). For instance, amendments to the Law on Religious Foundations in 2002 and 2003 allowed the foundations of non-Muslim religious minorities to acquire and dispose of property (Içduygu, Toktas, and Soner 2008; Soner 2010; Bayir 2013; Oran 2021). In 2008, a new Law on Foundations (Law No. 5737) entered into force. This law facilitated the acquisition and management of property owned by non-Muslim foundations. As another notable improvement, non-Muslim communities were allowed to open new places of worship, churches, and synagogues (Soner 2010). Furthermore, the Turkish government supported the renovation of many churches, synagogues, and religious sites in several cities and provinces, such as Ayvalık (Balıkesir), Diyarbakır, Edirne, Gaziantep, Gökçeada/İmroz (Çanakkale), Hatay, İstanbul, and Van (see also Grigoriadis 2021).

Official Regulation of Religious Holidays in Turkey

The existing studies acknowledge that national and religious public holidays might play important roles in national identity formation and nation

---

10. *Agos* is an Armenian bilingual newspaper published in Istanbul.

11. According to the Copenhagen Criteria, which were approved by the European Union in 1993 as the membership criteria, candidate countries are required to respect and protect their minorities. They are also required to achieve the stability of institutions guaranteeing democracy, the rule of law, human rights, and a functioning market economy. In 1999, the EU officially recognized Turkey as a candidate country for EU membership. This decision triggered an unprecedented reform process in Turkey in the early 2000s (e.g., see Tocci 2005; Sarigil 2007; Kaya 2013; Kızılkan-Kısacık 2013; Özdemir and Sarigil 2015).

building processes (e.g., see Çınar 2001; Guss 2001; Etzioni and Bloom 2004; Fuller 2004; Yanik 2006; McCrone and McPherson 2009; Adams 2010; Podeh 2011; Fox 2014; Qasmi 2017; Hintz and Quatrini 2021). Because public holidays are special occasions on which members of a particular nation come together around shared beliefs, values, norms, and traditions, such special days help reaffirm and reinforce the ideational and symbolic components of that nationality (Etzioni 2004, 8). Public holidays boost bonds and cohesion among the members of a nation and so reassert and reinforce national attachments and identities (Fox 2013). As McCrone and McPherson (2009, 8) also assert, national holidays "tell us much about who we are and who we want to be in national terms, as well as who is included and who excluded. National days are important commemorative devices which shed light on how national identity is imagined, shaped and mobilised." Hence, the religious holidays a given country officially recognizes and celebrates reveal not only state attitudes toward religious beliefs and groups but also national and state identity in that particular national setting. This observation is valid for the Turkish nation-state as well (e.g., see Özyürek 2006).

Table 5.1 presents a summary of key features of the official regulation of religious holidays and religious minority holidays in the Turkish setting. When we look at the formal rules and regulations, we see that the Turkish state recognizes only Sunni Islamic holidays (i.e., the Festival of Breaking the Fast, Eid al-Fitr, and the Feast of the Sacrifice, Eid al-Adha) as nationwide official religious holidays.[12] In other words, statutory religious holidays in Turkey are based on the dominant religious culture and identity in the country (i.e., Sunni Islam). Therefore, formal institutional arrangements reflect a majoritarian and monistic logic. The official recognition of only Sunni Islamic religious holidays indicates that, in official understandings and narratives, the Turkish national identity is associated with Sunni Islam. In other words, formal arrangements indicate that, as the majority religion, Sunni Islam constitutes the Turkish national identity, and thus it enjoys a privileged status within the Turkish sociopolitical landscape (see also Içduygu, Toktas, and Soner 2008; Tasch 2010; Bayir 2013; Bayar 2014; Lord 2017b, 2018, 2020; Oran 2021). Such official attitudes and understandings suggest that there is not much room for religious diversity and pluralism in

---

12. See the Law on National and Religious Holidays (Law No. 2429) (Ulusal Bayram ve Genel Tatiller Hakkında Kanun, Kanun No. 2429), https://www.mevzuat.gov.tr/MevzuatMetin/1.5.2429.pdf, accessed January 3, 2022.

TABLE 5.1. Formal Regulation of Religious Holidays and Religious Minority Holidays in Turkey

Type of institution	Institutional logic	Shared expectations	Behavioral regularities	Sources of legitimacy	Enforcement mechanisms
Religious majoritarianism					
Formal, officially embraced and recognized (de jure statutory)	Religious monism, majority belief and culture (i.e., Sunni Islam)	Official religious holidays to be based on Sunni Islamic beliefs	Nationally observing the Festival of Breaking the Fast and the Feast of the Sacrifice	State agencies, codified laws, and beliefs and norms of Sunni Islamic majority	Official, legal sanctions by formal courts
Religious minority holidays					
Informal, no official recognition and regulation (de facto)	Religious diversity and pluralism, minority beliefs and cultures	Various religious minority holidays to be observed and celebrated as well	Religious minority groups informally observing and celebrating their holidays	Beliefs, norms and traditions of respective religious minority group	Communal and social, such as naming and shaming, social exclusion

the formal domain. In other words, de jure arrangements construct and present a highly monolithic and homogenous religious field in the country, constituted and dominated by the majority religion (i.e., Sunni Islam). This implies that, although religious diversity and pluralism is a reality of the Turkish social landscape, formal institutional logic denies or ignores that reality.

Because Sunni Islamic religious holidays are formally recognized and sanctioned, they are enforced through official and legal mechanisms. For instance, it is a legal requirement that during state-sanctioned religious holidays, public businesses in the country must be closed in the observance of those holidays. Private businesses are also expected to follow formal rules and regulations. For instance, if a non-Muslim person runs a private business with Muslim employees, she or he has to allow Muslim employees to have those days off.

Because only religious holidays of the Sunni Muslim majority are officially recognized and sanctioned, the holidays observed and celebrated by religious minority groups (i.e., non-Muslims such as Christians and Muslims such as Alevis) have an informal, de facto status in the country. Although the Turkish state officially recognizes non-Muslim groups as minorities, their religious holidays are not formally recognized. This is also valid for Alevis, who are not even officially recognized. Therefore, Muslim and non-Muslim religious minority groups in Turkey informally observe and celebrate their holidays. In other words, since formal, legal regulations have excluded religious minority holidays, they exist only in the informal domain. Otherwise stated, religious minority holidays continue to function or operate in the informal sphere. By reflecting the beliefs, norms, and traditions of religious minority groups, those holidays display a much more diverse and pluralist religious field in the country. Regarding enforcement mechanisms, because they are not statutory, those religious holidays are enforced through communal and social mechanisms such as naming and shaming and social exclusion (see below).

Religious Minority Holidays in Turkey

This section briefly presents the major holidays observed by religious minority groups in Turkey (i.e., Christmas and Easter holidays celebrated by non-Muslim religious groups; the Day of Ashura celebrated by Turkish and Kurdish Alevi circles, and Gadir Hum celebrated by Arab Alevis) and the state attitude toward those minority holidays and rituals.

Non-Muslim Minority Holidays (Christmas and Easter)

The most important religious holidays among Christians in Turkey are the Christmas and Easter holidays. Christmas refers to the annual religious festival commemorating the birth of Jesus. While Catholic and Protestant Christians observe it on December 25, Orthodox circles observe it in early January. As another important religious holiday observed by Turkish Christians, Easter commemorates the resurrection of Jesus from the dead and it is observed in March and April.

Because these religious holidays are not officially recognized, when they overlap with a workday, non-Muslim employees or students who would like the day off must ask for a leave of absence. Interviewees emphasized that it is at the discretion of employers or school principals to allow non-Muslim employees or students to take the day off. The respondents added that they are usually allowed to take a leave of absence. However, some interviewees also noted that they sometimes face difficulties or problems when they want to take time off during their religious holidays. For instance, although public school' principals let their Christian students take these days off, the missed days are deducted from his or her right to an absence.[13] Non-Muslim civil servants might be required to use their annual leave to have the day off, or they might be forced to take a medical leave or compassionate leave. Despite these difficulties, it would be fair to conclude that such demands by non-Muslim employees or students are usually accommodated, but, of course, informally and at the discretion of relevant authorities.[14]

Is there any demand for formal recognition? The vast majority of the interviewees called for official recognition of their major religious holidays.[15] Some of them argued that this issue must be treated or understood as a matter of basic citizenship rights. For instance, Ayhan Gürkan, a priest at Mor Barsaumo Church (a Syriac Orthodox church in Midyat), stated to the author that "if I am a citizen of this country, the state should recognize my religious holidays because it is my basic citizenship right. . . . This is valid for the holidays of all minority groups. The state should respect their religious holidays. This is also a necessity of secularism principle." Similarly, Fadi Hurigil, the head of the Foundation of the Antioch Orthodox Church, stated:

> We do not consider ourselves as minorities or aliens. Actually, as autochthonous people, we are also the owners of these lands. We just have a different faith. . . . Besides, we are also citizens of the Turkish Republic. We also pay tax, do military service, and work for this country. . . . Thus, we should be able to enjoy the same rights that others [Muslims] enjoy. . . . If Muslims' religious holidays are officially recognized, then non-Muslim citizens' religious holidays, at least their most important holidays, should be an official holiday. This would certainly empower non-Muslims' feeling of belonging and attachment to the state.[16]

---

13. This is not an issue at private religious minority schools because those schools are usually closed during major religious holidays.

14. Author's interviews with Cem Çapar, Dimitri Doğum, Domenico Bertogli, Fadi Hurigil, Gabriel Akyuz, George Kacamonğlu, Nikola Dinç, and Tatul Avuşyan.

15. Some respondents stated that those holidays might be recognized as local holidays rather than as national holidays. For instance, it is suggested that in provinces with a substantial number of non-Muslims, local government officials (e.g., governors) might allow administrative leave for non-Muslim public employees and students during their religious holidays.

16. Similar ideas were expressed by several other interviewees, such as Gaffur Türkay, George Kocamanoğlu, Yusuf Akbulut, and Antonious Duma.

Muslim Minority Holidays (Day of Ashura and Gadir Hum)

With respect to the major religious holidays celebrated by Muslim minority groups, we might include the Day of Ashura, observed primarily by Turkish and Kurdish Alevis (who constitute around 15–25% of the Turkish population), and Gadir Hum, commemorated mainly by Arab Alevis (who comprise around 1.2% of the national population). Although Ramadan, the ninth month of the Islamic lunar calendar, is the holy month for the Sunni Muslim majority and many Sunni Muslims practice fasting from dawn to sunset during that month, the month of Muharram, the first month of the Islamic calendar, is relatively more significant in Turkish and Kurdish Alevi circles. Many Alevis fast for twelve days during the month of Muharram to commemorate and mourn the Twelve Imams (aka the fast of the Twelve Imams) (Hanoğlu 2017). The Day of Ashura (Aşure Günü)[17] is observed on the tenth day of the month of Muharram; on that day, Alevi circles in Turkey mourn the martyrdom of Husayn ibn Ali, a grandson of the Islamic prophet Muhammad, in 680 at Karbala. At the end of fasting, on the thirteenth day of Muharram, a feast is organized for family or community members[18] and a Cem congregation is held.

Gadir Hum, on the other hand, is celebrated primarily by the Arab Alevi community. There are little more than one million Arab Alevis (aka Nusayri) in Turkey, and they mostly reside in southern cities such as Adana, Mersin, and Hatay (see also Oran 2021). The holiday takes place on the eighteenth day of the twelfth and last month of the Islamic calendar (i.e., the month of Zu al-Hijjah, the Month of the Pilgrimage). During the Gadir Hum holiday, Arab Alevis commemorate Islamic prophet Muhammad's appointment of Ali ibn Abi Talib (his cousin and son-in-law) as his successor and the first Imam at Gadir Hum (aka Ghadir Khumm), an area between Mecca and Medina in Saudi Arabia, while he was returning from his last pilgrimage in 632. It is the most important religious holiday for Arab Alevis, and they do not work during that day.[19] Interviewees emphasized that many Arab Alevis consider working during the Gadir Hum holiday as a sin.

---

17. Ashura means the "tenth" in Arabic, and it refers to the tenth day of the month of Muharram.

18. This holiday feast involves traditions and practices such as sacrificing an animal and organizing a meal for family members, relatives, and neighbors and preparing *ashoura*, a wheat pudding with dried nuts and fruits.

19. Interviews during author's fieldwork in Hatay also confirm this point (e.g., author's interviews with Ali Yeral, Nasreddin Eskiocak, and Ali Mansuroglu).

Thus, if it coincides with a workday, private businesses and shops are closed; many students do not go to school; and civil servants request time off for the holiday or they work for half the day. Similar to Turkish Alevis, Arab Alevis also organize feasts for family and community members and Cem congregations during the Gadir Hum holiday.

As is the case with non-Muslims, Alevi civil servants and students might request a day off during their religious holidays. Interviewees noted that supervisors and school principals usually accommodate such demands.[20] Similar to non-Muslim communities, both Turkish and Arab Alevis also express their demand for formal, official recognition of their faith, culture, and institutions, including their most important religious holidays.[21] For instance, in the last decade, several civil society organizations of Arab Alevis[22] have organized conferences, meetings, petition campaigns, and press statements to express their demand for formal recognition of the Gadir Hum holiday. Turkish Alevi civil society organizations also articulate their demand for official recognition of the Day of Ashura.[23]

We also see some efforts and initiatives in the national parliament for legalizing Alevi religious holidays like Gadir Hum. For example, Tülay Hatimoğlulları Oruç, a deputy from the Peoples' Democratic Party (Halkların Demokratik Partisi) representing Adana Province and originally from Hatay Province, submitted a bill of law to the parliament in August 2018. By proposing an amendment to the law on national holidays (Law No. 2429), the draft law aimed at defining Gadir Hum as an official religious holiday. She also submitted multiple parliamentary questions inquiring about the government's position on Arab Alevis' demand for the official recognition of the Gadir Hum holiday.[24] Such attempts and initiatives, however, have (so far) failed to produce any change in state attitude.

---

20. Authors interviews with Ali Ekber Yurt, Nesimi Öz, Ali Yeral, Ali Mansuroğlu, and Nasreddin Eskiocak.

21. Author's interviews with Ali Ekber Yurt, Nesimi Öz, Zeynel Batar, and Ali Yeral.

22. Some of them were as follows: the Foundation for Ahl al-bayt Culture and Solidarity (Ehlibeyt Kültür ve Dayanışma Vakfı), the Association for Researching Alevi Culture (Alevi Kültürünü Araştırma Derneği), the Association for the Solidarity of Arab Alevis (Arap Halkı Alevileri Dayanışma Derneği), and the Association for Mediterranean Culture and Solidarity (Akdeniz Kültür ve Dayanışma Derneği).

23. See for instance, "Alevi kurumları: Aşure Günü resmi tatil olsun" [Alevi organizations want the Day of Ashura to be recognized as a public holiday], Hürriyet, August 16, 2016, https://www.hurriyet.com.tr/gundem/alevi-kurumlari-asure-gunu-resmi-tatil-olsun-40196110, accessed January 5, 2022.

24. Some other deputies from the region, for instance Serkan Topal and Mehmet Güzelmansur from the People's Republican Party (Cumhuriyet Halk Partisi, CHP) also raised similar demands.

It is important to acknowledge that Muslim and non-Muslim minority groups do not question the state's formal recognition of only Sunni Islamic religious holidays. Many non-Sunni Muslim groups also observe and celebrate those official holidays and abide by the formal rules regulating them. For instance, Nesimi Öz, an Alevi dede from the Tunceli cemevi, emphasized that they also observe and celebrate both the Eid-al-Fitr and Eid al-Adha holidays and follow various holiday traditions such as visiting relatives and organizing feasts for family members. He added that during those holidays, they also organize a large communal feast at the Tunceli cemevi. Non-Muslim interviewees emphasized that they happily accept the invitations of public officials (e.g., the office of mufti in provinces and districts) to join and celebrate Sunni Muslim holidays. Furthermore, because Sunni Muslim holidays are official national holidays, all the members of Muslim and non-Muslim religious minorities who work or attend school are also entitled to a vacation during those statutory holidays. Otherwise stated, religious minority groups also enjoy any benefits associated with those officially recognized religious holidays.

However, religious minority groups are critical of the nonrecognition of any religious holiday other than Sunni Islamic holidays. Thus, they consider the restrictive and exclusionary nature of formal institutions as inappropriate and unjust. In other words, in the eyes of religious minority groups, the existing formal arrangements of religious holidays, which are based on majoritarian and monistic logic, have limited legitimacy and approval. This particular case indicates that even if formal institutions do not directly damage or undermine the interests of social groups, those formal arrangements may still lack social approval and legitimacy.

State Attitudes toward Religious Minority Holidays: De Facto Recognition and Accommodation

What has been the state attitude and policy toward those informal religious minority holidays? Although several Muslim-majority countries (such as Iraq, Syria, Jordan, Lebanon, Egypt, Sudan, Chad, Niger, Mali, and Indonesia) officially recognize major Christian holidays such as Christmas and Easter, Turkey has not officially recognized Christian holidays. As noted above, Sunni Islamic religious holidays remain as the only statutory religious holidays in the country.

Even if the Turkish state has not formally recognized religious holidays celebrated and observed by Muslim and non-Muslim minority groups in the country, the state did not suppress or prohibit them either. In other words, formal arrangements neither acknowledge religious minority holidays nor prohibit those traditions and practices. Rather, government and state officials and dignitaries (e.g., president, ministers, and deputies at the national level; governors, mayors, and muftis at the provincial and district levels) have been *informally* celebrating the religious holidays of non-Muslims by making press statements, visiting minority religious sites and leaders during their holidays, and attending their celebrations. In other words, despite the absence of formal codification and recognition, state officials and political elites at national and local levels have been informally acknowledging and celebrating minority groups' religious holidays.[25] Some interviewees indicated that the state's informal recognition and celebration of religious minority holidays was triggered by EU reforms in the early 2000s.[26]

In terms of Alevi religious holidays, it is interesting that certain countries with a substantial number of Alevi migrants from Turkey officially recognize Alevi religious holidays. Alevi migrant communities in several European countries have achieved major rights and freedoms in the last decades (see also Özyürek 2009; Massicard 2013; Gedik, Birkalan-Gedik, and Madera 2020; Lord 2020). For instance, some European countries (e.g., Germany, the United Kingdom, Austria, Switzerland, and Denmark) have formally recognized Alevilik as a distinct religious faith and culture and so granted Alevi communities several rights and freedoms. The gains and achievements of Alevi migrants in Europe include the following:

> i) official recognition as a distinct belief group; ii) teaching of Alevism in schools and universities since the 2000s; iii) recognition of *Cemevis* (Cem Houses) as places of worship; iv) legal right for Alevi *dedes* (community elders with religious authority) to conduct marriages; v) legal allowance for Alevi cemeteries; vi) the right to collect taxes or allocate percentage of taxes toward Alevi faith organizations; vii) official recognition of Alevi sacred days as public holidays; viii) official recognition of Alevi faith leaders; and ix) the right for Alevi organizations to deliver religious services in hospitals, student residences, prisons, and police education centers. (Lord 2020, 15)

---

25. Author's interviews with Cem Çapar, Dimitri Doğum, Domenico Bertogli, Fadi Hurigil, George Kocamanoğlu, Tatul Avuşyan, Yakup Chang, and Antonios Duma.
26. Author's interviews with Fadi Hurigil and George Kocamanoğlu.

Thus, as a direct result of the official recognition of Alevilik as a religious faith and culture, Alevi migrants' religious holidays were formally recognized in several European countries. This suggests that Alevi workers and students in those countries (especially in several federal states in Germany) can take a leave of absence during their major religious holidays (e.g., the Day of Ashura).

However, in ironic contrast to several European countries hosting Alevi migrants from Turkey, the Turkish state has avoided de jure recognition of Alevis as a religious community and cemevis as a place of worship. Instead, Turkish authorities have preferred de facto recognition of Alevi faith and culture (see also Soner and Toktaş 2011; Massicard 2013). For instance, in the post-1980 period, government officials and dignitaries have been attending major Alevi religious festivals (e.g., Hacı Bektaş Veli Festival) and holiday celebrations, and visiting cemevis and attending Cem congregations in various provinces. As a case in point, since 2008, the leaders of the ruling conservative AKP have hosted *iftars* (evening meals that breaks the daily fast) during the month of Muharram. We see *iftars* being organized at the local level as well. For instance, the governors of Tunceli, a province with a substantial Alevi population, have been hosting *iftars* at Tunceli cemevi for Alevi community members.[27] Interviewees in Hatay noted that national and local political elites, such as ministers, deputies, governors, and mayors, have made congratulatory addresses and participating in the celebrations of Gadir Hum holiday in the last few decades.[28] The Turkish governments have also provided financial support for certain Alevi organizations, Alevi festivals and publications, and cultural activities organized by Alevi civil society organizations (Massicard 2013, 2014; Lord 2018).

One interesting attempt at dialogue and rapprochement between the Turkish state and the Alevi minority is the famous Alevi Initiative or Alevi Opening, launched by the conservative AKP government in 2009. This unprecedented initiative was a significant development in state-Alevi relations because government officials publicly met with Alevi circles to determine and accommodate their claims and demands.[29] The initiative

---

27. Author's interviews with Ali Ekber Yurt and Nesimi Öz.

28. Author's interviews with Ali Yeral, Ali Mansuroglu, and Nasreddin Eskiocak.

29. It is suggested that EU pressure and European Court of Human Rights decisions against Turkey were among the major factors that encouraged or forced the conservative AKP government to come up with such an initiative for the Alevi religious minority in the country (e.g., see Massicard 2013; Bardakci et al. 2017; Göner 2017; Gedik, Birkalan-Gedik, and Madera 2020).

involved seven workshops between June 2009 and January 2010 and hundreds of people with various backgrounds (e.g., representatives of civil-society organizations, academics, public opinion leaders, theology specialists, writers, intellectuals, artists, bureaucrats, and politicians) participated in those workshops.[30] At the end of the workshops, a report was prepared and submitted to the Office of Prime Ministry in March 2011. The report recommended various measures to meet Alevi demands, such as converting Diyanet into an independent body to represent various interpretations of Islam, removing compulsory religious courses from the national education curriculum, granting official status to cemevis as Alevis' places of worship, allocating public funds to all places of worship, educating and employing Alevi religious leaders (i.e., dedes), and establishing a research institute on Alevilik.

However, other than some symbolic and cosmetic steps (e.g., confiscating the Madımak Hotel in Sivas[31] and converting it into a Centre for Science and Culture, renaming Nevşehir University as Nevşehir Hacı Bektaş Veli University,[32] broadcasting publicly about Alevi faith and culture during the month of Muharram, and slightly modifying the curriculum of compulsory courses on religion), this rapprochement attempt failed to produce any substantial improvement (see also Soner and Toktaş 2011; Massicard 2014; Özkul 2015; Üşenmez and Duman 2015; Borovali and Boyraz 2015; Bardakci et al. 2017; Lord 2017a; Çarkoğlu and Elçi 2018; Karakaya-Stump 2018).[33] In 2022, the conservative AKP govern-

---

30. Having strong distrust and skeptical attitudes toward the conservative AKP government, many Alevi groups rejected participating in those workshops (Soner and Toktaş 2011; Lord 2017a; Çarkoğlu and Elçi 2018).

31. Madimak Hotel reminds Alevis of a highly tragic event. In July 1993, 37 people, most of whom were Alevi intellectuals, were killed at the Madimak Hotel in Sivas. The victims had gathered in the hotel to attend an Alevi religious festival. A conservative mob, after attending Friday prayers, attacked the hotel and set the building on fire. It was finally confiscated in 2011 and converted into a center for science and culture. The center has a corner devoted to those who were killed during the arson.

32. The main motivation behind this change was to honor Hacı Bektaş Veli (1209–71), a historically important figure for Alevi-Bektaşi circles.

33. Possible reasons for the failure of this initiative are as follows: the dominance of Sunni Islam within the Turkish sociopolitical landscape (e.g., Diyanet's strong opposition to formal recognition of the Alevi faith); AKP's conservative ideology, with limited room for religious beliefs and traditions other than Sunni-Hanefi Islam; and AKP's electoral calculations and concerns (i.e., the possibility of offending Sunni-Hanefi supporters and low expectation of Alevi support in return for the reforms) (see also Soner and

ment took a new step to accommodate certain Alevi demands. The government decided to establish a new public agency within the Ministry of Culture and Tourism to coordinate Alevi places of worship (i.e., cemevis) and also to conduct research about Alevi-Bektashi culture in Turkey. This new agency is named as the Directorate for Alevi-Bektashi Culture and Cemevis (Alevi-Bektaşi Kültür ve Cemevi Başkanlığı). As part of this new initiative, the state will also pay for the utilities of cemevis such as water and electricity expenses. However, many Alevi circles responded conservative government's this new initiative with harsh criticisms. They claimed that the initiative proved that the state treats Alevi minority as a cultural community rather than as a religious community. Thus, despite such unprecedented and bold initiatives, the Turkish state has avoided official, legal recognition of Alevi faith and institutions, and so has failed to accommodate Alevis' major religious needs and demands.

Given that Turkey differs from many European and Muslim-majority countries in terms of formal recognition of religious minority holidays, one might raise the following question: Why do we see informal/de facto recognition and accommodation but not formal/de jure recognition of religious minority holidays in Turkey? It appears that there are both ideational/symbolic and security-related concerns and calculations behind such state behavior. Regarding the formal recognition of the beliefs, practices, and institutions of Muslim religious minority groups (e.g., Alevis), as acknowledged above, similar to the Ottoman Empire, the Sunni-Hanefi version of Islam has shaped national and state identity during the Republican period. Given the fact that the Republican Turkish state embraced and promoted Sunni Islam and that Sunni Muslims constitute the majority in Turkish society, Sunni Islam has enjoyed dominant and privileged status within the Turkish sociopolitical landscape (Lord 2017b, 2018). As a result, many conservative Sunni Muslim circles consider the legal recognition of Alevi belief and institutions a threat to the privileged and dominant status of Sunni Islamic beliefs, norms, and values.

Related to this, those who oppose official recognition of Alevi religious belief, culture, and institutions assert that such an action would lead to divisions within Islam. For instance, claiming that Alevism should be understood as a particular interpretation of Islam, the Diyanet has subsumed

Toktaş 2011; Borovali and Boyraz 2015; Üşenmez and Duman 2015; Bardakci et al. 2017; Lord 2017a; Çarkoğlu and Elçi 2018).

Alevism under Islam, especially since the early 1980s (Lord 2017b, 2018). As a result, Diyanet officials strongly oppose the official recognition of Alevi belief as a distinct religious conviction and identity (see also Massicard 2013; Hurd 2014; Lord 2017b, 2018; Çarkoğlu and Elçi 2018). Believing that the mosque is the only legitimate place of worship in Islam, officials from the Diyanet assert that granting official status to cemevis as places of worship would undermine Islamic unity. For example, Mehmet Görmez, former head of the Diyanet, objected to the official recognition of cemevis as places of worship:

> We have always had two red lines and we have never abandoned them. The first is the definition of Alevism as a path outside Islam, which contradicts 1,000 years of history. The second is defining cemevis as alternatives to mosques as a place of worship.[34]

In terms of non-Muslim religious minority groups, as presented above, the Turkish state officially recognized the existence of religious minority groups (i.e., Armenians, Greeks, and Jews) and granted them certain rights. However, their religious holidays are not formally recognized. National security and survival concerns appear to shape policy toward non-Muslim religious minority groups. As noted above, the Turkish state conventionally treats minority rights and demands as a matter of national security and survival (see also Oran 2011). Given the securitization of minority issues, the state prefers to keep minority rights and freedoms to a minimum. This restrictive and security-based logic applies to religious minority holidays as well. Compared to formal recognition, informal recognition and accommodation provides greater flexibility and the space that the state needs in its relations with Muslim and non-Muslim religious minority groups.

That being said, in January 2021, officials of the conservative AKP government revealed that they plan to recognize the religious holidays of Muslim and non-Muslim minority groups as official holidays.[35] Because several

---

34. See "Legal Status to Alevi Worship Houses a 'Red Line,' Says Turkey's Religious Body Head," *Hurriyet Daily News*, January 3, 2016, https://www.hurriyetdailynews.com/legal-status-to-alevi-worship-houses-a-red-line-says-turkeys-religious-body-head-93366, accessed March 15, 2022.

35. "AKP'li Cahit Özcan: Farklı din ve inançta olan vatandaşlarımızın bayramlarının olduğu günlerde resmi tatil getiriyoruz" [Cahit Özcan from the AKP: We will recognize the holidays of religious minorities as official holidays], *T24*, January 27, 2021, https://

non-Muslim religious groups (i.e., Armenians, Greeks, and Jews) are already defined and treated as official religious minorities, the Turkish governments might also formalize their religious holidays. However, given the strong Sunni objection to the official recognition of Alevi faith, culture, and institutions, there are bigger hurdles in front of the inclusion of Alevi religious holidays (such as the Day of Ashura and Gadir Hum) into the list of statutory holidays. Nevertheless, the formalization of religious holidays of Muslim and non-Muslim minorities would be a major change to state–minority relations in the country. Moving religious minority holidays from informal to formal terrain would mean the official acknowledgment of religious diversity and pluralism in the Turkish social landscape. Such a shift in state attitude is also likely to empower religious minority groups' attachment to the Turkish state.[36]

Conclusions and Implications

This chapter examines religious minority holidays in Turkey as an emblematic case of layered informal institutions. What are the broad ramifications of this particular case? As the case of religious minority holidays in the Turkish setting shows, social groups might view formal institutional arrangements as beneficial or at least innocuous in terms of their self-interests. However, even if formal rules may not threaten or harm their self-interests, they may still consider those formal arrangements as illegitimate or as having a low level of legitimacy. This happens especially when formal rules and regulations are based on beliefs, norms, and values that diverge from their beliefs, norms, and values. Otherwise stated, formal arrangements might be exclusionary and discriminatory toward the beliefs and traditions of ethnic and religious minority groups. As a direct result of the exclusionary and biased nature of formal rules and regulations, those

t24.com.tr/haber/akp-li-cahit-ozcan-farkli-din-ve-inancta-olan-vatandaslarimizin-bayramlarinin-oldugu-gunlerde-resmi-tatil-getiriyoruz,929370, accessed March 15, 2022.

36. We should, however, acknowledge the presence of a striking variance in state attitudes toward minority holidays. While the Turkish state has been accommodative toward *religious* minority holidays to a certain extent, we do not really see the same attitude toward *ethnic* minority holidays such as the Newruz holiday celebrated by the Kurdish ethnic minority (for more on ethnic minority holidays such as Newruz, see Yanık 2006; Hintz and Quatrini 2021).

minority institutions would function in the informal domain. Having a different institutional logic and being layered onto the existing formal structures, those informal institutions operate in parallel to formal rules and regulations. Under those conditions, formal and informal institutions would constitute a multilayered institutional structure. In such multilayered institutional terrains, there might be occasional tensions or frictions between those formal and informal institutional layers.

Layered informal institutions differ substantially from symbiotic, superseding, and subversive informal institutions. As noted above, layered informal institutions are based on norms, values, and ideas that are different from those of the formal institutions. In other words, their logics differ from formal institutional logics. As a result, they do not have mutually beneficial relations with formal arrangements. Likewise, due to their diverging logics, they also do not supersede the existing formal institutions. Metaphorically speaking, they operate as different but overlapping layers. Regarding its key difference from the subversive type, as illustrated above, actors do not adhere to or utilize these informal arrangements to contest or subvert formal rules and regulations.

This particular case has also some implications for the analyses of holidays. The literature acknowledges that holidays might play various roles in societies. As summarized by Etzioni (2004), the Durkheimian approach emphasizes the *integrative* function of holidays and rituals for whole societies. Etzioni (2004), however, suggests that holidays are not necessarily unifiers of societies. He draws attention to their *disintegrative* and *conflictual* function by stating that "some group celebrations are disintegrative for the society as a whole, are openly oppositional and challenge the societal mores and symbols, or even serve as outright expression of a breakaway from the societal whole or from some other group" (2004, 19). Similarly, Hintz and Quatrini (2021) suggest that holidays can be sites of contentious politics, especially in authoritarian political regimes with suppressed or excluded minority groups. They note that "holidays are particularly effective sites of identity contestation through forms of celebration determined by citizens in defiance of the state as a method of reconstituting and reinforcing minority group identity" (2021, 290). The case of religious minority holidays in the Turkish context, however, suggests that there is a third option: those holidays might play a largely inert or neutral role at the societal level. In other words, they may have neither an integrative nor a disintegrative effect on the society as a whole. Rather than operating as a unifier of the whole society, their integrative effect and mechanism might be limited to certain social groups, such as ethnic and religious minorities. As they play a unifying or integrative role at the group level, they may also avoid operating in confrontational, contentious, and subversive ways at the societal level. One reason for the nonconfrontational operation of minority holidays at the national level might be the state's informal recognition and accommodation of those minority holidays and rituals. In other words, the state's accommodative attitude toward minority holidays is likely to prevent their use as an instrument of transgressive contentious politics.

This particular case further suggests that formal actors (unitary or collective) might be involved in various forms of informal politics. Recognizing only the Sunni Muslim majority's holidays, the Turkish state has preferred to keep the religious holidays of Muslim and non-Muslim minority groups in the informal domain. However, instead of banning or suppressing those minority religious traditions, rituals, and practices, the Turkish state has informally acknowledged and engaged with them. In other words, the state has allowed those institutions to operate in the twilight or in the shadows (Lund 2006; Peters 2011; Peters and Pierre 2020). Informal recognition of and engagement with minority groups might be a state strategy to contain or restrain antistate attitudes and orientations within those minority groups. Whatever motivations state officials and dignitaries might have, this particular case hints that informal governance might be pervasive in various sociopolitical settings across the globe. This implies that, as formal organizational actors, states might have multiple faces (formal and informal). Therefore, raising questions such as when, why, and how *formal* organizational actors engage in *informal* politics at the global, national, and local levels would be highly rewarding in terms of advancing our theoretical knowledge and understanding of diverse forms or styles of governance (see also Peters 2006; Christiansen and Neuhold 2012; Hummel 2021; Polese 2021).

Appendix 5.A. A List of Interviewees (Religious Minority Holidays)

No.	Name and Surname	Job/Position	Date	Location
Christian				
1	Antonios Duma	Priest, Roman Catholic Church, Santa Maria Draperis	July 10, 2019	İstanbul
2	Ayhan Gürkan	Priest, Teacher, Mor Barsaumo Church (Midyat) (Syriac Orthodox)	June 16, 2019	Mardin
3	Cem Çapar	Head of the Foundation of Armenian Orthodox Church (Samandağ, Vakıflı Village)	June 25, 2019	Hatay
4	Dimitri Doğum	Priest, Antioch Orthodox Church	June 22, 2019	Hatay
5	Domenico Bertogli	Church father, Antioch Catholic Church	June 20, 2019	Hatay
6	Fadi Hurigil	Head of the Foundation of Antioch Orthodox Church	June 24, 2019	Hatay
7	Gabriel Akyüz	Priest, Mardin Mor Behnam (Kirklar) Church	June 15, 2019	Mardin
8	Gaffur Türkay	Armenian community member	June 11, 2019	Diyarbakır
9	George Kocamanoğlu	Head of the Community of Antioch Protestant Church	June 24, 2019	Hatay
10	Nikola Dinç	Priest, İzmir Saint Polycarp Church	March 23, 2019	İzmir
11	Tatul Avuşyan	Armenian Patriarchate of Istanbul	July 9, 2019	İstanbul
12	Yakup Chang	Priest, Antioch Protestant Church	June 22, 2019	Hatay
13	Yılmaz Ümit	Catholic community member, İzmir St. Helena Church	March 22, 2019	İzmir
14	Yusuf Akbulut	Priest, St. Mary Church (Syriac Orthodox)	June 8, 2019	Diyarbakır
Muslim				
15	Ali Ekber Yurt	Dede, Tunceli Cemevi (Cem house)	June 5, 2019	Tunceli
16	Ali Mansuroğlu	Lawyer, Municipality of Defne	June 26, 2019	Hatay
17	Ali Yeral	Head of Ehlibeyt Kültür ve Dayanışma Vakfı (EHDAV)	June 19, 2019	Hatay
18	Nasreddin Eskiocak	Sheikh	June 18, 2019	Hatay
19	Nesimi Öz	Dede, Tunceli Cemevi (Cem house)	June 4, 2019	Tunceli
20	Zeycan Saltık Koçuk	Ana	June 4, 2019	Tunceli
21	Zeynel Batar	Dede	June 4, 2019	Tunceli

CHAPTER 6

A Subversive Informal Institution

"Multilingual Municipalism" of the Kurdish Movement

This chapter elucidates subversive informal institutions by examining an engrossing initiative in local governance by Turkey's Kurdish ethnopolitical movement. As presented in the theoretical chapter, certain actors (individual or collective) might view the existing formal arrangements as "illegitimate" and "harmful" in terms of their material or ideational interests. Failing to remove or amend those illegitimate and detrimental formal institutions, they might establish or resort to informal arrangements and practices. One might expect such informal institutions to be widespread especially among groups or movements excluded or marginalized by the existing sociopolitical system. As Clemens (1993, 755) observes, "groups marginalized by existing political institutions have an incentive to develop alternative models of organization." Similarly, Helmke and Levitsky (2006, 280) note that

> many developing countries are characterized by severe socioeconomic, eth-
> nic, and/or regional stratification, which makes it more likely that certain
> groups—for example, ethnic minorities—will be denied access to (or pro-
> tection from) formal state institutions. . . . such exclusion may lead these
> groups to maintain or (re)create substitutive informal institutions at the
> margins of the state legal system.

Excluded or marginalized groups (e.g., ethnic, religious, ideological) might resort to not only complementary or substitutive informal institutions but also to more contentious and subversive ones. They might resort to subversive informal arrangements, whose logics diverge from the logics

131

of the existing formal arrangements, to challenge or contest the existing undesirable formal rules and regulations.

This theoretical expectation is valid especially for peripheral and anti-systemic minority movements in authoritarian settings such as the Kurdish ethnopolitical movement in Turkey.[1] In its struggle to enhance the rights and freedoms of the suppressed Kurdish ethnic minority, the Kurdish movement has established several contentious informal institutions to resist, challenge, and undermine the existing exclusionary and suppressive formal rules and regulations. This chapter illustrates the notion of "subversive informal institution" by analyzing an interesting drive by the Kurdish ethnopolitical movement in municipal governance: multilingual municipalism (*çok dilli belediyecilik*). The empirical analysis of this case is based on quantitative and qualitative data derived from public opinion surveys; some in-depth interviews with Kurdish political actors and activists; election data (on national and local elections); official documents and reports from state agencies, political parties, and local governments; and newspapers.

The following section briefly introduces state attitudes and policies toward minority groups and languages and the resultant formal rules and regulations in order to gain a better understanding of the subversive nature of the informal arrangements initiated by the Kurdish movement. Next, the chapter briefly introduces the key features of Turkey's Kurdish ethnopolitical movement. The chapter then focuses on the Kurdish movement's initiative of multilingual municipalism as an emblematic case of a subversive informal institution. The concluding section restates the main points and arguments and presents the broader implications of this particular case of subversive informal institution.

---

1. In this chapter, I use the terms "Kurdish movement" and "Kurdish ethnopolitical movement" interchangeably. They refer to secular and left-oriented pro-Kurdish formations, including both legal pro-Kurdish political parties and civil society organizations and the illegal and armed Kurdistan Workers' Party (Partîya Karkerên Kurdistan, PKK). Although there are several other pro-Kurdish formations and movements (e.g., right oriented or pro-Islamic ones), the secular and left-oriented pro-Kurdish actors constitute the dominant wing within Turkey's Kurds.

The Turkish State's Attitudes and Policies toward Minority Languages

Before discussing the Turkish state's language policy, it would be helpful to have a brief look at the general state attitude toward minority groups and minority rights. As noted before, according to the Treaty of Lausanne, the Turkish Republican state accepted only certain non-Muslim groups (Armenians, Greeks, and Jews) as official minorities and granted them certain rights and freedoms. All Muslim ethnic groups (mainly Kurds), however, were excluded from the official definition of minority and referred to as constitutive elements of the Turkish nation (see also Yegen 1996, 2009; Icduygu and Soner 2006; Kizilkan-Kisacik 2013). As is widely acknowledged, the main objective of the founding fathers of the Turkish Republic was to establish a secular, centralized, and nationally homogenous nation-state, based on Turkishness. As a result, Turkish nation-building efforts and policies involved the Turkification of ethnically, linguistically, and culturally distinct groups (e.g., see Aslan 2007, 2021; Bozarslan 2008; Yegen 2009; Zeydanlıoğlu 2012, 2013; Bayir 2013; Kaya 2013; Bayar 2014; Gunes 2021; Oran 2021). It is worth to quoting Bayir (2013, 97) at length to illustrate the general features of cultural nationalism embraced and promoted by the Turkish Republic:

> From the outset, the Turkish state officially promoted "cultural nationalism" (kültür milliyetçiliği). This nationalism is defined as being based on culture and not on race or ethnie. The mythic claim behind this "cultural nationalism" is that it leaves the doors of the national community open to all, regardless of their ethnic, religious and other origins. Meanwhile, it trivializes the demand of this cultural nationalism for a coercive adaptation to a homogeneous culture, defined with reference to the Turkish language, culture, history and common ideals at the expense of other cultures, languages, histories, and so on. Indeed, state officials and many commentators have interpreted the possibility of being accepted into Turkishness as evidence of its civic and "legalist-voluntarist" nature. In reality, however, the discourse of "cultural nationalism" has been very exclusionary since access by non-Turks into the national community is conditioned upon their capacity for Turkification, that is, their unconditional acceptance to be Turks by culture.

Compared to individual rights and freedoms, the state elites have attributed much more importance to national and state interests (e.g., national security and unity) (Cizre 2003; İçduygu and Soner 2006; Oran 2021). Hence, ethnic, linguistic, and cultural diversity and multiculturalism have been viewed as potential threats to national solidarity, integrity, and survival. As a result, the Turkish state has considered minority issues as a matter of national integrity and security, rather than as a matter of human rights and freedoms (Bozarslan 2008; Cemiloglu 2009; Soner 2010; Bayir 2013; Kaya 2013; Atlas 2014; Gourlay 2018; Oran 2021). Due to such official understandings and tendencies, the Turkish state has even denied the existence of ethnic and cultural groups and identities other than Turkish ones. For instance, in official state discourse, the Kurds, who constituted the second largest ethnic group after the Turks, were referred to as Mountain Turks (McDowall 2004; Entessar 2010; Zeydanlıoğlu 2012; Bayir 2013; Oran 2021).[2] Thus, the state has been reluctant to recognize ethnic, linguistic, and cultural diversity in the country. Claiming the existence of ethnic groups and identities other than Turkish or demanding official status for those ethnic groups, cultures, and languages has been treated as separatism and can result in legal punishments such as imprisonment (Oran 2011; Gunes 2018). As Oran (2011, 45) notes:

> In Turkey, a monolithic concept of nation was employed in the early days of the Republic, and that authoritarian and oppressive attitude was [reinforced] by subsequent military interventions. . . . The approach not only denies the existence of minorities or minority rights, other than *what were deemed to be articulated in the Lausanne Treaty*, but also punishes those who make contrary claims and suggestions.

From the mid-1920s until the early 2000s, the politics of denial and suppression dominated Turkey's Kurdish policy. During each military regime, we see an increase in the repression of Kurdish ethnic identity and the Kurdish movement. Denying the ethnopolitical aspects of the problem, the state elites preferred to treat the Kurdish issue as a problem of socioeco-

---

2. Kurds constitute a multistate ethnic group in the Middle East. They are spread across four neighboring countries: Turkey, Iraq, Iran, and Syria. The majority of Kurds reside in Turkey, corresponding to around 15% to 20% of the Turkish population. In Iraq, Kurds constitute around 20% of the total population, and in Iran and Syria the Kurdish population corresponds to around 10% of the total.

nomic underdevelopment, security, and terrorism (Imset 1996; Yeğen 1996, 2007, 2011; van Bruinessen 2000; Romano 2006; Marcus 2007; Watts 2010; Romano and Gurses 2014; Aydin and Emrence 2015). As a result, the state primarily relied on military and socioeconomic measures to deal with this problem. Having said that, beginning in the early 2000s, the Turkish state adopted a (relatively) more moderate attitude toward the Kurdish issue and initiated certain legal and institutional changes to grant some cultural rights to Kurds (see below).

Regarding the state's language policy, it had two main objectives. First, in line with the official understandings and attitudes summarized above, state elites attempted to build a purified, standardized, and modernized Turkish language. Second, and related to the first objective, official language policy aimed to protect and promote purified Turkish as the common and dominant language in all spheres of sociopolitical life, and thus achieve linguistic homogeneity in the country (see also Aslan 2007, 2009; Cemiloglu 2009; Ucarlar 2009; Bayir 2013; Atlas 2014; Bouquet 2017; Oran 2021). As a result, the Turkish state tried to exclude, suppress, and, if possible, eliminate minority languages (e.g., Kurdish, Lazuri, Armenian, and Syriac) (İçduygu and Soner 2006; Cemiloglu 2009; Zeydanlıoğlu 2012, 2013; Bayir 2013; Atlas 2014; Arslan 2015; Sheyholislami 2015). Until the early 2000s, the state generally maintained its exclusionary and suppressive attitudes toward minority languages, in particular the Kurdish language.[3] As O'Neil (2011, 72) also suggests,

> for much of the history of the Republic of Turkey, a major contention between the state and its Kurdish population has been the use of the Kurdish language, the cornerstone of Kurdish culture. On various occasions, the Republic has banned its use in private and public, and some state officials and Turkish citizens have gone so far as to deny the very existence of Kurds and the Kurdish language.

---

3. The Kurdish language is treated as a member of the Iranian languages, which is a part of the Indo-European family (Entessar 1992, 4; White 2000, 16; Jwaideh 2006, 11). The most widely spoken dialects are Kurmanji, Sorani, Gorani, and Kirmanshani (van Bruinessen 2000; Romano 2006, 3; Sheyholislami 2015, 30). Regarding the status of Zazaki, although some circles consider it a dialect of Kurdish, others treat it as a separate language (e.g., Izady 1992) (for more on this debate, see Ucarlar 2009). Kurdish is the fourth most spoken language in the Middle East (after Arabic, Persian, and Turkish). In Turkey, it is the second most spoken language after Turkish. Only Iraq recognizes Kurdish as an official language.

It is useful to illustrate the state's exclusion and suppression of the Kurdish language with some specific examples. Beginning in the mid-1920s, the Republican state denied the existence of a separate Kurdish ethnic identity and language. Instead, Kurds were believed to be ancient Turks and so the Kurdish language was treated as a perverted dialect of Turkish. Thus, as part of its general policy of promoting Turkishness and the Turkish language, the state banned publications in the Kurdish language (see Hassanpour 1992; Romano 2006; Aslan 2007; Cemiloglu 2009; Ucarlar 2009; Casier 2010; O'Neil 2011; Hassanpour, Sheyholislami, and Skutnabb-Kangas 2012; Zeydanlıoğlu 2012; Bayir 2013; Arslan 2015; Sheyholislami 2015; Oran 2021). We also see several efforts to ban or limit the use of the Kurdish language in public spaces. For instance, in 1928, the students of Istanbul University initiated the campaign "Citizen! Speak Turkish." This campaign was approved and supported by the government. The main motivation of this initiative was to discourage the use of other languages in public realms (Aslan 2007; Bayir 2013).[4] The Press Law of 1931 banned publications in non-Turkish languages such as Kurdish, Arabic, and Laz. The 1934 Surname Law (Soyadı Kanunu) required citizens to adopt Turkish family names (Bayir 2013; Oran 2021). The state also converted thousands of non-Turkish place names (e.g., the names of villages, towns, and cities in Kurdish, Laz, Armenian, Greek, and Arabic) into Turkish. As Tunçel (2000, 27) shows, since the early Republic, around 35% of village names have been converted into Turkish. The Registration Law (Nüfus Kanunu) of 1972 required parents to give Turkish names to their children, which meant banning Kurdish names (Aslan 2009, 2021; Bayir 2013; Oran 2021). The 1961 Electoral Law banned the use of any language other than Turkish in electoral propaganda and campaigns. Furthermore, the 1982 Constitution (written under the military regime of 1980–83) also included suppressive provisions. For instance, Article 26 banned the use of Kurdish in the expression and dissemination of thought, and Article 28 prohibited publication and broadcasting in Kurdish. Article 42, which regulated the right and duty of education, asserted that "no language other than Turkish shall be taught as a mother tongue to Turkish citizens at any institution of education." The military regime also passed a law in 1983 (Law on Publications and Broadcasts in Languages Other Than Turkish, Law No. 2932) banning even speaking Kurdish in the public realm.

---

4. These campaigns also targeted non-Muslims (e.g., Jews, Greeks, and Armenians) in major cities such as Istanbul and Izmir (Aslan 2007).

Quite strikingly, this law also claimed that Turkish was the mother tongue of all Turkish citizens and banned the use of any language other than Turkish as a mother tongue. Although this law was repealed in 1991, the ban on broadcasting and publishing in Kurdish and using Kurdish in education or political activities persisted in the 1990s. Fearing that folk songs in Kurdish-majority provinces might be abused for ethnonationalist and separatist purposes, the state also banned singing folk songs in Kurdish in public spaces in the 1980s (see Scalbert-Yücel 2009).[5]

However, in the early 2000s, as part of the Europeanization process, the Turkish state softened its repressive attitude toward the Kurdish language. As a result, the state granted several linguistic rights to Kurds, such as legalizing publishing and broadcasting in Kurdish, legalizing learning the Kurdish language, allowing parents to give their children Kurdish names,[6] allowing political party campaigns to be in Kurdish, allowing defendants to use their mother language during court trials, and introducing elective Kurdish courses into the public education curriculum (see also Aslan 2009; Cemiloglu 2009; Ucarlar 2009; Bayir 2013; Kizilkan-Kisacik 2013; Zeydanlıoğlu 2013; Atlas 2014; Arslan 2015; Ozdemir and Sarigil 2015; Gourlay 2018; Gunes 2021). Nevertheless, the Turkish state has *still* avoided recognizing Kurdish as an official language.

In sum, formal rules and regulations are based on a strongly homogenous and monolithic understanding of national identity, which is based on Turkishness and Turkish nationalism. The principle of "One nation, one state, one language, one flag!" (*Tek millet, tek devlet, tek dil, tek bayrak!*) has been strictly protected. As the only official language, Turkish has been treated as one of the constitutive elements of Turkish national identity. As Aydıngün and Aydıngün (2004, 415) observe,

---

5. We should also acknowledge that the Turkish state's repressive policies and measures against the Kurdish language violated the Treaty of Lausanne, which marked the international recognition of the Turkish Republic. For instance, Article 39 of the Treaty stipulated that "no restrictions shall be imposed on the free use by any Turkish national of any language in private intercourse, in commerce, religion, in the press, or in publications of any kind or at public meetings."

6. In June 2003, the parliament amended Article 16 of the Registration Law by removing the statement that children could not be given names that conflict with the national culture and Turkish customs and traditions. However, names including the letters 'Q', 'W', or 'X', which exist in Kurdish but not in Turkish, are still not allowed. In other words, only Kurdish names that can be spelled in the official Turkish alphabet are allowed (Aslan 2009, 2021; Bayir 2013; Zeydanlıoğlu 2013; Oran 2021).

the Turkish Republic was founded with the modernist idea of a nation-state, and therefore it required a common culture. As a result, language and education were standardized to create a Turkish national identity. Adoption of a language policy was one of the most important strategies used by the founders of the Turkish Republic during the process of transition from an empire to a nation state.

Similarly, Zeydanlıoğlu (2013, 164) notes that

since the creation of the Republic of Turkey, language has been the crucial ingredient in the construction of the modern Turkish identity and the primary marker of what it means to be a Turk. From early on, being able to speak Turkish has been intimately linked to the notion of being a Turk and being a "civilised" citizen of the republic (see also Cemiloglu 2009; Ucarlar 2009; Bayir 2013; Atlas 2014).

Denying official recognition and status to the languages spoken by Muslim ethnic minority groups (e.g., Kurdish, Arabic, and Lazuri), the Turkish state recognizes only Turkish as its official language. For instance, Article 3 of the 1982 Constitution, which was written during the military regime (1980–83), states that "the State of Turkey, with its territory and nation, is an indivisible entity. Its language is Turkish." Thus, the official language policy has been based on the principle of monolingualism rather than multilingualism, and this principle has been one of the constitutive elements of the Turkish state and national identity. This constitutional principle has also determined various laws, rules, and regulations. For instance, since the Turkish language remains as the only official language, it is a formal and legal requirement that all kinds of administrative activities and official transactions and correspondence in national and local governance must take place in Turkish. Furthermore, in line with these constitutional norms and principles, the Law on Political Parties (Siyasi Partiler Kanunu, Law No. 2820), which was enacted in 1983 during the military regime (1980–83), states that political parties "cannot aim and involve in activities to disrupt the integrity of the nation by creating minorities within the country of the Republic of Turkey by means of preserving, developing or spreading languages and cultures other than the Turkish language and culture" (Article 81).

The Kurdish Ethnopolitical Movement in Turkey

Before turning to a subversive informal institution initiated by the Kurdish ethnopolitical movement, a brief look at the main characteristics of this movement will be useful. A quick overview of Turkey's Kurdish movement will also help us better contextualize the disruptive and subversive nature of the informal institutional arrangements initiated and promoted by this antisystemic ethnic minority movement in the Turkish context.

As summarized above, the state had intolerant, exclusionary, and repressive attitudes and policies toward the Kurdish ethnic minority. As one would expect, such exclusionary and suppressive state policies triggered violent as well as peaceful Kurdish ethnopolitical mobilization against the central state. For instance, as one study indicates, in the period from 1924 to 1938, there were 18 uprisings in Turkey and 17 of them took place in eastern Anatolia; 16 of them involved Kurds (Kirişçi and Winrow 1997).[7] These rural and tribal Kurdish revolts were severely suppressed by the Turkish state. After a decline in Kurdish ethnopolitical mobilization in the 1940s and 1950s, we see a major increase in Kurdish ethnopolitical activism in the 1960s and 1970s (Bozarslan 2008; Gunes 2021). In this period, the Kurdish movement had relatively much more urban, educated, secular, and leftist features with Marxist-Leninist orientations.

During the second half of the 1970s, there were several pro-Kurdish, leftist formations in Turkey. However, the Kurdistan Workers' Party (Partiya Karkaren Kurdistan, PKK), which was established in 1978 by Abdullah Öcalan and his friends, became the dominant and hegemonic Kurdish ethnonationalist group by the 1980s. The PKK declared its ultimate objective as establishing an independent, socialist Kurdish state. To achieve that objective, the PKK adopted the strategy of a "protracted people's war." As a result, in August 1984, the PKK initiated its first major armed attack on military installations near Eruh (Siirt) and Şemdinli (Hakkari) in the southeastern part of Turkey. Beginning in the early 1990s, the PKK-led Kurdish movement became much more organized, violent, and challenging. As a result, the armed conflict between Turkish security forces and the PKK intensified and reached its peak in the first half of the 1990s. The Kurdish conflict in Turkey, which has been one of the most prolonged ethnic con-

---

7. Major Kurdish revolts during the early Republican era were the Sheikh Said Rebellion (1925), the Ağrı Revolt (1926–30), and the Dersim (Tunceli) Revolt (1936–38).

flicts in the post–World War II era, has resulted in around 40,000 casualties, the destruction of about 3,000 villages, and the internal displacement of at least three million people (e.g., see Marcus 2007; Bozarslan 2008; Watts 2010; Aydin and Emrence 2015). By the mid-1990s, the PKK revised its ideological outlook and thus its political objectives. Distancing itself from Marxist and separatist ideals and goals, the PKK started to advocate a democratic political solution to the Kurdish conflict and demanded the expansion of democratic rights and freedoms of minority groups and political and administrative restructuring based on multiculturalism, decentralization, and democratic autonomy within national boundaries (see also Imset 1996; White 2000; Yavuz 2001; Romano 2006; Ucarlar 2009; Akkaya and Jongerden 2012; Gunes 2012, 2021; Dinc 2020).

Beginning in the early 1990s, the Kurdish ethnopolitical movement also established several legally operating pro-Kurdish political parties.[8] These pro-Kurdish parties have defended a peaceful and democratic solution for Turkey's Kurdish problem and called for several cultural and political rights and freedoms such as speaking, publishing, and broadcasting in Kurdish; public education in Kurdish; official status for the Kurdish language; constitutional recognition of Kurdish ethnic identity; general amnesty for PKK members; and increased socioeconomic investments in the eastern and southeastern regions. They have also called for power-sharing arrangements such as decentralization and democratic autonomy or self-rule (*demokratik özerklik* or *öz yönetim*). These antisystemic and peripheral political parties (Watts 2006, 2010; Wuthrich 2013; Gunes 2021), however, were accused of supporting terrorism and separatism and of creating propaganda against the indivisible integrity or unity of the Turkish territory and nation. As a result, Turkey's Constitutional Court has banned most of those successive pro-Kurdish political parties, several party officials and members have been murdered, and thousands of party members and activists have been jailed (see also Bayir 2013; Gunes 2021).

---

8. The major pro-Kurdish political parties are as follows: the People's Labor Party (Halkın Emek Partisi, HEP, 1990–93, the first legal Kurdish party); the Freedom and Democracy Party (Özgürlük ve Demokrasi Partisi, ÖZDEP, 1992–93); the Democracy Party (Demokrasi Partisi, DEP, 1993–94); the Democracy Party of the People (Halkın Demokrasi Partisi, HADEP, 1994–2003); the Democratic People's Party (Demokratik Halk Partisi DEHAP, 1997–2005); the Democratic Society Party (Demokratik Toplum Partisi, DTP, 2005–9); the Peace and Democracy Party (Barış ve Demokrasi Partisi, BDP, 2008–14); the Democratic Regions Party (Demokratik Bölgeler Partisi DBP, 2008 onward); and the Peoples' Democratic Party([Halkların Demokratik Partisi, HDP, 2012 onward).

TABLE 6.1. Electoral Support for the Pro-Kurdish Political Parties in *General* Elections (1991-2018)

Elections	Party	National vote (%)	Avg. regional vote (%)c	Seats
1991	HEP/SHPa	—		22
1995	· HADEP	4.2	28.06	—
1999	HADEP	4.8	30.47	—
2002	DEHAP	6.2	40.19	—
2007	DTP/Independentb	5.2	39.30	20
2011	BDP/Independentb	6.6	52.97	36
2015 (January)	HDP	13.1	69.40	80
2015 (November)	HDP	10.76	64.20	59
2018	HDP	11.70	57.6	67

Source: Compiled by the author from the TUIK (www.tuik.gov.tr) and the YSK (www.ysk.gov.tr).

a During the October 1991 general elections, the pro-Kurdish HEP and the social-democratic SHP entered an electoral alliance. The HEP candidates were included in the SHP's list. In 1992, they resigned from the SHP and joined the HEP. (See note 8 for the full names of the Kurdish parties.)

b The DTP and the BDP supported independent candidates in general elections to avoid the 10% national electoral threshold.

c The following provinces, which are mostly inhabited by Kurds, are included: Batman, Bitlis, Diyarbakır, Hakkari, Mardin, Muş, Siirt, Şanlıurfa, Şırnak, and Van.

When we look at the electoral performance of those pro-Kurdish political parties, despite some fluctuations, we see an increasing trend in their electoral popularity. For instance, table 6.1 and figure 6.1 show that, since the 2011 general elections, pro-Kurdish ethnic parties have received the majority of votes in Kurdish-majority provinces. It is also striking that since the June 2015 general elections, these political parties have passed the 10% national electoral threshold and attained several seats in the national parliament.

As table 6.2 shows, pro-Kurdish political parties also increased their electoral support during the local elections, and thus controlled an increasing number of municipalities (district, city, and metropolitan) in Kurdish-majority provinces in the eastern and southeastern regions. For instance, during the April 1999 local elections, the Democracy Party of the People (Halkın Demokrasi Partisi, HADEP) won 37 municipalities in those regions, including major cities such as Diyarbakır and Van. This was an unprecedented development in Kurdish electoral politics because, for the first time, an openly pro-Kurdish political party took control of local governmental organizations. Since then, the number of municipalities controlled by the Kurdish ethnopolitical movement has increased and reached 102 municipalities in the March 2014 local elections.

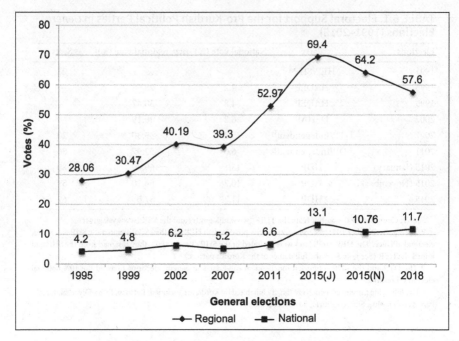

Figure 6.1. Electoral Popularity of Pro-Kurdish Political Parties during General Elections (Comparing National and Regional Levels) (1995–2018)

Multilingual Municipalism (Çok Dilli Belediyecilik)

The increasing electoral popularity of pro-Kurdish political parties during the local and general elections since the early 1990s has further empowered the Kurdish movement in Turkey (Watts 2010; Akkaya and Jongerden 2012; Öztürk 2013; Sarigil 2018a; Gunes 2020, 2021). In her analysis of Kurdish party politics, Watts (2010, 13) rightly notes that

> by working within electoral politics, Kurdish challengers gained access to state-allocated material, legal, and political resources that were unavailable to those using armed contention. . . . Entering governmental institutions and participating in formal political arenas created a durable platform for activism that helped the movement withstand failing fortunes on other fronts, created new social and political facts on the ground in Kurdish-majority provinces of the southeast, and helped legitimize the movement through votes. In sum, it furthered the movement in ways that armed struggle could not.

TABLE 6.2. Electoral Popularity of Pro-Kurdish Political Parties in *Local (Municipal)* Elections (1994–2019)

Local elections	Party	National vote (%)	Number of municipalities
1994	DEP[a]	—	—
1999	HADEP	3.82	37
2004	DEHAP/SHP[b]	5.15	54
2009	DTP	5.7	99
2014	BDP/HDP[c]	6.4	102
2019	HDP[d]	5.6	65

Source: Compiled by the author from the TUIK (www.tuik.gov.tr) and the YSK (www.ysk.gov.tr).

[a] Due to attacks on DEP party buildings and offices and armed assaults on its candidates, the DEP decided to boycott the March local elections.

[b] The DEHAP entered an electoral coalition with the SHP.

[c] The BDP competed in the eastern and the HDP in the western provinces, but the HDP failed to earn any municipality.

[d] The HDP did not nominate any candidate in most of western provinces and supported the candidates of the National Alliance (Millet İttifakı) in several western provinces.

Gaining the control of local governments in Kurdish-majority provinces is a particularly important achievement for the movement. Given the size of the Kurdish ethnic minority in Turkey (around 15% to 20% of the total population), it is unlikely pro-Kurdish political parties could seize a parliamentary majority and, as a result, governmental power at the national level. Hence, controlling municipal or local governments in the Kurdish-inhabited areas becomes a much more attainable objective for the movement in legal party politics.

As the literature on contentious politics also acknowledges, political opportunity structures (i.e., the features of regimes and institutions) matter in terms of the effectiveness and success of opponent groups' contention. As McAdam, Tarrow, and Tilly (2004, 41) note, "Though challengers habitually face resource deficits and are excluded from routine decision making, the political environment at any time is not immutable; the political opportunities for a challenger to engage in successful collective action vary over time. These variations shape the ebb and flow of a movement's activity" (see also Tilly and Tarrow 2015). From this perspective, access to local government should be interpreted as a major political opportunity for an antisystemic ethnic minority movement. This is valid for Turkey's Kurdish movement as well. Having control of local governments brings various ideational and material openings and benefits to the Kurdish movement at multiple levels (i.e., local, national, and transnational). Ideationally, it brings social recognition, approval, and legitimacy. As Watts (2010, 85) notes, given that the

Kurdish movement in Turkey has been an antisystemic political movement, one of the main tasks of pro-Kurdish political parties was to establish and maintain legitimacy and approval within the existing political system. As "activists in office" (Watts 2010), mayors are political actors elected by local people, and therefore they enjoy legal and democratic legitimacy across local, national, and transnational politics.

Pro-Kurdish political parties' status as legitimate political actors also brings them some material opportunities, advantages, and benefits. For instance, having control of local governments enables them to access various sociopolitical organizations, networks, platforms, and resources at the national and transnational levels (see also Casier 2010; Watts 2010). Working within the system allows the Kurdish movement to access public resources and authority at regional and national levels (e.g., controlling the budget of municipalities, managing public properties and businesses, and enforcing municipal rules and regulations) (see also Watts 2006, 2010; Öztürk 2013).[9] Furthermore, municipal control provides several opportunities for the Kurdish movement to apply for external funding (e.g., grants from the European Union and other international funding bodies) (see Watts 2010; Flader and Gürer 2019).

The control of local governments in Kurdish regions has also provided an opportunity for the Kurdish movement to achieve some of its political objectives such as challenging, contesting, and subverting official understandings, principles, rules, and regulations, which have been shaped by Turkish nationalism (see also Gambetti 2009; Scalbert-Yücel 2009; Dorronsoro and Watts 2012; Flader and Gürer 2019). In other words, by implementing its own understanding of local governance, which has been relatively much more multiculturalist and pluralist, the Kurdish movement has questioned and challenged the mentality of official governance (which is based on highly monolithic and centralizing understandings) as well as the state's suppressive and exclusionary attitudes, rules, and regulations toward non-Turkish cultures, languages, and identities. As Scalbert-Yücel (2009, 2)

9. In the Turkish administrative system, municipalities are authorized with providing a wide range of public services at the local level such as supporting local commerce; organizing private job courses for the unemployed; taking care of infrastructure (water supply, drainage, and sewage systems); solid waste, environmental cleanup, and health; emergency rescue services; local traffic and roads; cemeteries, parks, and green areas; housing; cultural and artistic activities; tourism; and various welfare services (see Tutkal 2021).

also notes, through municipal control "Kurdish contention enters the state's offices. The municipality is thus situated in an in-between space." The control of local governments means that the Kurdish movement has been enabled to work within the formal political system. This official status or position has provided the antisystemic and peripheral Kurdish movement various opportunities to contest, disrupt, and subvert the existing formal rules and regulations. As Watts (2010, 25) observes:

> Although the [pro-Kurdish] parties were circumscribed in their debate about administrative and political reform, they could try to create a competing "governmentality" to that of the Turkish state and to create a new kind of Kurdish national subject. Specifically, they did this through modernist administrative projects as well as through symbolic politics, such as the promotion and officialization of the Kurdish language, "Kurdification" of public space, and use of spectacle (fairs and festivals). Such activities served simultaneously to challenge the norms and practices of the Turkish state and to create a nationalized Kurdish citizen who might legitimize and demand a new, specifically Kurdish representation (see also Gambetti 2009).

One specific and absorbing case is the principle and practice of *multilingual municipalism* (or *multilingual local governance*), initiated and promoted by the municipalities controlled by pro-Kurdish political parties in the eastern and southeastern regions. In early 2007, the municipality of Sur district in the city of Diyarbakır initiated multilingual municipalism (see also Casier 2010; Akkaya and Jongerden 2012; Gunes 2012; Yücel 2016; Gourlay 2018). This unprecedented initiative was justified by the multicultural social structure of the region. In 2005, Sur municipality conducted a large survey that included all the households within the borders of Sur district (more than 8,000 households). According to the results of the survey, 72% of the residents of Sur district stated that their mother tongue was Kurdish, while 24% responded that Turkish was their first language. The remaining respondents identified Arabic, Syriac, and Armenian as their mother tongue. This heterogeneous social structure encouraged the municipal council of Sur district to adopt a multilingual approach to municipal services by passing a resolution on "Multilingual Municipality Service" in January 2007. In a later period, other municipalities controlled by pro-Kurdish political parties also adopted this principle and practice in their respective districts and cities.

Regarding the timing of this initiative, one might rightly raise the following question: Although the Kurdish movement has controlled several municipalities in the region since the 1999 local elections, why did the movement introduce multilingual municipalism in 2007? One possible reason might be Europeanization reforms. As indicated above, in the early 2000s, as part of the Europeanization process, the Turkish state adopted a relatively more moderate attitude toward the Kurdish issue and granted several cultural and linguistic rights to the Kurdish ethnic minority. The Kurdish movement seems to have taken advantage of this relatively liberal political environment brought about by EU reforms. As Gunes (2021, 47) also notes, "the legal reforms the government carried out to meet the EU accession conditions have increased the democratic space for the pro-Kurdish political movement to broaden its activities and become [a] more effective political actor." Thus, the Europeanization process created a window of opportunity for the Kurdish movement to achieve some of its social and political objectives.

Table 6.3 presents a summary of the similarities and differences between the existing formal arrangements and the Kurdish movement's multilingual municipalism. As summarized, as an informal arrangement, multilingual

TABLE 6.3. A Comparison of Formal Rules and Regulations with Informal Multilingual Municipalism

Type of institution	Institutional logic	Shared expectations	Behavioral regularities	Sources of legitimacy	Enforcement mechanisms
Monolingualism					
Formal, officially recognized and regulated (de jure)	Homogeneity, uniformity, centralization, majoritarianism, Turkishness	Formal governance (national and local) to take place only in official language (i.e., Turkish)	All public services to be delivered only in Turkish	State agencies, codified laws and norms	Official, legal sanctions by formal courts
Multilingual municipalism (*çok dilli belediyecilik*)					
Informal, no official recognition and regulation (de facto)	Diversity (cultural, ethnic, linguistic), regionalism, minority empowerment, intercultural dialogue	Local governance to accommodate ethnic, cultural, and linguistic diversity	Municipal services to be delivered in multiple languages	Beliefs, norms, and values of an antisystemic and peripheral minority movement	Communal and social (such as naming and shaming)

municipalism substantially differs from the existing formal rules and regulations. To begin with, the logic of multilingual municipalism directly contradicts the formal institutional logic. While the rationale of official rules and regulations is shaped by uniformity, homogeneity, and centralization and based on the majority identity (i.e., Turkishness), multilingual municipalism is constituted by the principles of diversity, pluralism, multiculturalism, regionalism, and minority empowerment. Criticizing the Turkish state's homogenizing and monolithic understandings and orientations, the Kurdish movement has emphasized the ethnic, linguistic, religious, and regional diversity in the country. As a result, the movement has demanded that formal rules and regulations (e.g., the constitution and laws) should acknowledge the multicultural nature of society and protect and promote minority groups and their rights and freedoms. Regarding governance, as noted above, the Kurdish movement has been demanding power-sharing arrangements such as decentralization, regional autonomy, or self-rule. For instance, the party program of pro-Kurdish Peoples' Democratic Party (Halkların Demokratik Partisi, HDP) states (quoted in Gunes 2018, 263):

> Our party believes that a fundamental solution to all identity and cultural problems is possible with the adoption of a new democratic and pluralistic constitution that promotes freedom and equality. Our party struggles for the realisation of the constitutional assurance of equality of rights of different identities, languages, beliefs and cultures, and the definition of a constitutional citizenship shaped on this understanding; education in mother tongue and the application of the right of using mother tongue in every area of life including the public sphere; and democratic autonomy operating on the basis of local self-governance.

Given these political values, preferences, and objectives of the Kurdish movement, it is not surprising that the rationale of multilingual municipalism initiated and promoted by the movement is based on diversity (cultural, ethnic, linguistic, and regional), pluralism, and regionalism.

As one would expect, multilingual municipalism differs from the formal arrangements in terms of expectations and behavioral regularities as well. While formal rules and regulations require that municipal services are delivered only in the official language (i.e., Turkish), multilingual municipalism advocates for the use of several other languages (e.g., Kurdish, Arabic, Armenian, and Syriac), depending on the social structure of a particular region. Thus, the expectation is that local governments should consider linguistic diversity in their regions. In the case of multilingual municipalism, municipal services are provided in multiple languages (see below).

Which specific policies, arrangements, and practices are involved in multilingual local governance?

Providing municipal services in multiple languages. In addition to Turkish, which is the only official language in Turkey, several other languages (such as Kurdish, Arabic, Syriac, and Armenian) were used in the provision of municipal services (e.g., using local languages when communicating with residents in public buildings; performing civil marriages in multiple languages; and providing preschool/childcare services in Kurdish). Municipalities employed civil servants who could speak the local languages and deliver municipal services to local people in their mother tongues.

Using local languages in municipal publications and communications. The municipalities started to publish leaflets, magazines, newsletters, CDs, and books in several regional languages. The books published by the municipalities included children's books, tourist books, public-health pamphlets, and books of baby names in local languages. In addition, the municipalities controlled by pro-Kurdish political parties designed their websites and released promotional videos in languages other than Turkish. Finally, these municipalities also started to post billboards in Kurdish.

Naming and renaming public spaces. Another initiative of multilingual municipalism was related to naming public spaces. The practice of naming and renaming public spaces (e.g., public buildings, cultural centers, public squares, parks, roads, and streets) has taken two forms. First, municipalities run by pro-Kurdish parties replaced several Turkish names with Kurdish names. Second, Kurdish translations were added to the existing Turkish street and road names and written in the Kurdish alphabet (i.e., multilingual signs).[10] It is claimed that one of the goals of the policy of naming and renaming public spaces was to reinsert Kurdishness into the public sphere and so re-Kurdify public spaces (see Jongerden 2009; Watts 2010; Atlas 2014).[11]

Organizing and supporting cultural events and projects. As part of multi-

---

10. One key difference between the Kurdish and Turkish alphabets is that the Kurdish alphabet includes the letters 'Q', 'W', and 'X', which are commonly used letters in Kurdish.

11. All the interviewees also acknowledged such a motivation behind multilingual municipalism.

lingual municipalism, pro-Kurdish municipalities also provided financial and logistical support for various cultural events and activities for children and adults (e.g., art, theater, literature, film and music festivals and performances) that were organized in various local languages. To promote local language and culture, the municipalities took part in several cultural projects, such as launching language courses and children's choirs. For instance, the pro-Kurdish Diyarbakır Metropolitan Municipality supported the Dengbêj and Dengbêji Tradition Project (Dengbêj ve Dengbêjlik Geleneği Projesi).[12] The project was funded by the European Union's grant scheme for the promotion of cultural rights, cultural diversity, and intercultural dialogue in Turkey. One specific objective of this program was to support and enrich the daily use of languages and dialects other than Turkish (see Scalbert-Yücel 2009).[13] Such a motivation was compatible with the objectives of multilingual municipalism as well. As part of this project, the Diyarbakır Metropolitan Municipality funded the opening of the House of Dengbêj in Diyarbakır in 2007.

Multilingual municipalism has several specific functions and objectives. First, as former Sur mayor Abdullah Demirbaş stated, delivering municipal services in the mother tongue of local people would contribute to the efficiency and effectiveness of municipal services.[14] Thus, one objective of multilingual municipalism was to increase the quality of local governance.

Beyond improving local governance, this initiative, Demirbaş emphasized, also had several social and political objectives. To begin with, it challenged the formal state rules and regulations, practices, and narratives. The principle of multilingual municipalism was based on ideas such as cultural, ethnic, and linguistic diversity and plurality and intercultural dialogue and understanding. Thus, through multilingual municipalism, the Kurdish ethnopolitical movement resisted and contested the state's homogenizing and centralizing understandings, attitudes, narratives, and policies and tried to increase the public's knowledge and awareness of ethnic, cultural, and linguistic diversity in the country. In other words, beyond improving local governance, another main motivation of multilingual municipalism was to contest and subvert official rules, principles, and regulations such as the

---

12. The term "*dengbêj*" refers to a Kurdish singer and storyteller.

13. Some governmental institutions, such as the Office of the Prime Minister, Directorate General of Press and Information, and the Ministry of Culture and Tourism, also got involved in this project.

14. Author's interview with Abdullah Demirbaş, Istanbul, July 10, 2019.

rule of monolingualism. As Flader and Gürer (2019, 190) observe, "The municipalities have clearly managed to push the boundaries of institutional politics by integrating norms and practices of [the Kurdish movement] into municipal policies and have thereby challenged the state on its own terrain." Similarly, Watts (2010, 165) remarks that

> pro-Kurdish parties and politicians working at the level of local government built nationalized and "Kurdified" public spaces. This served to construct a public narrative of Kurdishness and broaden the field of contestation in Turkey, even though this field was in some ways fragile. In essence they created new facts on the ground, crafting nonconventional moments and cracks of alternative practice within a Turkish administrative and ideological edifice (see also Scalbert-Yücel 2009; Gourlay 2018).

Second, by promoting and mobilizing the Kurdish language and culture in the public sphere, the initiative aimed to boost ethnic consciousness, fraternity, and solidarity among members of the Kurdish ethnic minority. Through such mechanisms, multilingual municipalism served to build a novel and more national Kurdish identity. As Watts (2010, 142) notes, "pro-Kurdish parties and officials used the resources of local office to try to establish an alternative Kurdish governmental presence and to construct a new Kurdish subject or collective community." Thus, in addition to its contentious and oppositional features, multilingual municipalism also had constitutive aspects. Vahap Coşkun, an academic from Dicle University (Diyarbakır), also acknowledged the multiple motivations behind this initiative and emphasized its identity-building and identity-asserting functions:

> For sure, this initiative had multiple objectives. First, local people, especially those who could not speak the Turkish language, used to have such a need and demand. Thus, this initiative was positive in terms of improving municipal services. Second, and more importantly, by increasing the visibility of the Kurdish language in the public realm, the Kurdish movement also aimed at inscribing Kurdishness into the public sphere. . . . And, this was something welcomed and supported by all other Kurdish political circles in the region, including Islamist Kurds.[15]

---

15. Author's interview, Diyarbakır, September 27, 2019. Other interviewees (e.g., Mahmut Bozarslan, a journalist, Diyarbakır, June 7, 2019; Muhammed Akar, a lawyer

Third, Demirbaş notes that by incorporating local languages and dialects (other than Kurdish) into local governance, this informal institutional arrangement seeks to protect and empower other local cultures, identities, and languages in Turkey's eastern and southeastern regions (e.g., Arabic, Armenian, and Syriac) (see also Gourlay 2018; Flader and Gürer 2019). In a separate interview, Demirbaş acknowledged this aspect of multilingual municipalism: "I'm not just fighting for Kurds but for the diversity of this region. Assyrians, Christians, the Armenians, the Arabs—for the last 85 years we've been told there are only Turks and only one religion. And people who challenge this are always declared to be terrorists, enemies of the state, criminals" (see Jones 2013). These statements suggest that the promotion of ethnic and cultural identities other than Kurdish serves the Kurdish movement's broader strategy of contesting official rules and regulations based on Turkishness. As Gourlay (2018, 477) also observes, "As Kurds acknowledge and promote Turkey's religious and ethnic diversity they are presenting an alternative politics, one that is not exclusively Kurdish but that creates spaces for the minorities that hegemonic Turkish politics seek to deny."

What has been the public opinion on such issues? One might expect such initiatives of the municipalities controlled by pro-Kurdish political parties to be welcomed and supported by the local people. Indeed, the results of the existing surveys indicate that while the Turkish majority lends limited support to the Kurds' linguistic demands, the Kurdish minority articulates strong linguistic demands.[16] As figure 6.2 shows, on average,

---

and politician, Diyarbakır, June 8, 2019; Mehmet Emin Aktar, a lawyer, Diyarbakır, September 27, 2019) also emphasized the same political motivations behind multilingual municipalism.

16. As part of a broader research project on Turkey's Kurdish issue, three public opinion surveys were conducted in 2011, 2013, and 2015. The surveys were funded by the Economic Policy Research Foundation of Turkey (Türkiye Ekonomi Politikaları Araştırma Vakfı, TEPAV). The main objective of the surveys was to detect Kurdish demands and Turkish attitudes toward those demands. All the surveys were conducted by a private research company, based in Istanbul, through face-to-face interviews with participants, aged 18 or above. In 2011, 6,516 randomly chosen respondents from 48 provinces participated in the first survey. The same survey was repeated in 2013 with 7,103 participants from 50 provinces. After making some slight changes to the survey, we readministered it in 2015. The third round of the survey had 7,100 participants from 50 provinces. A multistage, stratified, cluster-sampling procedure was utilized to identify households. Once households were selected, age and gender quotes were applied to identify one respondent from each household.

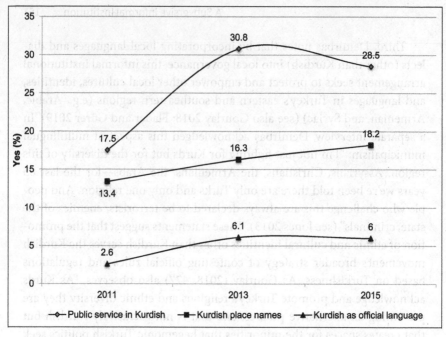

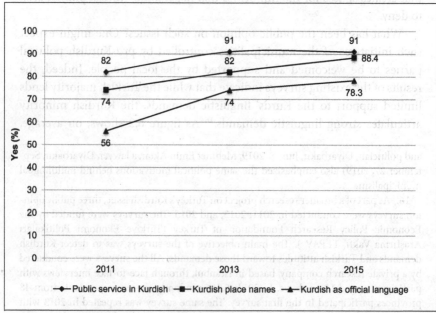

Figure 6.2. Turkish and Kurdish Mass Support for Some Linguistic Demands (2011, 2013, 2015)

around one-quarter of the Turkish majority supports delivering public services in Kurdish, 16% approves of place names in Kurdish, and only 5% accepts the recognition of Kurdish as an official language. On the other hand, on average, the vast majority of Kurds express their support for delivering public services in Kurdish (88%), allowing place names in Kurdish (81.5%), and recognizing Kurdish as an official language (69%). One might claim that strong Kurdish support for such linguistic rights and demands constitutes another motivation behind the Kurdish movement's initiative of multilingual municipalism.

State Response to Multilingual Local Governance

How did the state respond to the contentious and subversive informal institution initiated by the antisystemic Kurdish ethnopolitical movement? Regarding regime response to contentious claims, Tilly and Tarrow (2015, 112) note that

> every regime divides known claim-making performances into prescribed, tolerated, and forbidden. A regime's government and other authorities enforce the prescribed performances, facilitate or at least do not block the tolerated performances, and act to suppress forbidden performances. Contained contention occurs within the limits set by prescribed and tolerated performances. Transgressive contention breaks out of those institutional limits into forbidden or previously unknown territory.

As stated above, the Turkish state has been promoting a highly monolithic and homogenous understanding of national and state identity based on Turkishness. In addition, according to official rules and regulations, municipalities are required to provide public services in Turkish. Given those formal institutional rules and regulations, the principle of multilingual municipalism adopted and promoted by the Kurdish ethnopolitical movement in local governance is perceived as a major threat to the principle of national and territorial integrity. As a result, the state responded to these transgressive and subversive informal arrangements with coercive and repressive measures (see also Watts 2010; Bayir 2013). For instance, many name changes were overruled by provincial governors[17] and by administrative

_____

17. In the Turkish administrative system, although mayors are locally elected, gover-

courts.[18] Kurdish mayors have also faced prosecution and imprisonment for their efforts to promote multilingual municipalism and campaign for greater Kurdish linguistic rights and freedoms. As a case in point, the Ministry of Internal Affairs filed a lawsuit against Sur Municipality at the Council of State (Danıştay), the highest administrative court in the country. The mayor of Sur municipality, Abdullah Demirbaş, was accused of violating constitutional principles, misusing his authority, municipal facilities, and resources, and assisting the "separatist" and "terrorist" PKK (Toumani 2008; Bayir 2013; Jones 2013). In June 2007, the Eighth Chamber of the Council of State removed Demirbaş from office due to multilingual municipal services initiated by Sur municipality.[19] Stating that municipal services could not be delivered in any language other than Turkish, the court dissolved the elected municipal council. Similarly, the mayor of Diyarbakir Metropolitan Municipality, Osman Baydemir, was also prosecuted for sending celebration cards in the Kurdish language.

Especially after the collapse of the Peace Process (2013–15), the state increased pressure and repression on the Kurdish movement in general and on pro-Kurdish political parties in particular (see also Gunes 2021). For instance, the government formally took over several municipalities and most of the mayors removed from office were detained and imprisoned (see also Tutkal 2021; Whiting and Kaya 2021).[20] By 2019, the vast majority of

nors are centrally appointed by the government and they represent the state in provinces and districts. Provincial governors are called *vali* and district governors are named *kaymakam* in Turkish.

18. For instance, see "19 parkın Kürtçe isimlerini, 'bölücü ve ahlaka aykırı' sayılarak kaldırıldı!" [19 park names in Kurdish were viewed as separatist and immoral, and thus removed], *T24*, July 22, 2012, https://t24.com.tr/haber/19-parkin-kurtce-isimleri-bolucu-ve-ahlaka-aykiri-sayilarak-kaldirildi,208985, accessed July 16, 2022.

19. During the local elections of March 2009, Abdullah Demirbaş was reelected as the mayor of Sur district with increasing popularity (from 56% to 66%). His increasing electoral popularity is interpreted as evidence of Sur residents' support for multilingual municipal services. However, in May 2009, he was sentenced to two years of imprisonment. In May 2010, he was released on medical grounds.

20. The AKP government based such a repressive measure on Decree 674, introduced by the government in September 2016, during the state of emergency (July 2016–July 2018). Article 38 of the emergency decree enabled the Ministry of Internal Affairs to remove elected mayors from office if they were "accused" of a criminal act and instead appoint a trustee. Interestingly, the government continued to utilize such an extraordinary power even after the end of the state of emergency in July 2018. The decree is available at https://www.resmigazete.gov.tr/eskiler/2016/09/20160901M2-2.htm, accessed July 25, 2022.

municipalities controlled by pro-Kurdish political parties during the March 2014 local elections were taken over by the government (around 95 out of 102 municipalities). As a result, government-appointed trustees (*kayyum*) replaced mayors from pro-Kurdish political parties who had been elected by local people. However, during the March 2019 local elections, most of the municipalities taken over by the government were regained by the pro-Kurdish HDP. The HDP won around 65 municipalities during those local elections. Despite this electoral outcome, the central government followed the same strategy even after the March 2019 local elections and took over almost all of the municipalities won by the pro-Kurdish HDP, including three metropolitan municipalities: Diyarbakır, Mardin, and Van.[21] In brief, when the subversive informal institution promoted by the Kurdish movement began to undermine and threaten official rules and regulations, the state responded by cracking down on those informal initiatives and arrangements.[22]

Having said that, this initiative by the Kurdish movement did lead to some changes in the state's attitude toward the use of the Kurdish language in local governance. It is still the case that the Turkish state formally recognizes only one language as the official language (i.e., the Turkish language and nothing else). Hence, the Kurdish language is still not allowed in formal governance. However, to a certain extent, Kurdish is *informally* accommodated in local governance. For instance, although many government-appointed trustees removed Kurdish signboards, plaques, and banners from public buildings and spaces, some municipalities that were taken over by the government maintained the use of Kurdish signboards, plaques, and banners at public buildings and squares. In other words, the subversive informal institution initiated by the Kurdish movement has led to some shifts in local governance. If not de jure, we see government's de facto recognition and approval of the use of Kurdish in local governance. Thus, the Kurdish movement's informal subversive arrangements triggered some shifts in the attitudes of a formal actor (i.e., the central state) in an informal domain.

----

21. By the end of 2020, only five district municipalities remained in the hands of the HDP.

22. Another motivation behind such a repressive state policy was to prevent the Kurdish movement from accessing and controlling public resources through local governments (see also Whiting and Kaya 2021).

Conclusions and Implications

This chapter examines the multilingual municipalism initiated and promoted by Turkey's Kurdish ethnopolitical movement as a representative case of a subversive informal institution. This particular case suggests that when actors (individual or collective) face illegitimate *and* harmful formal rules and regulations, they are likely to resort to subversive informal arrangements and practices. More specifically, when minority groups or movements face exclusionary and suppressive formal institutional arrangements, they are likely to resort to informal means and mechanisms to promote their cause and to confront, contest, and resist the existing disadvantageous formal rules and regulations. This suggests that state authoritarianism is likely to facilitate the creation and maintenance of destructive informal institutional arrangements and mechanisms. In authoritarian regimes in particular, informal institutions can be tools of civil disobedience, political mobilization, and resistance against the existing exclusionary or repressive formal arrangements. By utilizing such informal arrangements, opposition movements try to "disrupt 'normal' political routines, articulating highly contentious identity claims and challenging the nationalist basis of the state" (Watts 2006, 129; see also Hintz and Quatrini 2021).

This case also constitutes an illustrative example of deliberate, intentional, and strategic design and use of informal institutions. The case of multilingual municipalism confirms that informal rules and arrangements can become a political instrument used by disadvantaged and discriminated opposition groups to publicly assert certain social or political facts and to confront, contest, and undermine the legal and moral authority of the existing suppressive formal rules and regulations. In other words, informal institutions can be a strategic instrument of antisystemic and antagonistic politics, especially in authoritarian and suppressive sociopolitical settings.

This case also has some implications for contentious politics in authoritarian settings. As opponent groups contest authoritarian rules, policies, and practices, they use various conventional and nonconventional strategies and means such as strikes, protests, rallies, demonstrations, occupations, public meetings, boycotts, petition, litigation, and awareness-raising campaigns, both online and offline (e.g., see McAdam, Tarrow and Tilly 2004; Tilly and Tarrow 2015; Borsuk et al. 2022). This particular case suggests that opposition groups, which do not have enough resources and power to remove or reform the existing suppressive and exclusionary formal rules and regulations, might struggle against those formal arrangements by utilizing various informal means and mechanisms (see also Metinsoy 2021). McAdam, Tarrow, and Tilly (2004, 2009) also acknowledge that institutionalization constitutes one of the mechanisms of contentious politics. However, institutionalization should not be limited to formal arrangements. As this particular case confirms, contending sociopolitical movements and groups such as ethnic minorities might consciously devise informal institutions to challenge or contest the existing formal rules and regulations. Otherwise stated, opponent groups might resort to informal institutionalization to achieve formal deinstitutionalization. Contending groups might employ informal arrangements in their peaceful struggle against the existing authoritarian regime because the de facto, amorphous, and less visible nature of informal arrangements and formations provides opposition groups various opportunities to resist, contest, and disrupt the existing suppressive and exclusionary formal rules and regulations. In brief, the repertoire of contention in authoritarian settings also includes informal institutional arrangements and initiatives. This implies that contentious politics in repressive sociopolitical settings usually involves informal components as well. One might even claim that, in authoritarian settings, informal aspects of contentious politics are likely to occupy a larger space than its formal aspects. Therefore, a better understanding of contentious politics in authoritarian settings requires one to pay due attention to the formal and informal faces of resistance and contention.

CHAPTER 7
Conclusions and Implications

Earlier institutional analyses paid greater attention to the role of formal rules and regulations in sociopolitical life, treating informal institutions as something residual or epiphenomenal. Given the plethora of strong and influential informal institutions in the social and political spheres, it is surprising that, until recently, informal institutions have not been a central focus of institutional theory. As Azari and Smith (2012, 39) observe, one habit in the existing institutional literature is an inclination to treat informal institutions as a "residual category, a backstop source of explanation where others [formal ones] have failed" (see also K. Tsai 2006, 124). Similarly, Radnitz (2011, 351) detects that "much of political science implicitly or explicitly begins from a premise of functioning formal institutions, and sees deviations from expectations stemming from that model as aberrant—both normatively and empirically." Finally, Brie and Stölting (2012, 19) note that

> the informal is simultaneously the unwanted stepchild of the social sciences and something that continues to enthrall them. Accessible only in a limited fashion to qualitative empirical research, rarely able to be grasped in elegant formal models, and still morally suspect, the informal sphere has the aura of the irrational and the irregular. Standard works of institutional analysis still have the tendency to push the informal to the margins of institutional analysis.

However, as the empirical chapters of this study show, a good deal happens in the informal domain of sociopolitical life and those developments might have direct or indirect consequences, or both, for the formal realm. This suggests that as long as we ignore the role of informal institutional factors, we have limited knowledge and understanding of sociopolitical life. As Helmke and Levitsky (2004, 725) suggest, in many contexts, informal institutions, ranging from bureaucratic and legislative norms to clientelism and patrimonialism, shape even more strongly political behavior and outcomes. Scholars who fail to consider these informal rules of the game risk missing many of the most important incentives and constraints that underlie political behavior.

Similarly, Peters (2019, 202) notes that

informal institutions . . . constitute a very real part of political life. They arise in a variety of circumstances and can play a variety of roles. As well as being important on their own, they are perhaps most important in the manner in which they interact with formal institutions and contribute to, or detract from, the achievement of goals through the processes of governing.

Therefore, it is comforting to see that recent institutional studies pay more attention to the role of informal institutional factors and dynamics. However, the existing institutional literature does not really provide a comprehensive conceptual and theoretical framework of informal institutions. Compared to formal institutions, informal institutions still remain underexplored and undertheorized in the institutional literature. As Lauth (2015, 56) observes, "institutionalist approaches fell short of incorporating informal rules and institutions in a coherent theoretical manner."

Given this lacuna in the institutional literature, this study offers a conceptual and theoretical framework for the role of informal institutions in the social and political spheres. The theoretical framework is based on a new, improved typology of informal institutions, which is based on the following three dimensions: (1) formal institutional legitimacy, (2) formal institutional utility, and (3) the compatibility between formal and informal institutional logics. This three-dimensional typology identifies new forms of formal-informal interaction and four novel types of informal institutions: (1) *symbiotic*, (2) *superseding*, (3) *layered*, and (4) *subversive*. This new multidimensional typology of informal institutions adds to our knowledge and understanding of the role of informal institutions in sociopolitical life. Thus, this typology has a strong potential to trigger novel research questions, questions that have been neglected by the existing underspecified, and thus incomplete, typological analyses.

In sociopolitical life, informal institutions can emerge as a result of either intentional design or evolutionary processes. In terms of intentional design, the following conditions and factors enhance the likelihood of informal institutions emerging: the failure or reluctance of human agents to establish a formal institution; the incomplete nature of the existing formal rules and regulations; the complexity, rigidity, or inefficiency of formal institutions; the ambiguity of the existing formal rules and regulations; the presence of exclusionary and discriminatory formal institutions; and the legitimacy deficit of formal institutions. Informal institutions might also emerge through relatively more decentralized, unintentional, evolutionary, and spontaneous processes and practices, such as habituation. Additionally, the emergence of informal institutions might be an unintended consequence of abrupt formal institutional change. In the aftermath of sudden and dramatic changes to formal institutional rules and regulations, certain formal institutions might persist and continue their lives as an informal institution under the newly established sociopolitical system.

In terms of informal institutional change, factors such as changes in the efficiency and legitimacy of formal institutions, shifts in the surrounding sociopolitical culture, and changing power structures among institutional actors are likely to trigger informal institutional change.

To illustrate each type of informal institution and the conceptual and theoretical points, this study examines several empirical cases of informal institutions as derived from various issue areas in the Turkish sociopolitical context: civil law, conflict resolution, minority rights, and local governance. The Turkish case, which is characterized by an abundance of strong and influential informal institutions, provides a highly useful and valuable sociopolitical context in terms of getting fresh insights into informal institutions and thus in constructing novel hypotheses on the role of informal institutions in the sociopolitical world. The following cases in the Turkish context are analyzed: *religious marriage* (as a symbiotic informal institution); the *Cem courts* of the Alevi religious minority (as a superseding informal institution); the *holidays of religious minority groups* (i.e., Christians and Alevis) (as a layered informal institution); and *multilingual municipalism* initiated by the Kurdish ethnopolitical movement (as a subversive informal institution) (summarized in table 7.1). Empirical analyses are based on original quantitative and qualitative data derived from several focus groups, in-depth interviews, and a nationwide survey (Informal Institutions in Turkey Survey, TEKA 2019) (see Sarigil 2019), among others.

TABLE 7.1. A Summary of the Empirical Cases of Informal Institutions

Cases	Type	Institutional logic	Majority vs. minority institution	Issue areas
Religious marriage	Symbiotic	Concordant	Majority	Family, marriage
Cem courts	Superseding/ complementary	Concordant	Religious minority	Conflict resolution, justice
Religious minority holidays	Layered	Discordant	Religious minority	Religious traditions, religious minority rights
Multilingual municipalism	Subversive	Discordant	Ethnic minority	Local governance, ethnic minority rights, linguistic rights

Implications

The study has major theoretical implications for institutional theory in general and for research on informal institutions in particular.

The empirical analyses of this study confirm that informal institutions are indispensable elements of sociopolitical life. Although informal institutions are relatively more amorphous and inconspicuous than formal institutional structures, they are real and prevalent entities. Informal institutions may even occupy more space in certain social and political domains. To use the analogy of an iceberg, if formal institutions correspond to the tip of the iceberg (the visible part above the surface of the sea), informal institutions constitute its invisible part, below sea level. Other than their considerable direct impact, informal institutions indirectly shape sociopolitical processes, behaviors, and outcomes by interacting with formal rules and regulations in myriad ways (cooperative or competitive). The empirical analyses of this study confirm that as major building blocks of sociopolitical life, informal institutions substantially affect not only the efficiency and effectiveness of formal institutions but also their social approval and legitimacy. Therefore, studying informal institutions and conducting a systematic analysis of formal-informal institutional interactions and configurations is quite rewarding for institutional perspectives. As Helmke and Levitsky (2004, 726) suggest,

> good institutional analysis requires rigorous attention to both formal and informal rules. Careful attention to informal institutions is critical to

understanding the incentives that enable and constrain political behavior. Political actors respond to a mix of formal and informal incentives, and in some instances, informal incentives trump the formal ones.

The empirical chapters of this study analyze four interesting cases of informal institutions derived from the Turkish sociopolitical landscape. As summarized in table 7.1, three of those informal institutions (Cem courts, religious minority holidays, and multilingual municipalism) belong to religious and ethnic minority groups. Such distribution is probably not surprising because, especially in restrictive, authoritarian regimes, formal legal systems tend to reflect the norms and values of the dominant majority group and so exclude minority cultures and identities (see also Lord 2018). The restrictive and exclusionary nature of formal state rules and regulations in repressive regimes forces excluded and marginalized ethnic and religious minority groups to set up or resort to various institutions that operate in the informal domain. These minority institutions might either conflict or cooperate with the existing formal arrangements. The fourth case (religious marriage), however, is an informal institution adhered to by the majority of Turkish society; this particular case shows that we should not limit informal institutions to minority groups or movements. In other words, majority groups might resort to nonstate, informal rules and regulations as well.

Regarding the role of informal institutions in sociopolitical life, we see two different treatments or perspectives in the extant literature: pessimistic and optimistic. The pessimistic view expects informal structures to impede, weaken, or paralyze formal rules and regulations (e.g., see North 1990; O'Donnell 1996; Böröcz 2000; Collins 2002; Ganev 2007; Hertog 2010; Mattingly 2016). K. Tsai (2006, 124) observes that in the pessimistic view "informal institutions are blamed for inhibiting the normal functioning of formal institutions. Cultural explanations for why certain countries are neither more developed nor more democratic are often cited as cogent examples of how informal institutions may undermine formal ones." Peters (2019, 213) makes a similar observation regarding the skeptical approach: "To the extent that informal institutions do have normative content, it is generally negative and they are seen as undermining the formal institutions of government." Thus, the pessimistic view generally assumes that the formal is good, while the informal is bad.

A relatively more optimistic perspective, however, suggests that informal institutions might enhance the performance of formal rules and regulations and thus contribute through problem solving, public goods provision, governance, democratization, and socioeconomic development (e.g., see Axelrod 1986; Wang 2000; Hu 2007; L Tsai 2007; C. Williamson 2009; Xu and Yao 2015; Seidler 2018; Levitsky and Ziblatt 2018). For instance, C. Williamson (2009, 377) indicates that "countries that have stronger informal institutions, regardless of the strength of formal institutions, achieve higher levels of economic development than those countries with lower informal institutional scores."

The current study suggests that both views have some truth and validity. As the in-depth analyses of several empirical cases of informal institutions in the Turkish sociopolitical context confirm, the interaction between formal and informal institutions might be either competitive or cooperative. For instance, as the analysis of subversive informal institutions indicate, excluded or suppressed groups (ethnic, religious, or ideological) in authoritarian regimes are likely to contest or challenge the existing formal rules and regulations by setting up various contentious and destructive informal institutions. However, as the case of symbiotic informal institution (informal religious marriage) suggests, there might also be cooperative or mutually supportive relations between formal and informal institutions. Informal institutions might not only enhance the efficiency of formal institutions but their social approval and legitimacy as well. Therefore, as Peters (2019, 215) warns, "informal institutions are neither inherently positive or negative but must be evaluated individually" (see also Lauth 2000; Helmke and Levitsky 2004; Ledeneva 2018; Polese 2021). From that perspective, it is not worthwhile to spend time on the question of whether informal institutions empower or undermine formal rules and regulations. A theoretically more fruitful question to ask would be the following: How and through what mechanisms and processes might an informal institution undermine or empower a formal institution? When and under what conditions might a cooperative informal institution turn into a competitive one, and a competitive one become a cooperative one?

This study further implies that institutional analyses should not underestimate the importance of the legitimacy aspect of institutions. Existing institutional analyses pay a great deal of attention to the efficiency and effectiveness of formal institutions (e.g., see Helmke and Levitsky 2004, 2006). However, the in-depth analyses of several empirical cases of institutions in the Turkish sociopolitical context show that the legitimacy aspect of formal institutions matters as well. Despite a high degree of efficiency and effectiveness, formal institutions might still be limited in terms of legitimacy and appropriateness. The empirical analyses indicate that formal rules and regulations such as official civil marriage, official regulation of religious holidays, formal state courts, and the principle of monolingualism in governance have enjoyed limited legitimacy in the eyes of several social groups. The legitimacy deficit of formal institutions in return has encouraged human agents to resort to informal arrangements. In other words, as the empirical analyses of this study confirm, the limited legitimacy of formal institutional arrangements constitutes one of the major motivations behind actors' appeal and adherence to informal rules and regulations. Thus, the legitimacy aspect of formal institutions is highly consequential not only for formal institutional performance and thus compliance but also for the emergence and subsequent development of informal institutions. Therefore, it is fair to conclude that, as long as we ignore or neglect actors' legitimacy concerns, we will have limited knowledge and comprehension of the rise and evolution of informal institutions in the social and political worlds.

Future Research

When we focus on formal-informal institutional interactions, we tend to reify both formal and informal institutions. However, formal and informal arrangements are not frozen entities. Rather, their status might shift across time. Accordingly, an informal institution or practice might get codified and so turn into a formal institution (e.g., see Farrel and Heritier 2003; Stacey and Rittberger 2003; K. Tsai 2006; Van Cott 2006; Levitsky and Ziblatt 2018; Hummel 2021). For instance, in her analysis of private sector development in China since the late 1970s, K. Tsai (2006) shows that to avoid the restrictions of constraining formal institutions, local actors devised certain informal coping strategies. For instance, in China, "wearing a red hat" stands for the practice of registering a business as a collective enterprise despite its being privately owned and managed. How did this institution emerge? Tsai shows that during the first decade of economic reform, private enterprises with more than eight employees were not legally allowed. To avoid this formal restriction, private enterprises adopted the practice of "wearing a red hat," which meant registering the business as a collective enterprise. Thus, many of the collective enterprises were bigger private businesses wearing red hats as a disguise or camouflage. Over time, this informal practice became institutionalized, and it emerged as a standard practice for private entrepreneurs. The use of the red hat disguise facilitated the expansion of a number of larger private enterprises. Tsai further shows that the expansion of those informal institutions and practices undermined the legitimacy and validity of restrictive formal rules, regulations, and policies and motivated or encouraged political elites to reform these rules, regulations, and policies. This reform process also involved the legalization and formalization of informal institutions (i.e., larger private enterprises). Accordingly, in the late 1980s, private enterprises were officially recognized and permitted; this reform further boosted the growth of the private sector.

Another striking example of formal recognition is how, as part of broader efforts to recognize ethnic diversity and collective rights for native peoples in the 1990s, many Latin American countries revised their constitutions and officially recognized informal, native legal institutions, such as *rondas campesinas* and indigenous customary law (see Van Cott 2006).

Presidential term limits in US politics constitute another illustrative example. Until 1951, it was a de facto, informal rule that presidents step down after serving two terms in the office of the presidency (the US constitution did not specify any limit on presidential terms). Thus, US presidents generally respected this unwritten law and retired from office after two terms. This informal rule was codified with the Twenty-Second Amendment to the US Constitution in 1951 (see also Levitsky and Ziblatt 2018).

We should also acknowledge that an existing formal institution might become informalized. For instance, religious marriage in Turkey was a formal, legal institution during the Ottoman period but became informal during the Republican era. The strictly secular Republic, which was formally established in 1923, adopted a new Civic Law in 1926 that introduced entirely secular formal civil marriage that was registered and licensed by municipalities. However, Turkish society continued to conduct religious marriages informally. Thus, religious marriage, which was a formal institution during the Ottoman era, persisted and continued as a widespread informal institution under the secular Republican regime.

If so, then why, when, and how do formal institutions become informal and informal institutions get formalized? To ask this differently, why do agents keep certain institutions in the informal sphere and move others to the formal realm, or vice versa? This study provides one possible answer to this important question. The case of religious marriage, for instance, suggests that when an abrupt and radical transition to a new social or political order takes place, certain formal institutional rules and regulations of the old system might persist and maintain themselves as informal institutions under the new regime. In other words, some formal institutions might get informalized in the aftermath of a sudden and dramatic formal institutional transformation. In such cases, informalization appears to be an unintended and unpredicted consequence of abrupt formal institutional change. Having said that, the issue of formalization and informalization of institutions remains an undertheorized issue.[1] Hence, investigating such processes through further theoretical and empirical research would certainly benefit institutional theory.

Finally, another possible extension of this study would be applying the conceptual and theoretical framework to different sociopolitical settings. This naturally begs the following question: To what extent might the conceptual and theoretical framework presented in this study travel across different sociopolitical settings? The theoretical framework of this study offers novel types of informal institutions and propositions on the emergence and transformation of informal institutions. The concepts and propositions that this study advances have potential to stimulate further substantive research on informal institutions, especially in sociopolitical contexts where informal institutions are pervasive and influential. Informal rules and regulations substantially shape sociopolitical processes and outcomes across the world, especially in regions such as Latin America, Africa, the Middle East, the post-Soviet region, and Asia.[2] Thus, putting the theoretical concepts and propositions of this study into empirical operation in different sociopolitical settings would in return refine and improve the conceptual and theoretical framework developed in this study.

In brief, it would be still useful and profitable to conduct further scholarly research about the emergence and evolution of informal institutions, the interplay between formal and informal institutions, and (in)formalization processes. The following specific questions especially warrant further

1. For some initial studies on the formalization of informal rules and practices, see Hix 2002; Farrell and Heritier 2003; Stacey and Rittberger 2003; and Heritier 2012.

2. This statement, however, does not mean that informal institutions are absent from the social and political spheres in developed countries (see, for instance, Heritier 2012). As Böröcz (2000, 352) also states, "Social life is simply impossible, even in the West, without a serious, reliable and comfortably available informal component."

investigation through additional case studies or large-N research: When and how do the limitations of existing formal institutions (e.g., inefficiency, complexity, rigidity, ambiguity, illegitimacy, and exclusionary and discriminatory features) trigger the rise of informal institutions? How and through what mechanisms do informal institutions undermine or empower formal institutions? Why, when, and how do the existing informal institutions change? How does informal institutional change affect formal arrangements? Finally, regarding (in)formalization processes, why, when, and how do actors formalize an existing informal practice or rule? And why and how do the existing formal arrangements become informalized?

BIBLIOGRAPHY

Acemoglu, Daron, Simon Johnson, and James A. Robinson. 2005. "Institutions as a Fundamental Cause of Long-Run Growth." In *Handbook of Economic Growth*, edited by Aghion Philippe and Steven N. Durlauf, 385–472. Netherlands: Elsevier.

Acikalin, Mehmet, and Hamide Kilic. 2017. "The Role of Turkish National Holidays in Promoting Character and Citizenship Education." *Journal of Social Science Education* 16 (3): 74–83.

Adams, Laura L. 2010. *The Spectacular State: Culture and National Identity in Uzbekistan*. Durham, NC: Duke University Press.

Akgönül, Samim. 2019. "Religious Minorities." In *The Routledge Handbook of Turkish Politics*, edited by Alpaslan Özerdem and Matthew Whiting, 328–39. New York: Routledge.

Akkaya, Ahmet H., and Joost Jongerden. 2012. "Reassembling the Political: The PKK and the Project of Radical Democracy." *European Journal of Turkish Studies* 14.

Alford, Robert R., and Roger Friedland. 1985. *Powers of Theory: Capitalism, the State, and Democracy*. Cambridge: Cambridge University Press.

Aliyev, Huseyn. 2017. *When Informal Institutions Change: Institutional Reforms and Informal Practices in the Former Soviet Union*. Ann Arbor: University of Michigan Press.

Apaydın, H. Yunus. 2000. "Nikah Akdinin Mahiyeti ve İmam Nikahı Uygulaması" [The importance of the marriage contract and religious marriage]. *Erciyes Üniversitesi Sosyal Bilimler Enstitüsü Dergisi* 1 (9): 373–80.

Arat, Yeşim. 2021. "Democratic Backsliding and the Instrumentalization of Women's Rights in Turkey." *Politics & Gender* (August): 1–31. https://doi.org/10.1017/S1743923X21000192

Arslan, Sevda. 2015. "Language Policy in Turkey and Its Effect on the Kurdish Language." Master's thesis, Department of Political Science, Western Michigan University.

Aslan, Senem. 2007. "'Citizen, Speak Turkish!' A Nation in the Making." *Nationalism and Ethnic Politics* 13 (2): 245–72.

Aslan, Senem. 2009. "Incoherent State: The Controversy over Kurdish Naming in Turkey." *European Journal of Turkish Studies* 10.

Aslan, Senem. 2021. "Legal Contention and Minorities in Turkey: The Case of the Kurds and Alevis." In *Negotiating Democracy and Religious Pluralism: India, Pakistan, and Turkey*, edited by Karen Barkey, Sudipta Kaviraj, and Vatsal Naresh, 301–21. Oxford: Oxford University Press.

Atlas, Duygu. 2014. "The Role of Language in the Evolution of Kurdish National Identity in Turkey." In *Kurdish Awakening: Nation Building in a Fragmented Homeland*, edited by Ofra Bengio, 155–75. Austin: University of Texas Press.

Aubert, Vilhelm. 1967. "Courts and Conflict Resolution." *Journal of Conflict Resolution* 11 (1): 40–51.

Axelrod, Robert M. 1984. *The Evolution of Cooperation*. New York: Basic Books.

Axelrod, Robert. 1986. "An Evolutionary Approach to Norms." *American Political Science Review* 80 (4): 1095–1111.

Aydin, Aysegul, and Cem Emrence. 2015. *Zones of Rebellion: Kurdish Insurgents and the Turkish State*. Ithaca, NY: Cornell University Press.

Aydingün, Ayşegül, and Ismail Aydingün. 2004. "The Role of Language in the Formation of Turkish National Identity and Turkishness." *Nationalism and Ethnic Politics* 10 (3): 415–32.

Azari, Julia R., and Jennifer K. Smith. 2012. "Unwritten Rules: Informal Institutions in Established Democracies." *Perspectives on Politics* 10 (1): 37–55.

Balkız, Ali. 2007. *Kent Koşullarında Sosyolojik Olgu Olarak Alevilik* [Alevism as a Sociological Fact in Urban Settings]. İstanbul: Alev Yayınları.

Bardach, Eugene, and Robert A. Kagan. 2017. *Going by the Book: The Problem of Regulatory Unreasonableness*. New York: Routledge.

Bardakci, Mehmet, Annette Freyberg-Inan, Christoph Giesel, and Olaf Leisse. 2017. *Religious Minorities in Turkey: Alevi, Armenians, and Syriacs and the Struggle to Desecuritize Religious Freedom*. London: Palgrave Macmillan.

Bates, Robert H. 1988. "Contra Contractarianism: Some Reflections on the New Institutionalism." *Politics & Society* 16 (2–3): 387–401.

Bayar, Yeşim. 2014. "In Pursuit of Homogeneity: The Lausanne Conference, Minorities and the Turkish Nation." *Nationalities Papers* 42 (1): 108–25.

Bayir, Derya. 2013. *Minorities and Nationalism in Turkish Law*. Burlington, VT: Ashgate.

Beetham, David. 2011. "Legitimacy." In *International Encyclopedia of Political Science*, edited by Bertrand Badie, Dirk Berg-Schlosser, and Leonardo Morlino. Thousand Oaks, CA: Sage.

Behar, Cem. 2004. "Neighborhood Nuptials: Islamic Personal Law and Local Customs—Marriage Records in a Mahalle of Traditional Istanbul (1864–1907)." *International Journal of Middle East Studies* 36 (4): 537–59.

Belge, Ceren. 2006. "Friends of the Court: The Republican Alliance and Selective Activism of the Constitutional Court of Turkey." *Law & Society Review* 40 (3): 653–92.

Berger, Peter L., and Thomas Luckmann. 1967. *The Social Construction of Reality*. New York: Doubleday Anchor.

Beylunioğlu, Anna Maria. 2017. "Recasting the Parameters of Freedom of Religion in Turkey: Non-Muslims and the AKP." In *Authoritarian Politics in Turkey: Elections, Resistance and the AKP*, edited by Bahar Baser and Ahmet Erdi Öztürk, 141–56. London: I.B. Tauris.

Bloor, Michael, Jane Frankland, Michelle Thomas, and Kate Robson. 2001. *Focus Groups in Social Research*. Thousand Oaks, CA: Sage.

Bó, Pedro Dal. 2005. "Cooperation under the Shadow of the Future: Experimental Evidence from Infinitely Repeated Games." *American Economic Review* 95 (5): 1591–1604.

Böröcz, József. 2000. "Informality Rules." *East European Politics & Societies* 14 (2): 348–80.

Borovali, Murat, and Cemil Boyraz. 2015. "The Alevi Workshops: An Opening without an Outcome?" *Turkish Studies* 16 (2): 145–60.

Borsuk, İmren, Pınar Dinç, Sinem Kavak, and Pınar Sayan. 2022. *Authoritarian Neoliberalism and Resistance in Turkey: Construction, Consolidation, and Contestation*. Singapore: Palgrave Macmillan.

Bottoni, Rossella. 2013. "The Legal Treatment of Religious Minorities: Non-Muslims in Turkey and Muslims in Germany." In *Religion, Identity and Politics: Germany and Turkey in Interaction*, edited by Haldun Gülalp and Günter Seufert, 128–43. New York: Routledge.

Boudon, Raymond. 2003. "Beyond Rational Choice Theory." *Annual Review of Sociology* 29 (1): 1–21.

Bouquet, Olivier. 2017. "Non-Muslim Citizens as Foreigners Within: How Ecnebi Became Yabancı from the Ottoman Empire to the Turkish Republic." *Middle Eastern Studies* 53 (3): 486–99.

Bozarslan, Hamit. 2008. "Kurds and the Turkish State." In *The Cambridge History of Turkey, Volume 4: Turkey in the Modern World*, edited by Reşat Kasaba, 333–56. Cambridge: Cambridge University Press.

Bozkurt, Fuat. 1998. "State–Community Relations in the Restructuring of Alevism." In *Alevi Identity: Cultural, Religious and Social Perspectives*, edited by Tord Olsson, Elisabeth Özdalga, and Catharina Raudvere, 100–114. Istanbul: Swedish Research Institute.

Bratton, Michael. 2007. "Formal versus Informal Institutions in Africa." *Journal of Democracy* 18 (3): 96–110.

Brie, Michael, and Erhard Stölting. 2012. "Formal Institutions and Informal Institutional Arrangements." In *International Handbook on Informal Governance*, edited by Thomas Christiansen and Christine Neuhold, 19–39. Cheltenham, UK: Edward Elgar.

Brinks, Daniel M. 2003. "Informal Institutions and the Rule of Law: The Judicial Response to State Killings in Buenos Aires and São Paulo in the 1990s." *Comparative Politics* 36 (1): 1–19.

Brint, Steven, and Jerome Karabel. 1991. "Institutional Origins and Transformations: The Case of American Community Colleges." In *The New Institutionalism in Organizational Analysis*, edited by Walter W. Powel and Paul J. Dimaggio, 337–60. Chicago: University of Chicago Press.

Brunsson, Nils, and Johan P. Olsen. 1993. *The Reforming Organization*. London: Routledge.

Campbell, John L. 1997. "Mechanisms of Evolutionary Change in Economic Governance: Interaction, Interpretation and Bricolage." In *Evolutionary Economics and Path Dependence*, edited by Jan Ottosson and Lars Magnusson, 10–32. Cheltenham, UK: Edward Elgar.

Campbell, John L. 2004. *Institutional Change and Globalization*. Princeton, NJ: Princeton University Press.

Campbell, John L. 2010. "Institutional Reproduction and Change." In *Oxford Handbook of Comparative Institutional Analysis*, edited by Glenn Morgan, John L. Campbell, Colin Crouch, Peer H. Kristensen, Ove K. Pedersen, and Richard Whitley, 87–115. Oxford: Oxford University Press.

Çamuroğlu, Reha. 1998. "Alevi Revivalism in Turkey." In *Alevi Identity: Cultural, Religious and Social Perspectives*, edited by Tord Olsson, Eli Ozdalga and Catharina Raudvere, 79–84. Istanbul: Swedish Research Institute.

Carey, John M. 2000. "Parchment, Equilibria, and Institutions." *Comparative Political Studies* 33 (6–7): 735–61.

Çarkoğlu, Ali. 1998. "The Turkish Party System in Transition: Party Performance and Agenda Change." *Political Studies* 46 (3): 544–71.

Çarkoğlu, Ali. 2005. "Political Preferences of the Turkish Electorate: Reflections of an Alevi–Sunni Cleavage." *Turkish Studies* 6 (2): 273–92.

Çarkoğlu, Ali, and Ezgi Elçi. 2018. "Alevis in Turkey." In *Routledge Handbook of Minorities in the Middle East*, edited by Paul S. Rowe, 212–24. London: Routledge.

Casier, Marlies. 2010. "Turkey's Kurds and the Quest for Recognition: Transnational Politics and the EU—Turkey Accession Negotiations." *Ethnicities* 10 (1): 3–25.

Casson, Mark C., Marina Della Giusta, and Uma S. Kambhampati. 2010. "Formal and Informal Institutions and Development." *World Development* 38 (2): 137–41.

Çelik, Ayşe Betül, Rezarta Bilali, and Yeshim Iqbal. 2017. "Patterns of 'Othering' in Turkey: A Study of Ethnic, Ideological, and Sectarian Polarisation." *South European Society and Politics* 22 (2): 217–38.

Cemiloglu, Dicle. 2009. "Language Policy and National Unity: The Dilemma of the Kurdish Language in Turkey." Senior honors thesis, Political Science, University of Pennsylvania. https://core.ac.uk/reader/76393840

Cetinsaya, Gokhan. 1999. "Rethinking Nationalism and Islam Some: Preliminary Notes on the Roots of Turkish-Islamic Synthesis in Modern Turkish Political Thought." *Muslim World* 89 (3–4): 350–76.

Checkel, Jeffrey T., ed. 2013. *Transnational Dynamics of Civil War*. New York: Cambridge University Press.

Christensen, Johan. 2021. "Expert Knowledge and Policymaking: A Multi-Disciplinary Research Agenda." *Policy & Politics* 49 (3): 455–71.

Christiansen, Thomas, and Christine Neuhold, eds. 2012. *International Handbook on Informal Governance*. Northampton, MA: Edward Elgar.

Çınar, Alev. 2001. "National History as a Contested Site: The Conquest of Istanbul and Islamist Negotiations of the Nation." *Comparative Studies in Society and History* 43 (2): 364–91.

Cizre, Ümit. 2003. "Demythologyzing the National Security Concept: The Case of Turkey." *Middle East Journal* 57 (2): 213–29.

Cizre, Ümit, ed. 2008. *Secular and Islamic Politics in Turkey: The Making of the Justice and Development Party*. New York: Routledge.

Cleaver, Frances. 2012. *Development through Bricolage: Rethinking Institutions for Natural Resource Management*. Abingdon, UK: Routledge.

Clemens, Elisabeth S. 1993. "Organizational Repertoires and Institutional Change: Women's Groups and the Transformation of US Politics, 1890–1920." *American Journal of Sociology* 98 (4): 755–98.

Collier, David, Jody Laporte, and Jason Seawright. 2008. "Typologies: Forming Concepts and Creating Categorical Variables." In *The Oxford Handbook of Political Methodology*, edited by Janet M. Box-Steffensmeier, Henry E. Brady, and David Collier, 152–73. New York: Oxford University Press.

Collins, Kathleen. 2002. "Clans, Pacts, and Politics in Central Asia." *Journal of Democracy* 13 (3): 137–52.

Collins, Kathleen. 2004. "The Logic of Clan Politics: Evidence from the Central Asian Trajectories." *World Politics* 56 (2): 224–61.

Colomy, Paul. 1998. "Neofunctionalism and Neoinstitutionalism: Human Agency and Interest in Institutional Change." *Sociological Forum* 13: 265–300.

Conway, Steve, and Louise Westmarland. 2021. "The Blue Wall of Silence: Police Integrity and Corruption." In *Silence of Organizations: How Organizations Cover Up Wrongdoing*, edited by Sebastian Starystach and Kristina Höly, 105–33. Heidelberg: Heidelberg Bibliothek.

Cyr, Jennifer. 2019. *Focus Groups for the Social Science Researcher*. Cambridge: Cambridge University Press.

Deephouse, David L., Jonathan Bundy, Leigh Plunkett Tost, and Mark C. Suchman. 2017. "Organizational Legitimacy: Six Key Questions." In *The Sage Handbook of Organizational Institutionalism*, edited by Royston Greenwood, Christine Oliver, Thomas B. Lawrance, and Renate E. Meyer, 27–54. Thousand Oaks, CA: Sage.

DeMeritt, Jacqueline H. R. 2012. "International Organizations and Government Killing: Does Naming and Shaming Save Lives?" *International Interactions* 38 (5): 597–621.

Dimaggio, Paul J., and Walter W. Powell. 1991. "Introduction." In *The New Institutionalism in Organizational Analysis*, edited by Walter W. Powell and Paul J. Dimaggio, 1–38. Chicago: University of Chicago Press.

Dinc, Pinar. 2020. "The Kurdish Movement and the Democratic Federation of Northern Syria: An Alternative to the (Nation-) State Model?" *Journal of Balkan and Near Eastern Studies* 22 (1): 47–67.

Dorronsoro, Gilles, and Nicole F. Watts. 2012. "The Collective Production of Challenge: Civil Society, Parties, and Pro-Kurdish Politics in Diyarbakır." In *Negotiating Political Power in Turkey*, edited by Elise Massicard and Nicole F. Watts, 115–33. New York: Routledge.

Doty, D. Harold, and William H. Glick. 1994. "Typologies as a Unique Form of Theory Building: Toward Improved Understanding and Modeling." *Academy of Management Review* 19 (2): 230–51.

Dressler, Markus. 2006. "The Modern Dede: Changing Parameters for Religious Authority in Contemporary Turkish Alevism." In *Speaking for Islam: Religious Authorities in Muslim Societies*, edited by Gudrun Kramer and Sabine Schmidtke, 269–94. Leiden: Brill.

Dressler, Markus. 2008. "Religio-Secular Metamorphoses: The Re-making of Turkish Alevism." *Journal of the American Academy of Religion* 76 (2): 280–311.

Dressler, Markus. 2015. "Turkish Politics of Doxa: Otherizing the Alevis as Heterodox." *Philosophy & Social Criticism* 41 (4–5): 445–51.

Eckstein, Harry. 1975. "Case Studies and Theory in Political Science." In *Handbook of Political Science*, edited by Fred I. Greenstein and Nelson W. Polsby, 79–138. Reading, MA: Addison-Wesley.

Eisenstadt, Shmuel Noah. 1964. "Institutionalization and Change." *American Sociological Review* 29 (2): 235–47.

Eisenstadt, Todd A. 2003. "Thinking outside the (Ballot) Box: Informal Electoral Institutions and Mexico's Political Opening." *Latin American Politics and Society* 45 (1): 25–54.

Ellickson, Robert C. 1986. "Of Coase and Cattle: Dispute Resolution among Neighbors in Shasta County." *Stanford Law Review* 38 (3): 623–87.

Ellickson, Robert C. 1991. *Order without Law: How Neighbors Settle Disputes*. Cambridge, MA: Harvard University Press.

Elman, Colin. 2009. "Explanatory Typologies in Qualitative Analysis." In *The Sage Handbook of Case-Based Methods*, edited by David Byrne and Charles C. Ragin, 121–31. Thousand Oaks, CA: Sage.

Entessar, Nader. 1992. *Kurdish Ethnonationalism*. Boulder, CO: Lynn Rienner.

Entessar, Nader. 2010. *Kurdish Politics in the Middle East*. London: Lexington Books.

Erdemir, Aykan. 2005. "Tradition and Modernity: Alevis' Ambiguous Terms and Turkey's Ambivalent Subjects." *Middle Eastern Studies* 41 (6): 937–51.

Erinç, Muhammed. 2017. "Dini Nikah-Resmi Nikah Karşılaştırması ve Müftülere Nikah Görevinin Verilmesi" [A comparison of religious marriage and formal civil marriage, and the authorization of muftis in civil marriage]. *İslam Hukuku Araştırmaları Dergisi* 30: 299–336.

Erman, Tahire, and Emrah Göker. 2000. "Alevi Politics in Contemporary Turkey." *Middle Eastern Studies* 36 (4): 99–118.

Erol, Ayhan. 2010. "Re-imagining Identity: The Transformation of the Alevi Semah." *Middle Eastern Studies* 46 (3): 375–87.

Eş, Murat. 2013. "Alevis in Cemevis: Religion and Secularism in Turkey." In *Topog-

raphies of Faith.: Religion in Urban Spaces, edited by Irene Becci, Marian Burchardt, and Jose Casanova, 25–44. Leiden: Brill.

Etzioni, Amitai. 2004. "Holidays and Rituals: Neglected Seedbeds of Virtue." In *We Are What We Celebrate: Understanding Holidays and Rituals*, edited by Amitai Etzioni and Jared Bloom, 1–42. New York: New York University Press.

Etzioni, Amitai, and Jared Bloom, eds. 2004. *We Are What We Celebrate: Understanding Holidays and Rituals*. New York: New York University Press.

Farrell, Henry, and Adrienne Héritier. 2003. "Formal and Informal Institutions under Codecision: Continuous Constitution-Building in Europe." *Governance* 16 (4): 577–600.

Flader, Ulrike, and Çetin Gürer. 2019. "Building Alternative Communities within the State: The Kurdish Movement, Local Municipalities and Democratic Autonomy." In *Funding, Power and Community Development*, edited by Niamh McCrea and Fergal Finnegan, 177–92. Bristol, UK: Policy Press.

Fleetwood, Steve. 2008. "Institutions and Social Structures." *Journal for the Theory of Social Behaviour* 38 (3): 241–65.

Fligstein, Neil. 1991. "The Structural Transformation of American Industry: An Institutional Account of the Causes of Diversification in the Largest Firms, 1919–1979." In *The New Institutionalism in Organizational Analysis*, edited by Walter W. Powel and Paul J. Dimaggio, 311–36. Chicago: University of Chicago Press.

Fox, Jon E. 2013. "National Holiday Commemorations: The View from Below." In *The Cultural Politics of Nationalism and Nation-Building: Ritual and Performance in the Forging of Nations*, edited by Rachel Tsang and Eric Taylor Woods, 50–64. New York: Routledge.

Friedland, Roger, and Robert R. Alford. 1991. "Bringing Society Back In: Symbols, Practices, and Institutional Contradictions." In *The New Institutionalism in Organizational Analysis*, edited by Walter W. Powel and Paul J. DiMaggio, 232–63. Chicago: University of Chicago Press.

Fuller, Linda K., ed. 2004. *National Days/National Ways: Historical, Political, and Religious Celebrations around the World*. Westport, CT: Praeger.

Galvan, Dennis C. 2004. *The State Must Be Our Master of Fire: How Peasants Craft Culturally Sustainable Development in Senegal*. Berkeley: University of California Press.

Gambetti, Zeynep. 2009. "Decolonizing Diyarbakir: Culture, Identity and the Struggle to Appropriate Urban Space." In *Comparing Cities: The Middle East and South Asia*, edited by Kamran Asdar Ali and Martina Rieker, 97–129. Oxford: Oxford University Press.

Ganev, Venelin I. 2007. *Preying on the State: The Transformation of Bulgaria after 1989*. Ithaca, NY: Cornell University Press.

Gedik, Erdoğan, Hande Birkalan-Gedik, and Adelaide Madera. 2020. "Alevism in Turkey and in Transnational Space: Negotiated Identities between Religion, Culture and Law." *Stato, Chiese e Pluralismo Confessionale*. https://doi.org/10.13130/1971-8543/14392

George, Alexander L., and Andrew Bennett. 2005. *Case Studies and Theory Development in the Social Sciences*. Cambridge, MA: MIT Press.

Gerring, John. 2017. *Case Study Research: Principles and Practices*. 2nd ed. *Cambridge*. Cambridge: Cambridge University Press.

Gilley, Bruce. 2008. "Legitimacy and Institutional Change: The Case of China." *Comparative Political Studies* 41 (3): 259–84.

Göle, Nilüfer. 1997. "Secularism and Islamism in Turkey: The Making of Elites and Counter-elites." *Middle East Journal* 51 (1): 46–58.

Göner, Özlem. 2017. "Alevi-State Relations in Turkey: Recognition and Re-Marginalisation." In *Alevis in Europe: Voices of Migration, Culture and Identity*, edited by Tözün Issa, 115–29. London: Routledge.

Goodin, Robert E. 1996. "Institutions and Their Design." In *The Theory of Institutional Design*, edited by Robert E Goodin, 1–53. New York: Cambridge University Press.

Gourlay, William. 2018. "The Kurds and the 'Others': Kurdish Politics as an Inclusive, Multi-ethnic Vehicle in Turkey." *Journal of Muslim Minority Affairs* 38 (4): 475–92.

Gözaydın, İştar. 2009. *Diyanet: Türkiye Cumhuriyeti'nde Dinin Tanzimi* [Diyanet: The regulation of religion in the Turkish Republic]. İstanbul: İletişim Yayınları.

Gözler, Kemal. 2020. "İslam Hukukunun Değeri-2: Lâik Hukukun Kemirilmesi, İslâm Hukukunun Eleştirisi ve Savunulması" [The erosion of secular law, critique and defense of Islamic law]. www.anayasa.gen.tr

Griffiths, John. 1986. "What Is Legal Pluralism?" *Journal of Legal Pluralism and Unofficial Law* 18 (24): 1–55.

Grigoriadis, Ioannis N. 2008. "On the Europeanization of Minority Rights Protection: Comparing the Cases of Greece and Turkey." *Mediterranean Politics* 13 (1): 23–41.

Grigoriadis, Ioannis N. 2012. "Minorities." In *The Routledge Handbook of Modern Turkey*, edited by Metin Heper and Sabri Sayarı, 282–92. New York: Routledge.

Grigoriadis, Ioannis N. 2021. "Between Citizenship and the Millet: The Greek Minority in Republican Turkey." *Middle Eastern Studies* 57 (5): 741–57. https://doi.org/10.1080/00263206.2021.1894553

Grzymala-Busse, Anna. 2006. *Informal Institutions and the Post-Communist State*. Washington, DC: National Council for Eurasian and East European Research.

Grzymala-Busse, Anna. 2010. "The Best Laid Plans: The Impact of Informal Rules on Formal Institutions in Transitional Regimes." *Studies in Comparative International Development* 45 (3): 311–33.

Gunes, Cengiz. 2012. *The Kurdish National Movement in Turkey: From Protest to Resistance*. New York: Routledge.

Gunes, Cengiz. 2018. "The Rise of the Pro-Kurdish Democratic Movement in Turkey." In *Routledge Handbook on the Kurds*, edited by Michael M. Gunter, 259–70. New York: Routledge.

Gunes, Cengiz. 2020. "Kurdish Political Representation in Turkey: The Changing

Context and New Trends." In *The Kurds in the Middle East: Enduring Problems and New Dynamics*, edited by Mehmet Gurses, David Romano, and Michael M. Gunter, 3–19. New York: Lexington Books.

Gunes, Cengiz. 2021. *The Political Representation of Kurds in Turkey: New Actors and Modes of Participation in a Changing Society*. London: I.B. Tauris.

Gunes-Ayata, Ayse. 1992. "The Turkish Alevis." *Innovation: The European Journal of Social Science Research* 5 (3): 109–14.

Guss, David M. 2001. *The Festive State: Race, Ethnicity, and Nationalism as Cultural Performance*. Berkeley: University of California Press.

Hall, Peter A. 1986. *Governing the Economy: The Politics of State Intervention in Britain and France*. New York: Oxford University Press.

Hall, Peter A., ed. 1989. *The Political Power of Economic Ideas: Keynesianism across Nations*. Princeton, NJ: Princeton University Press.

Hall, Peter A. 1992. "The Movement from Keynesianism to Monetarism: Institutional Analysis and British Economic Policy in the 1970s." In *Structuring Politics: Historical Institutionalism in Comparative Analysis*, edited by Sven Steinmo, Kathleen Thelen, and Frank Longstreth, 90–113. Cambridge: Cambridge University Press.

Hall, Peter A. 1993. "Policy Paradigms, Social Learning, and the State: The Case of Economic Policymaking in Britain." *Comparative Politics* 25 (3): 275–96.

Hall, Peter A. 2010. "Historical Institutionalism in Rationalist and Sociological Perspective." In *Explaining Institutional Change: Ambiguity, Agency and Power*, edited by James Mahoney and Kathleen Thelen, 204–25. Cambridge: Cambridge University Press.

Hall, Peter A., and Rosemary C. R. Taylor. 1996. "Political Science and the Three New Institutionalisms." *Political Studies* 44 (5): 936–57.

Hanoğlu, Hayal. 2017. "An Introduction to Alevism: Roots and Practices." In *Alevis in Europe: Voices of Migration, Culture and Identity*, edited by Tözün Issa, 14–25. London: Routledge.

Hardin, Garrett. 1968. "The Tragedy of the Commons." *Science* 162 (3859): 1243–48.

Hassanpour, Amir. 1992. *Nationalism and Language in Kurdistan, 1918–1985*. San Francisco: Mellen Research University Press.

Hassanpour, Amir, Jaffer Sheyholislami, and Tove Skutnabb-Kangas. 2012. "Introduction: Kurdish: Linguicide, Resistance and Hope." *International Journal of the Sociology of Language*: 1–18. https://doi.org/10.1515/ijsl-2012-0047

Helmke, Gretchen, and Steven Levitsky. 2004. "Informal Institutions and Comparative Politics: A Research Agenda." *Perspectives on Politics* 2 (4): 725–40.

Helmke, Gretchen, and Steven Levitsky, eds. 2006. *Informal Institutions and Democracy: Lessons from Latin America*. Baltimore: John Hopkins University Press.

Hensler, Deborah R. 2003. "Our Courts, Ourselves: How the Alternative Dispute Resolution Movement Is Re-shaping Our Legal System." *Penn State Law Review* 108: 165–98.

Héritier, Adrienne. 2007. *Explaining Institutional Change in Europe*. Oxford: Oxford University Press.

Heritier, Adrienne. 2012. "Formal and Informal Institutions in the EU's Legislative Process." In *International Handbook on Informal Governance*, edited by Thomas Christiansen and Christine Neuhold, 335–53. Cheltenham, UK: Edward Elgar.

Hertog, Steffen. 2010. *Princes, Brokers, and Bureaucrats: Oil and the State in Saudi Arabia*. Ithaca, NY: Cornell University Press.

Hintz, Lisel, and Allison L. Quatrini. 2021. "Subversive Celebrations: Holidays as Sites of Minority Identity Contestation in Repressive Regimes." *Nationalities Papers* 49 (2): 289–307.

Hira, Anil, and Ron Hira. 2000. "The New Institutionalism: Contradictory Notions of Change." *American Journal of Economics and Sociology* 59 (2): 267–82.

Hix, Simon. 2002. "Constitutional Agenda-Setting through Discretion in Rule Interpretation: Why the European Parliament Won at Amsterdam." *British Journal of Political Science* 32 (2): 259–80.

Hodgson, Geoffrey M. 2006. "What Are Institutions?" *Journal of Economic Issues* 40 (1): 1–25.

Hosmer, David W., Jr., Stanley Lemeshow, and Rodney X. Sturdivant. 2013. *Applied Logistic Regression*. 3rd ed. Hoboken, NJ: John Wiley and Sons.

Hu, Biliang. 2007. *Informal Institutions and Rural Development in China*. London: Routledge.

Hummel, Calla. 2021. *Why Informal Workers Organize: Contentious Politics, Enforcement, and the State*. Oxford: Oxford University Press.

Hurd, Elizabeth Shakman. 2014. "Alevis under Law: The Politics of Religious Freedom in Turkey." *Journal of Law and Religion* 29 (3): 416–35.

Hyden, Goran. 1983. *No Shortcuts to Progress: African Development Management in Perspective*. Berkeley: University of California Press.

Hyden, Goran. 2006. *African Politics in Comparative Perspective*. Cambridge: Cambridge University Press.

Icduygu, Ahmet, and B. Ali Soner. 2006. "Turkish Minority Rights Regime: Between Difference and Equality." *Middle Eastern Studies* 42 (3): 447–68.

İçduygu, Ahmet, Şule Toktas, and B. Ali Soner. 2008. "The Politics of Population in a Nation-Building Process: Emigration of Non-Muslims from Turkey." *Ethnic and Racial Studies* 31 (2): 358–89.

Ilkkaracan, Pinar. 1998. "Exploring the Context of Women's Sexuality in Eastern Turkey." *Reproductive Health Matters* 6 (12): 66–75.

Imerman, Dane. 2018. "Contested Legitimacy and Institutional Change: Unpacking the Dynamics of Institutional Legitimacy." *International Studies Review* 20 (1): 74–100.

Immergut, Ellen M. 2011. "Institutions and Institutionalism." In *International Encyclopedia of Political Science*, edited by Bertrand Badie, Dirk Berg-Schlosser, and Leonardo Morlino. Thousand Oaks, CA: Sage.

Imset, Ismet G. 1996. "The PKK: Terrorists or Freedom Fighters?" *International Journal of Kurdish Studies* 10 (1–2): 45–100.

Ingraham, Patricia W., Donald P. Moynihan, and Matthew Andrews. 2008. "Formal and Informal Institutions in Public Administration." In *Debating Institutionalism*, edited by Jon Pierre, B. Guy Peters, and Gerry Stoker, 66–85. Manchester: Manchester University Press.

Issa, Tözün, ed. 2017. *Alevis in Europe: Voices of Migration, Culture and Identity*. London: Routledge.

Izady, Mehrdad R. 1992. *The Kurds: A Concise Handbook*. New York: Taylor and Francis.

Jackall, Robert. 1988. *Moral Mazes: The World of Corporate Managers*. New York: Oxford University Press.

Johnson, Cathryn, Timothy J. Dowd, and Cecilia L. Ridgeway. 2006. "Legitimacy as a Social Process." *Annual Review of Sociology* 32: 53–78.

Jones, Dorian. 2013. "Jail Is Occupational Hazard for Kurdish Mayor." *Deutsche Welle*, January 16. Accessed December 27, 2020. https://www.dw.com/en/jail-is-occupational-hazard-for-kurdish-mayor/a-16494351

Jongerden, Joost. 2009. "Crafting Space, Making People: The Spatial Design of Nation in Modern Turkey." *European Journal of Turkish Studies* (10): 1 –25. https://doi.org/10.4000/ejts.4014

Jwaideh, Wadie. 2006. *The Kurdish National Movement: Its Origins and Development*. Syracuse, NY: Syracuse University Press.

Kalaycıoğlu, Ersin. 2012. "Kulturkampf in Turkey: The Constitutional Referendum of 12 September 2010." *South European Society and Politics* 17 (1): 1–22.

Karagöz, Hüseyin Mirza. 2017. "Alevism in Turkey: Tensions and Patterns of Migration." In *Alevis in Europe: Voices of Migration, Culture and Identity* edited by Tözün Issa, 71–82. London: Routledge.

Karakaya, Buket. 2018. "The Process of Marginalization of the Alevis in the Ottoman Empire: A Historical Perspective." Master's thesis, History of Religions, MF Norwegian School of Theology.

Karakaya-Stump, Ayfer. 2018. "The AKP, Sectarianism, and the Alevis' Struggle for Equal Rights in Turkey." *National Identities* 20 (1): 53–67.

Karakaya-Stump, Ayfer. 2020. *The Kizilbash/Alevis in Ottoman Anatolia: Sufism, Politics and Community*. Edinburgh: Edinburgh University Press.

Karakoç, Ekrem. 2013. "Ethnicity and Trust in National and International Institutions: Kurdish Attitudes toward Political Institutions in Turkey." *Turkish Studies* 14 (1): 92–114.

Karpat, Kemal. 1985. *Ottoman Population (1830–1914): Demographic and Social Characteristics*. Madison: University of Wisconsin Press.

Karpat, Kemal H. 1973. *Social Change and Politics in Turkey: A Structural-Historical Analysis*. Leiden: Brill.

Kaufmann, Chaim D., and Robert A. Pape. 1999. "Explaining Costly International Moral Action: Britain's Sixty-Year Campaign against the Atlantic Slave Trade." *International Organization* 53 (4): 631–68.

Kaufmann, Wesley, Reggy Hooghiemstra, and Mary K. Feeney. 2018. "Formal Institutions, Informal Institutions, and Red Tape: A Comparative Study." *Public Administration* 96 (2): 386–403.

Kaya, Ayhan. 2013. "Multiculturalism and Minorities in Turkey." In *Challenging Multiculturalism: European Models of Diversity*, edited by Raymond Taras, 297–317. Edinburgh: Edinburgh University Press.

Kehl-Bodrogi, Krisztina, Barbara Kellner Heinkele, and Anke Otter Beaujean. 1997. *Syncretistic Religious Communities in the Near East*. Vol. 76. Leiden: Brill.

Keohane, Robert O. 1984. *After Hegemony: Cooperation and Discord in the World Political Economy*. Princeton, NJ: Princeton University Press.

Khalil, Elias L. 1995. "Organizations versus Institutions." *Journal of Institutional and Theoretical Economics* 151 (3): 445–66.

Kılınç, Ramazan. 2019. *Alien Citizens: The State and Religious Minorities in Turkey and France*. Cambridge: Cambridge University Press.

Kirişçi, Kemal, and Gareth M. Winrow. 1997. *The Kurdish Question and Turkey: An Example of a Trans-State Ethnic Conflict*. Portland, OR: Frank Cass.

Kizilkan-Kisacik, Zelal B. 2013. "The Impact of the EU on Minority Rights: The Kurds as a Case." In *The Kurdish Question in Turkey: New Perspectives on Violence, Representation and Reconciliation*, edited by Cengiz Gunes and Welat Zeydanlioglu, 205–24. London: Routledge.

Knight, Jack. 1992. *Institutions and Social Conflict*. Cambridge: Cambridge University Press.

Knight, Jack. 2001. "Models, Interpretations, and Theories: Constructing Explanations of Institutional Emergence and Change." In *Explaining Social Institutions*, edited by Jack Knight and Itai Sened, 95–120. Ann Arbor: University of Michigan Press.

Knight, Jack, and Itai Sened. 2001. "Introduction." In *Explaining Social Institutions*, edited by Jack Knight and Itai Sened, 1–13. Ann Arbor: University of Michigan Press.

Korkmaz, Esat. 2008. *Dört Kapı Kırk Makam* [Four gateways, forty levels]. Istanbul: Anahtar Kitaplar Yayınevi.

Kose, Talha. 2013. "Between Nationalism, Modernism and Secularism: The Ambivalent Place of 'Alevi Identities'." *Middle Eastern Studies* 49 (4): 590–607.

Köse, Talha, and Nimet Beriker. 2012. "Islamic Mediation in Turkey: The Role of Ulema." *Negotiation and Conflict Management Research* 5 (2): 136–61.

Kraatz, Matthew S., and Emily S. Block. 2017. "Institutional Pluralism Revisited." In *The Sage Handbook of Organizational Institutionalism*, edited by Royston Greenwood, Christine Oliver, Thomas B. Lawrance, and Renate E. Meyer, 532–57. Thousand Oaks, CA: Sage.

Lauth, Hans-Joachim. 2000. "Informal Institutions and Democracy." *Democratization* 7 (4): 21–50.

Lauth, Hans-Joachim. 2004. "Formal and Informal Institutions: On Structuring Their Mutual Co-existence." *Romanian Journal of Political Science* 4 (1): 66–88.

Lauth, Hans-Joachim. 2015. "Formal and Informal Institutions." In *Routledge Handbook of Comparative Political Institutions*, edited by Jennifer Gandhi and Ruben Ruiz-Rufino, 56–70. London: Routledge.

Ledeneva, Alena V. 1998. *Russia's Economy of Favours: Blat, Networking and Informal Exchange*. Cambridge: Cambridge University Press.

Ledeneva, Alena, ed. 2018. *Global Encyclopedia of Informality: Towards Understanding of Social and Cultural Complexity*. Vol. 1. London: UCL Press.

Lenz, Tobias, and Lora Anne Viola. 2017. "Legitimacy and Institutional Change in International Organisations: A Cognitive Approach." *Review of International Studies* 43 (5): 939–61.

Levi, Margaret. 1990. "A Logic of Institutional Change." In *The Limits of Rationality*, edited by Karen S. Cook and Margaret Levi, 402–18. Chicago: University of Chicago Press.

Levi, Margaret. 1997. *Consent, Dissent, and Patriotism*. Cambridge: Cambridge University Press.

Levitsky, Steven, and María Victoria Murillo. 2009. "Variation in Institutional Strength." *Annual Review of Political Science* 12: 115–33.

Levitsky, Steven, and Daniel Ziblatt. 2018. *How Democracies Die*. New York: Broadway Books.

Levy, Jack S. 2008. "Case Studies: Types, Designs, and Logics of Inference." *Conflict Management and Peace Science* 25 (1): 1–18.

Lieberman, Robert C. 2002. "Ideas, Institutions, and Political Order: Explaining Political Change." *American Political Science Review* 96 (4): 697–712.

Long, J. Scott. 1997. *Regression Models for Categorical and Limited Dependent Variables*. Thousand Oaks, CA: Sage.

Lord, Ceren. 2017a. "Rethinking the Justice and Development Party's 'Alevi Openings.'" *Turkish Studies* 18 (2): 278–96.

Lord, Ceren. 2017b. "Between Islam and the Nation: Nation-Building, the Ulama and Alevi Identity in Turkey." *Nations and Nationalism* 23 (1): 48–67.

Lord, Ceren. 2018. *Religious Politics in Turkey: From the Birth of the Republic to the AKP*. Cambridge: Cambridge University Press.

Lord, Ceren. 2020. "The Transnational Mobilization of the Alevis of Turkey: From Invisibility to the Struggle for Equality." In *The Oxford Handbook of Turkish Politics*, edited by Güneş M. Tezcür. Oxford: Oxford University Press.

Lounsbury, Michael. 2007. "A Tale of Two Cities: Competing Logics and Practice Variation in the Professionalizing of Mutual Funds." *Academy of Management Journal* 50 (2): 289–307.

Lowndes, Vivien. 1996. "Varieties of New Institutionalism: A Critical Appraisal." *Public Administration* 74 (2): 181–97.

Lowndes, Vivien. 2018. "Institutionalism." In *Theory and Methods in Political Science*, edited by Vivien Lowndes, David Marsh, and Gerry Stoker, 54–74. London: Palgrave.

Lund, Christian. 2006. "Twilight Institutions: Public Authority and Local Politics in Africa." *Development and Change* 37 (4): 685–705.

MacLean, Lauren M. 2010. *Informal Institutions and Citizenship in Rural Africa: Risk and Reciprocity in Ghana and Côte d'Ivoire*. Cambridge: Cambridge University Press.

Magnarella, Paul J. 1973. "The Reception of Swiss Family Law in Turkey." *Anthropological Quarterly* 46 (2): 100–116.

Magnarella, Paul J. 1993. "East Meets West: The Reception of West European Law in the Ottoman Empire and the Modern Turkish Republic." *Journal of International Law and Practice* 2 (2): 281–306.

Mahoney, James. 2000. "Path Dependence in Historical Sociology." *Theory and Society* 29 (4): 507–48.

Mahoney, James, and Kathleen Thelen. 2010. *Explaining Institutional Change: Ambiguity, Agency and Power.* Cambridge: Cambridge University Press.

Mansbridge, Jane. 2014. "The Role of the State in Governing the Commons." *Environmental Science & Policy* 36: 8–10.

Mantzavinos, Chrysostomos. 2011. "Institutions." In *The Sage Handbook of the Philosophy of Social Sciences*, edited by Ian C. Jarvie and Jesus Zamora-Bonilla, 399–412. London: Sage.

March, James G., and Johan P. Olsen. 1984. "The New Institutionalism: Organizational Factors in Political Life." *American Political Science Review* 78 (3): 734–49.

March, James G., and Johan P. Olsen. 1989. *Rediscovering Institutions: The Organizational Basis of Politics.* New York: Free Press.

March, James G., and Johan P. Olsen. 1998. "The Institutional Dynamics of International Political Orders." *International Organization* 52 (4): 943–69.

March, James G., and Johan P. Olsen. 2006. "Elaborating the 'New Institutionalism.'" In *The Oxford Handbook of Political Institutions*, edited by R. A. W. Rhodes, Sarah A. Binder, and Bert A. Rockman, 3–20. New York: Oxford University Press.

Marcic, Sinisa. 2015. "Informal Institutions in the Western Balkans: An Obstacle to Democratic Consolidation." *Journal of Balkan and Near Eastern Studies* 17 (1): 1–14.

Marcus, Aliza. 2007. *Blood and Belief: The PKK and the Kurdish Fight for Independence.* New York: New York University Press.

Martykanova, Darina. 2009. "Matching Sharia and 'Governmentality': Muslim Marriage Legislation in the Late Ottoman Empire." In *Institutional Change and Stability: Conflicts, Transitions and Social Values*, edited by Andreas Gemes, Florencia Peyrou, and Ioannis Xydopoulos, 153–75. Pisa: Plus-Pisa University Press.

Massicard, Elise. 2013. *The Alevis in Turkey and Europe: Identity and Managing Territorial Diversity.* New York: Routledge.

Massicard, Elise. 2014. "Democratization in Turkey? Insights from the Alevi issue." In *Turkey's Democratization Process*, edited by Carmen Rodriguez, Antonio Avalos, Hakan Yılmaz, and Ana I. Planet, 376–90. New York: Routledge.

Mattingly, Daniel C. 2016. "Elite Capture: How Decentralization and Informal Institutions Weaken Property Rights in China." *World Politics* 68 (3): 383–412.

McAdam, Doug, Sidney Tarrow, and Charles Tilly. 2004. *Dynamics of Contention.* Cambridge: Cambridge University Press.

McAdam, Doug, Sidney Tarrow, and Charles Tilly. 2009. "Comparative Perspectives on Contentious Politics." In *Comparative Politics: Rationality, Culture, and*

Structure, edited by Mark I. Lichbach and Alan S. Zuckerman, 260–90. Cambridge: Cambridge University Press.

McCrone, David, and Gayle McPherson, eds. 2009. *National Days: Constructing and Mobilising National Identity*. New York: Palgrave.

McDowall, David. 2004. *A Modern History of the Kurds*. 3rd ed. London: I.B. Tauris.

Merry, Sally Engle. 1988. "Legal Pluralism." *Law & Society Review* 22 (5): 869–96.

Metin, Ismail. 1992. *Alevilerde Halk Mahkemeleri* [People's courts among Alevis]. Istanbul: Aydinlar.

Metinsoy, Murat. 2021. *The Power of the People: Everyday Resistance and Dissent in the Making of Modern Turkey, 1923–1938*. Cambridge: Cambridge University Press.

Meyer, John W., and Brian Rowan. 1977. "Institutionalized Organizations: Formal Structure as Myth and Ceremony." *American Journal of Sociology* 83 (2): 340–63.

Milgrom, Paul R., Douglass C. North, and Barry R. Weingast. 1990. "The Role of Institutions in the Revival of Trade: The Law Merchant, Private Judges, and the Champagne Fairs." *Economics & Politics* 2 (1): 1–23.

Moe, Terry M. 1990. "Political Institutions: The Neglected Side of the Story." *Journal of Law, Economics, & Organization* 6: 213–53.

Moe, Terry M. 2005. "Power and Political Institutions." *Perspectives on Politics* 3 (2): 215–33.

Moix, Bridget. 2006. "Matters of Faith: Religion, Conflict, and Conflict Resolution." In *The Handbook of Conflict Resolution: Theory and Practice*, edited by Morton Deutsch, Peter T. Coleman, and Eric C. Marcus, 582–601. San Francisco: Jossey-Bass.

Morgan, David L. 1996. "Focus Groups." *Annual Review of Sociology* 22 (1): 129–52.

Morris, Jeremy, and Abel Polese, eds. 2014. *The Informal Post-Socialist Economy: Embedded Practices and Livelihoods*. London: Routledge.

Navaro-Yashin, Yael. 2002. *Faces of the State: Secularism and Public Life in Turkey*. Princeton, NJ: Princeton University Press.

North, Douglass C. 1990. *Institutions, Institutional Change and Economic Performance*. New York: Cambridge University Press.

North, Douglass C. 1993a. "Institutions and Credible Commitment." *Journal of Institutional and Theoretical Economics* 149 (1): 11–23.

North, Douglass C. 1993b. *Institutions, Institutional Change and Economic Performance*. New York: Cambridge University Press.

North, Douglass C. 1998. "Economic Performance through Time." In *The New Institutionalism in Sociology*, edited by Mary C. Brintan and Victor Nee, 247–58. New York: Russell Sage Foundation.

North, Douglass C. 2001. "Five Propositions about Institutional Change." In *Explaining Social Institutions*, edited by Jack Knight and Itai Sened, 15–26. Ann Arbor: University of Michigan Press.

Ocasio, William, Patricia H. Thornton, and Michael Lounsbury. 2017. "Advances to the Institutional Logics Perspective." In *The Sage Handbook of Organizational Institutionalism*, edited by Royston Greenwood, Christine Oliver, Thomas B. Lawrance, and Renate E. Meyer, 509–31. Thousand Oaks, CA: Sage.

O'Donnell, Guillermo A. 1994. "Delegative Democracy." *Journal of Democracy* 5 (1): 55–69.

O'Donnell, Guillermo A. 1996. "Illusions about Consolidation." *Journal of Democracy* 7 (2): 34–51.

Olsen, Johan P. 2009. "Change and Continuity: An Institutional Approach to Institutions of Democratic Government." *European Political Science Review* 1 (1): 3–32.

Olson, Mancur. 1965. *The Logic of Collective Action: Public Goods and the Theory of Groups*. Cambridge, MA: Harvard University Press.

Olsson, Tord, Elisabeth Özdalga, and Catharina Raudvere, eds. 1998. *Alevi Identity: Cultural, Religious and Social Perspectives*. Istanbul: Swedish Research Institute.

O'Neil, Mary Lou. 2011. "Linguistic Human Rights and the Rights of Kurds." In *Human Rights in Turkey*, edited by Zehra F. Kabasakal Arat and Richard Falk, 72–86. Philadelphia: University of Pennsylvania Press.

Oran, Baskin. 2011. "The Minority Concept and Rights in Turkey: The Lausanne Peace Treaty and Current Issues." In *Human Rights in Turkey*, edited by Zehra F. Kabasakal Arat and Richard Falk, 35–57. Philadelphia: University of Pennsylvania Press.

Oran, Baskın. 2021. *Minorities and Minority Rights in Turkey: From Ottoman Empire to the Present State*. Boulder, CO: Lynne Rienner.

Ortayli, Ilber. 1994. *Studies on Ottoman Transformation*. Istanbul: ISIS Press.

Ortayli, Ilber. 2000. *Osmanlı Toplumunda Aile* [Family in Ottoman society]. Istanbul: Pan.

Orucu, Esin. 1987. "Turkey: Reconciling Traditional Society and Secular Demands." *Journal of Family Law* 26 (1): 221–36.

Ostrom, Elinor. 1990. *Governing the Commons: The Evolution of Institutions for Collective Action*. Cambridge: Cambridge University Press.

Özbudun, Ergun. 2000. *Contemporary Turkish Politics: Challenges to Democratic Consolidation*. London: Lynne Rienner.

Özbudun, Ergun. 2015. "Turkey's Judiciary and the Drift toward Competitive Authoritarianism." *International Spectator* 50 (2): 42–55.

Özbudun, Ergun. 2016. "Problems of Rule of Law and Horizontal Accountability in Turkey: Defective Democracy or Competitive Authoritarianism?" In *Democratic Consolidation in Turkey: Micro and Macro Challenges*, edited by Cengiz Erisen and Paul Kubicek, 144–66. New York: Routledge.

Özdemir, Burcu, and Zeki Sarigil. 2015. "Turkey's Europeanization Process and the Kurdish Issue." In *The Europeanization of Turkey: Polity and Politics*, edited by Ali Tekin and Aylin Guney, 180–94. New York: Routledge.

Ozen, Hayriye. 2013. "Informal Politics in Turkey during the Ozal Era (1983–1989)." *Alternatives: Turkish Journal of International Relations* 12 (4): 78–91.

Özkul, Derya. 2015. "Alevi 'Openings' and Politicization of the 'Alevi Issue' during the AKP Rule." *Turkish Studies* 16 (1): 80–96.

Öztürk, Duygu Canan. 2013. "Socio-Spatial Practices of the Pro-Kurdish Municipalities: The Case of Diyarbakır." Master's thesis, Urban Policy Planning and Local Governments, Middle East Technical University.

Öztürkmen, Arzu. 2001. "Celebrating National Holidays in Turkey: History and Memory." *New Perspectives on Turkey* 25 (Fall): 47–75.

Özyürek, Esra. 2006. *Nostalgia for the Modern: State Secularism and Everyday Politics in Turkey.* Durham, NC: Duke University Press.

Özyürek, Esra. 2009. "'The Light of the Alevi Fire Was Lit in Germany and Then Spread to Turkey': A Transnational Debate on the Boundaries of Islam." *Turkish Studies* 10 (2): 233–53.

Painter, Martin, and B. Guy Peters. 2010. *Tradition and Public Administration.* New York: Palgrave Macmillan.

Pejovich, Svetozar. 1999. "The Effects of the Interaction of Formal and Informal Institutions on Social Stability and Economic Development." *Journal of Markets & Morality* 2 (2): 164–81.

Peters, B. Guy. 1998. *Comparative Politics: Theory and Methods.* New York: New York University Press.

Peters, B. Guy. 2006. "Forms of Informality: Identifying Informal Governance in the European Union." *Perspectives on European Politics and Society* 7 (1): 25–40.

Peters, B. Guy. 2011. "Governing in the Shadows." *Asia Pacific Journal of Public Administration* 33 (1): 1–16.

Peters, B. Guy. 2012. *Institutional Theory in Political Science: The New Institutionalism.* 3rd ed. New York: Continuum.

Peters, B. Guy. 2019. *Institutional Theory in Political Science: The New Institutionalism.* 4th ed. Cheltenham, UK: Edward Elgar.

Peters, B. Guy, and Jon Pierre. 2020. "The New Institutionalism in Political Science." In *The Sage Handbook of Political Science*, edited by Dirk Berk-Schlosser, Bertrand Badie, and Leonardo Morlino, 133–52. London: Sage.

Pierre, Jon. 1993. "Legitimacy, Institutional Change, and the Politics of Public Administration in Sweden." *International Political Science Review* 14 (4): 387–401.

Pierson, Paul. 2000. "The Limits of Design: Explaining Institutional Origins and Change." *Governance* 13 (4): 475–99.

Podeh, Elie. 2011. *The Politics of National Celebrations in the Arab Middle East.* Cambridge: Cambridge University Press.

Polese, Abel. 2021. "What Is Informality: (Mapping) 'the Art of Bypassing the State' in Eurasian Spaces—and Beyond." *Eurasion Geography and Economics.* https://doi.org/10.1080/15387216.2021.1992791

Pop-Eleches, Grigore. 2007. "Historical Legacies and Post-communist Regime Change." *Journal of Politics* 69 (4): 908–26.

Poyraz, Bedriye. 2005. "The Turkish State and Alevis: Changing Parameters of an Uneasy Relationship." *Middle Eastern Studies* 41 (4): 503–16.

Qasmi, Ali Usman. 2017. "Identity Formation through National Calendar: Holidays and Commemorations in Pakistan." *Nations and Nationalism* 23 (3): 620–41.

Radnitz, Scott. 2011. "Informal Politics and the State." *Comparative Politics* 43 (3): 351–71.

Reh, Christine. 2012. "Informal Politics: The Normative Challenge." In *International Handbook on Informal Governance*, edited by Thomas Christiansen and Christine Neuhold, 65–84. Cheltenham, UK: Edward Elgar.

Romano, David. 2006. *The Kurdish Nationalist Movement: Opportunity, Mobilization and Identity*. Cambridge: Cambridge University Press.

Romano, David, and Mehmet Gurses, eds. 2014. *Conflict, Democratization and the Kurds in the Middle East: Turkey, Iran, Iraq and Syria*. New York: Palgrave Macmillan.

Roy, Srirupa. 2006. "Seeing a State: National Commemorations and the Public Sphere in India and Turkey." *Comparative Studies in Society and History* 48 (1): 200–232.

Ruggie, John Gerard. 1998. "What Makes the World Hang Together? Neo-utilitarianism and the Social Constructivist Challenge." *International Organization* 52 (4): 855–85.

Şahin, Şehriban. 2005. "The Rise of Alevism as a Public Religion." *Current Sociology* 53 (3): 465–85.

Sarigil, Zeki. 2007. "Europeanization as Institutional Change: The Case of the Turkish Military." *Mediterranean Politics* 12 (1): 39–57.

Sarigil, Zeki. 2015a. "Showing the Path to Path Dependence: The Habitual Path." *European Political Science Review* 7 (2): 221–42.

Sarigil, Zeki. 2015b. "Public Opinion and Attitude toward the Military and Democratic Consolidation in Turkey." *Armed Forces & Society* 41 (2): 282–306.

Sarigil, Zeki. 2018a. *Ethnic Boundaries in Turkish Politics: The Secular Kurdish Movement and Islam*. New York: New York University Press.

Sarigil, Zeki. 2018b. "Ethnic and Religious Prejudices in the Turkish Social Landscape." *European Sociological Review* 34 (6): 711–27. https://doi.org/10.1093/esr/jcy036

Sarigil, Zeki. 2019. "Türkiye'de Enformel Kurumlar Anketi" (TEKA 2019) [Informal institutions in Turkey survey], edited by Zeki Sarigil. Ankara: Bilkent University.

Scalbert-Yücel, Clémence. 2009. "The Invention of a Tradition: Diyarbakır's Dengbêj Project." *European Journal of Turkish Studies* 10.

Schmidt, Vivien A. 2008. "Discursive Institutionalism: The Explanatory Power of Ideas and Discourse." *Annual Review of Political Science* 11: 303–26.

Schmidt, Vivien A. 2010. "Taking Ideas and Discourse Seriously: Explaining Change through Discursive Institutionalism as the Fourth 'New Institutionalism.'" *European Political Science Review* 2 (1): 1–25.

Schoon, Eric W. 2022. "Operationalizing Legitimacy." *American Sociological Review* 87 (3): 478–503. https://doi.org/10.1177/00031224221081379

Scott, W. Richard. 2014. *Institutions and Organizations: Ideas, Interests, and Identities*. 4th ed. Thousand Oaks, CA: Sage.

Scott, W. Richard. 2017. "Institutional Theory: Onward and Upward." In *The Sage Handbook of Organizational Institutionalism*, edited by Royston Greenwood, Christine Oliver, Thomas B. Lawrance, and Renate E. Meyer, 853–72. Thousand Oaks, CA: Sage.

Sehring, Jenniver. 2009. "Path Dependencies and Institutional Bricolage in Post-Soviet Rural Water Governance." *Water Alternatives* 2 (1): 61–81.

Seidler, Valentin. 2018. "Copying Informal Institutions: The Role of British Colonial Officers during the Decolonization of British Africa." *Journal of Institutional Economics* 14 (2): 289–312.

Selznick, Philip. 1957. *Leadership in Administration: A Sociological Interpretation*. New York: Harper and Row.

Selznick, Philip. 1992. *The Moral Commonwealth: Social Theory and the Promise of Community*. Berkeley: University of California Press.

Şentürk, Burcu. 2017. "Urbanisation, Socialist Movements and the Emergence of Alevi Identity in the 1970s." In *Alevis in Europe: Voices of Migration, Culture and Identity*, edited by Tözün Issa, 82–96. London: Routledge.

Seufert, Günter. 1997. "Between Religion and Ethnicity: A Kurdish-Alevi Tribe in Globalizing Istanbul." In *Space, Culture and Power: New Identities in Globalizing Cities*, edited by Ayse Oncu and Petra Weyland, 157–76. London: Zed Books.

Shambayati, Hootan, and Esen Kirdiş. 2009. "In Pursuit of 'Contemporary Civilization': Judicial Empowerment in Turkey." *Political Research Quarterly* 62 (4): 767–80.

Shankland, David. 1998. "Anthropology and Ethnicity: The Place of Ethnography in the New Alevi Movement." In *Alevi Identity: Cultural, Religious and Social Perspectives*, edited by Tord Olsson, Elisabeth Özdalga, and Catharina Raudvere, 19–27. Istanbul: Swedish Research Institute.

Shankland, David. 2003. *The Alevis in Turkey: The Emergence of a Secular Islamic Tradition*. New York: Routledge.

Shaw, Stanford J. 1978. "The Ottoman Census System and Population, 1831–1914." *International Journal of Middle East Studies* 9 (3): 325–38.

Sheingate, Adam. 2010. "Rethinking Rules: Creativity and Constraint in the US House of Representatives." In *Explaining Institutional Change: Ambiguity, Agency and Power*, edited by James Mahoney and Kathleen Thelen, 168–203. Cambridge: Cambridge University Press.

Shepsle, Kenneth A. 2006. "Rational Choice Institutionalism." In *The Oxford Handbook of Political Institutions*, edited by R. A. W. Rhodes, Sarah A. Binder, and Bert A. Rockman, 23–38. Oxford: Oxford University Press.

Sheyholislami, Jaffer. 2015. "The Language Varieties of the Kurds." In *The Kurds: History, Religion, Language and Politics*, edited by Wolfgang Taucher, Mathias Vogl, and Peter Webinger, 30–52. Vienna: Austrian Federal Ministry of the Interior.

Şirin, Çiğdem V. 2013. "Analyzing the Determinants of Group Identity among Alevis in Turkey: A National Survey Study." *Turkish Studies* 14 (1): 74–91.

Sökefeld, Martin. 2002. "Alevi Dedes in the German Diaspora: The Transformation of a Religious Institution." *Zeitschrift für Ethnologie* 127 (2): 163–86.

Solomonovich, Nadav. 2021. "'Democracy and National Unity Day' in Turkey: The Invention of a New National Holiday." *New Perspectives on Turkey* 64: 55–80.

Soner, B. Ali. 2010. "The Justice and Development Party's Policies towards Non-Muslim Minorities in Turkey." *Journal of Balkan and Near Eastern Studies* 12 (1): 23–40.

Soner, Bayram Ali, and Şule Toktaş. 2011. "Alevis and Alevism in the Changing Context of Turkish Politics: The Justice and Development Party's Alevi Opening." *Turkish Studies* 12 (3): 419–34.

Soyler, Mehtap. 2013. "Informal Institutions, Forms of State and Democracy: The Turkish Deep State." *Democratization* 20 (2): 310–34.

Soyler, Mehtap. 2015. *The Turkish Deep State: State Consolidation, Civil-Military Relations and Democracy.* New York: Routledge.

Stacey, Jeffrey, and Berthold Rittberger. 2003. "Dynamics of Formal and Informal Institutional Change in the EU." *Journal of European Public Policy* 10 (6): 858–83.

Starn, Orin. 1999. *Nightwatch: The Politics of Protest in the Andes.* Durham, NC: Duke University Press.

Starr, June. 1978. *Dispute and Settlement in Rural Turkey: An Ethnography of Law.* Leiden: Brill.

Starr, June, and Jonathan Pool. 1974. "The Impact of a Legal Revolution in Rural Turkey." *Law & Society Review* 8: 533–60.

Stewart, Michael. 2007. "Modernity and the Alevis of Turkey: Identity, Challenges and Change." *Journal of International Relations* 9 (1): 50–60.

Stiglitz, Edward H., and Barry R. Weingast. 2011. "Rational Choice." In *International Encyclopedia of Political Science*, edited by Bertrand Badie, Dirk Berg-Schlosser, and Leonardo Morlino. Thousand Oaks, CA: Sage.

Stinchcombe, Arthur L. 1968. *Constructing Social Theories.* New York: Harcourt Brace.

Strang, David, and Wesley D. Sine. 2002. "Interorganizational Institutions." In *The Blackwell Companion to Organizations*, edited by Joel A. C. Baum, 497–519. Oxford: Blackwell.

Suchman, Mark C. 1995. "Managing Legitimacy: Strategic and Institutional Approaches." *Academy of Management Review* 20 (3): 571–610.

Tamanaha, Brian Z. 2021. *Legal Pluralism Explained: History, Theory, Consequences.* New York: Oxford University Press.

Tambar, Kabir. 2010. "The Aesthetics of Public Visibility: Alevi Semah and the Paradoxes of Pluralism in Turkey." *Comparative Studies in Society and History* 52 (3): 652–79.

Tambar, Kabir. 2014. *The Reckoning of Pluralism: Political Belonging and the Demands of History in Turkey.* Stanford, CA: Stanford University Press.

Tasch, Laman. 2010. "Defining Nation and Religious Minorities in Russia and Turkey: A Comparative Analysis." *Politics and Religion* 3 (2): 327–51.

Tezcür, Güneş Murat. 2009. "Judicial Activism in Perilous Times: The Turkish Case." *Law & Society Review* 43 (2): 305–36.

Thelen, Kathleen, and Sven Steinmo. 1992. "Historical Institutionalism in Comparative Politics." In *Structuring Politics: Historical Institutionalism in Comparative Analysis*, edited by Sven Steinmo, Kathleen Thelen, and Frank Longstreth, 1–33. Cambridge: Cambridge University Press.

Thornton, Patricia H., and William Ocasio. 1999. "Institutional Logics and the Historical Contingency of Power in Organizations: Executive Succession in the Higher Education Publishing Industry, 1958–1990." *American Journal of Sociology* 105 (3): 801–43.

Thornton, Patricia H., and William Ocasio. 2008. "Institutional Logics." In *The Sage Handbook of Organizational Institutionalism*, edited by Royston Greenwood, Christine Oliver, Thomas B. Lawrance, and Renate E. Meyer, 99–128. Thousand Oaks, CA: Sage.

Thornton, Patricia H., William Ocasio, and Michael Lounsbury. 2012. *The Institutional Logics Perspective: A New Approach to Culture, Structure, and Process*. Oxford: Oxford University Press.

Tilly, Charles, and Sidney G. Tarrow. 2015. *Contentious Politics*. Oxford: Oxford University Press.

Tocci, Nathalie. 2005. "Europeanization in Turkey: Trigger or Anchor for Reform?" *South European Society and Politics* 10 (1): 73–83.

Toktaş, Şule. 2006. "EU Enlargement Conditions and Minority Protection: A Reflection on Turkey's Non-Muslim Minorities." *East European Quarterly* 40 (4): 489–518.

Toktas, Sule, and Bulent Aras. 2009. "The EU and Minority Rights in Turkey." *Political Science Quarterly* 124 (4): 697–720.

Toumani, Meline. 2008. "Minority Rules." *New York Times*, February 17. Accessed December 12. https://www.nytimes.com/2008/02/17/magazine/17turkey-t.html

Tripp, Aili Mari. 1997. *Changing the Rules: The Politics of Liberalization and the Urban Informal Economy in Tanzania*. Berkeley: University of California Press.

Tsai, Kellee S. 2006. "Adaptive Informal Institutions and Endogenous Institutional Change in China." *World Politics* 59 (01): 116–41.

Tsai, Kellee S. 2007. *Capitalism without Democracy: The Private Sector in Contemporary China*. Ithaca, NY: Cornell University Press.

Tsai, Kellee S. 2016. "Adaptive Informal Institutions." In *The Oxford Handbook of Historical Institutionalism*, edited by Orfeo Fioretos, Tulia G. Falleti, and Adam Sheingate, 270–87. Oxford: Oxford University Press.

Tsai, Lily L. 2007. *Accountability without Democracy: How Solidary Groups Provide Public Goods in Rural China*. Cambridge: Cambridge University Press.

Tucker, Judith E. 1996. "Revisiting Reform: Women and the Ottoman Law of Family Rights, 1917." *Arab Studies Journal* 4 (2): 4–17.

Tunçel, Harun. 2000. "Türkiye'de İsmi Değiştirilen Köyler" [Renamed villages in Turkey]. *Fırat Üniversitesi Sosyal Bilimler Dergisi* 10 (2): 23–34.

Tutkal, Serhat. 2021. "Trustees Instead of Elected Mayors: Authoritarian Neoliberalism and the Removal of Kurdish Mayors in Turkey." *Nationalities Papers*: 1–23. https://doi.org/10.1017/nps.2021.42

Ucarlar, Nesrin. 2009. *Between Majority Power and Minority Resistance: Kurdish Linguistic Rights in Turkey*. Lund: Lund University.

Ury, William. 1999. *Getting to Peace: Transforming Conflict at Home, at Work, and in the World*. New York: Penguin.

Üşenmez, Özgür, and Levent Duman. 2015. "Identity Problems in Turkey: Alevis and AKP." *Alternative Politics/Alternatif Politika* 7 (3): 620–44.

Van Bruinessen, Martin. 2000. *Kurdish Ethno-nationalism versus Nation-Building States: Collected Articles*. Istanbul: Isis Press.

Van Cott, Donna Lee. 2006. "Dispensing Justice at the Margins of Formality." In *Informal Institutions and Democracy: Lessons from Latin America*, edited by Gretchen Helmke and Steven Levitsky, 249–73. Baltimore: Johns Hopkins University Press.

van Rossum, Wibo M. 2008. "Religious Courts alongside Secular State Courts: The Case of the Turkish Alevis." *Law, Social Justice & Global Development Journal* 12 (2).

Vergin, Nur. 1985. "Social Change and the Family in Turkey." *Current Anthropology* 26 (5): 571–74.

Voigt, Stefan. 2018. "How to Measure Informal Institutions." *Journal of Institutional Economics* 14 (1): 1–22.

Vorhoff, Karin. 1998. "'Let's Reclaim Our History and Culture!' Imagining Alevi Community in Contemporary Turkey." *Welt des Islams* 38 (2): 220–52.

Wall, James A., Jr., Nimet Beriker, and Sharon Wu. 2010. "Turkish Community Mediation." *Journal of Applied Social Psychology* 40 (8): 2019–42.

Wang, Hongying. 2000. "Informal Institutions and Foreign Investment in China." *Pacific Review* 13 (4): 525–56.

Wang, Peng, and Jingyi Wang. 2018. "How China Promotes Its Military Officers: Interactions between Formal and Informal Institutions." *China Quarterly* 234: 399–419.

Watts, Nicole F. 2006. "Activists in Office: Pro-Kurdish Contentious Politics in Turkey." *Ethnopolitics* 5 (2): 125–44.

Watts, Nicole F. 2010. *Activists in Office: Kurdish Politics and Protest in Turkey*. Seattle: University of Washington Press.

Waylen, Georgina. 2014. "Informal Institutions, Institutional Change, and Gender Equality." *Political Research Quarterly* 67 (1): 212–3.

Weingast, Barry R. 1996. "Political Institutions: Rational Choice Perspectives." In *A New Handbook of Political Science*, edited by Robert E. Goodin and Hans-Dieter Klingemann, 167–90. Oxford: Oxford University Press.

Weingast, Barry R. 2002. "Rational Choice Institutionalism." In *Political Science: The State of the Discipline*, edited by Ira Katznelson and Helen V. Milner, 660–92. New York: W. W. Norton.

White, Paul J. 2000. *Primitive Rebels or Revolutionary Modernizers? The Kurdish National Movement in Turkey*. London: Zed Books.

White, Paul Joseph, and Joost Jongerden. 2003. *Turkey's Alevi Enigma: A Compre-hensive Overview*. Leiden: Brill.

Whiting, Matthew, and Zeynep N. Kaya. 2021. "Autocratization, Permanent Emer-gency Rule and Local Politics: Lessons from the Kurds in Turkey." *Democratiza-tion* 28 (4): 1–19.

Williamson, Claudia R. 2009. "Informal Institutions Rule: Institutional Arrange-ments and Economic Performance." *Public Choice* 139 (3–4): 371–87.

Williamson, Oliver E. 1985. *The Economic Institutions of Capitalism*. New York: Free Press.

Williamson, Oliver E. 1993. "Transaction Cost Economics Meets Posnerian Law and Economics." *Journal of Institutional and Theoretical Economics* 149 (1): 99–118.

Wuthrich, F. Michael. 2013. "An Essential Center-Periphery Electoral Cleavage and the Turkish Party System." *International Journal of Middle East Studies* 45 (4): 751–73.

Wuthrich, F. Michael. 2015. *National Elections in Turkey: People, Politics, and the Party System*. Syracuse, NY: Syracuse University Press.

Xu, Xiaobing. 2005. "Different Mediation Traditions: A Comparison between China and the US." *American Review of International Arbitration* 16: 515–81.

Xu, Yiqing, and Yang Yao. 2015. "Informal Institutions, Collective Action, and Pub-lic Investment in Rural China." *American Political Science Review* 109 (2): 371–91.

Yanik, Lerna K. 2006. "'Nevruz'or 'Newroz'? Deconstructing the 'Invention' of a Contested Tradition in Contemporary Turkey." *Middle Eastern Studies* 42 (2): 285–302.

Yavuz, M. Hakan. 2001. "Five Stages of the Construction of Kurdish Nationalism in Turkey." *Nationalism and Ethnic Politics* 7 (3): 1–24.

Yavuz, M. Hakan. 2009. *Secularism and Muslim Democracy in Turkey*. Cambridge: Cambridge University Press.

Yeğen, Mesut. 1996. "The Turkish State Discourse and the Exclusion of Kurdish Identity." *Middle Eastern Studies* 32 (2): 216–29.

Yeğen, Mesut. 2007. "Turkish Nationalism and the Kurdish Question." *Ethnic and Racial Studies* 30 (1): 119–51.

Yegen, Mesut. 2009. "'Prospective-Turks' or 'Pseudo-Citizens': Kurds in Turkey." *Middle East Journal* 63 (4): 597–615.

Yeğen, Mesut. 2011. "The Kurdish Question in Turkey: Denial to Recognition." In *Nationalisms and Politics in Turkey: Political Islam, Kemalism and the Kurdish Issue*, edited by Marlies Casier and Joost Jongerden, 67–85. New York: Routledge.

Yıldırım, Ali. 1991. *Ali Özsoy Dede: Şiirleri ve Görüşleri* [The poems and views of Dede Ali Özsoy]. Istanbul: Alev Yayınları.

Yıldırım, Ali. 2013. *Alevi Hukuku* [Alevi law]. Ankara: Italik.

Yıldırım, Rıza. 2017. "A Genealogy of Modern Alevism, 1950–2000: Elements of Continuity and Discontinuity." In *Alevis In Europe: Voices of Migration, Culture and Identity*, edited by Tözün Issa, 96–114. London: Routledge.

Yıldırım, Rıza. 2018. *Geleneksel Alevilik: İnanç, İbadet, Kurumlar, Toplumsal Yapı, Kolektif Bellek* [Traditional Alevism: Belief, worship, institutions, social structure, and collective memory]. İstanbul: İletişim.

Yıldız, İlhan. 2007. "Minority Rights in Turkey." *Brigham Young University Law Review* 3: 791–812.

Yılmaz, Gözde. 2016. "From EU Conditionality to Domestic Choice for Change: Exploring Europeanisation of Minority Rights in Turkey." In *Turkey and the European Union: Processes of Europeanisation*, edited by Çiğdem Nas and Yonca Özer, 119–40. London: Routledge.

Yücel, Clémence Scalbert. 2016. "Common Ground or Battlefield? Deconstructing the Politics of Recognition in Turkey." *Nationalism and Ethnic Politics* 22 (1): 71–93.

Zelditch, Morris. 2001. "Theories of Legitimacy." In *The Psychology of Legitimacy: Emerging Perspectives on Ideology, Justice, and Intergroup Relations*, edited by John T. Jost and Brenda Major, 33–53. Cambridge: Cambridge University Press.

Zencirci, Gizem. 2012. "Secularism, Islam, and the National Public Sphere: Politics of Commemorative Practices in Turkey." In *Visualizing Secularism and Religion: Egypt, Lebanon, Turkey, India*, edited by Alev Çinar, Srirupa Roy, and Maha Yahya, 93–109. Ann Arbor: University of Michigan Press.

Zeydanlıoğlu, Welat. 2012. "Turkey's Kurdish Language Policy." *International Journal of the Sociology of Language* (217): 99–125.

Zeydanlioğlu, Welat. 2013. "Repression or Reform? An Analysis of the AKP's Kurdish Language Policy." In *The Kurdish Question in Turkey: New Perspectives on Violence, Representation and Reconciliation*, edited by Cengiz Gunes and Welat Zeydanlıoğlu, 162–85. London: Routledge.

Zgut, Edit. 2022. "Informal Exercise of Power: Undermining Democracy under the EU's Radar in Hungary and Poland." *Hague Journal on the Rule of Law*: 1–22.

INDEX

1982 Constitution, The, 136, 138

Accommodating informal institutions, 20
Agos newspaper, 114
AKP (*Adalet ve Kalkınma Partisi*), 67
Alevis (Alevi community): 70, 79–82; Alevi
Initiative (Opening), 123–124; Alevi
Revival (Renaissance), 98–102; Arab
(Nusayri), 119–120; *bağlama* (*saz*), 85;
belief, 79, 81; *cem* ceremony (congregation), 84; civil society organizations, 99–
100; collective amnesia, 102; *dar* (*meydan*),
86; *dede*, 84–88; demands, 81; *deyiş* (*nefes*),
84, 85; distrust of formal state institutions,
89, 97; Diyanet, 125–126; *düşkün*, 87, 90;
erkan, 86, 87; ethnic groups, 119; fasting,
119; *Gadir Hum*, 119–120; *Görüm*, 85, 94;
Karbala, 119; *Kızılbaş*, 90; *kirvelik* (*musa-
hiplik*), 90; leftist movements 97; lokma 84;
Madımak Hotel, 124; martyrdom of
Husayn ibn Ali, 119; Mehdi, 90; migration,
80; modernization, 93–98; Muharram, 119;
Ottoman persecution, 89; peripheral status,
92; *semah*, 84; *seyyid*, 84; size, 79; socialist
left, 97; state suppression, 91; *talip*, 85; the
Day of Ashura, 119; The Twelve Imams,
119
Armenians, 110

Baydemir, Osman, 154
Behavioral approach, 1; behavioralism, 1
Binary logit models, 69
Blat system, 6, 20, 38, 43
Blood feuds, 6, 10, 88
Blood money, 10, 37
Bribery, 6, 10
Brunissen, Pierre, 113

Case selection, 10
Cem courts (*Cem mahkemeleri*), 32, 82–102
Cemevis (Cem Houses): 81, 99–102; Tunceli,
121
Christmas, 16, 117, 121
Civil marriage (*resmi nikah, devlet nikahı,
belediye nikahı*): 31, 51–53; legitimacy defi-
cit, 54–57
Civil Registry Services Law, The (*Nüfus
Hizmetleri Kanunu*), 67
Clientelism, 6, 10, 20, 30, 34, 37
Collective action problems, 21, 37
Community justice institution, 84
Community mediation, 102
Competing informal institutions, 20
Complementary informal institutions, 19–20,
102, 104
Constructivist perspective, 17, 22
Contentious politics, 34, 143, 156–157
Converging institutional outcomes, 19
Copenhagen Criteria, 114
Coping strategies, 38
Cost-benefit calculus, 22
Council of State, The (*Danıştay*), 154
Court of Cassation, The (*Yargıtay*), 113
Critical moments (junctures), 41
Cultural nationalism (*kültür milliyetçiliği*), 133
Cyprus crisis, 113

Data availability, 12
De facto practice, 9
Demirbaş, Abdullah, 149, 151, 154
Demirel, Süleyman, 8
Dengbej and Dengbeji Tradition Project, 149
Derin devlet, 8
Developing world, 8
Dink, Hrant, 114

Directorate for Alevi-Bektashi Culture and Cemevis, The (*Alevi-Bektaşi Külter ve Cemevi Başkanlığı*), 125
Dispute resolution, 78
Diverging institutional outcomes, 19
Diyanet (*Diyanet İşleri Başkanlığı*), 52, 70, 91–92
Diyarbakir Metropolitan Municipality, 149, 154

Easter, 16, 117, 121
Electoral Law, The (1961), 136
Ethnic identity, 59, 63
EU reforms, 114, 137, 146

Factor analysis, 77
Family tradition, 55
Favoritism (*kayırma/torpil*), 9, 10, 30, 37
First Gulf War, The (1990–1991), 8
Focus groups, 12, 47–48, 53
Formal vs informal institutions, 6–7
Formal institutions (rules): ambiguity, 38; change, 67; definition, 6; effectiveness, 19, 21; inefficiency, 37; legitimacy, 13, 26–27, 35, 163–164; legitimacy deficit, 39, 51; restrictive, suppressive types, 39; utility, 13, 27–28; weakness, 8
Formal reality, 10
Formalization, 164–165
Forms of governance, 129
Foundation of the Antioch Orthodox Church, The, 118
Francini, Adriano, 114

Greeks, 110

Habituation, 13, 40
Hanefi school of Sunni Islamic jurisprudence, 70, 89, 124–125
Hatimoğulları-Oruç, Tülay, 120
HDP (*Halkların Demokratik Partisi*), 120, 147, 155
Holidays: 107, 115; Durkheimian approach, 128
Honor killing (crime), 10, 88
Hypotheses, 58–60

Identity politics, 98
Ideology politics, 97
Ideology, 60, 63

Informal institutions: change, 42–45; decay, 104; definition, 6; emergence, 36–41; evolutionary emergence, 40–42; Helmke and Levitsky typology, 19–20; incomplete nature, 37; intentional design, 13, 36–40, 156; measurement, 11; multidimensional typology, 13, 25–36; optimistic view, 163; pessimistic view, 162; partial typologies, 21; theoretical framework, 17–45; theorizing, 10–12; two dimensional typologies, 18–19
Informal: economy 10; justice mechanisms, 82–93; politics, 9, 129; reality, 10
Informalization, 165
Informational costs, 96–97
Institutional logic: definition, 13, 25–26, 28–30, 32–33; compatibility between formal and informal institutional logics, 29–30
Institutional: approaches, 1; compliance, 21–25; heterogeneity, 29; strength, 5; theory, 4; layers, 128
Institutions: definition, 5; distributional consequences, 44; elements, 5
Intensive fieldwork, 12
Interviews, 12, 49, 53–54, 83, 108
Islamization of secular civil marriage, 67

Jews, 110
Judiciary: confidence, 103; governmental control, 103; judge, 82; juristocracy (judicial tutelage), 102; judicial independence, 103

Kadı, 32, 50, 89
Kayyum, 155
Kurdish: demands, 140; ethnopolitical movement, 139–142; *meles*, 88; revolts, 139; suppression of Kurdish language, 136–138

Labor camps, 112
Language campaigns, 112
Law on Capital Tax, The (*Varlık Vergisi*) (1942–1944), 112
Law on Civil Servants, The (1926), 112
Law on National and Religious Holidays, The, 115
Law on Political Parties, The (*Siyasi Partiler Kanunu*) (1983), 138
Law on Religious Foundations, The, 114
Layered informal institutions, 32–33, 107–131
Layering, 13
Legal legitimacy, 55

Legal pluralism, 103
Legitimacy, 26
Legitimation, 74
Litigation costs, 92
logic of appropriateness, The, 22
logic of consequentiality, The, 22

Madrasa, 88
Majoritarian logic, 115
Matrimonial contracts, 51
Measurement of variables, 60–62
Men of religion, 51, 52
Methodological challenges, 11
Minorities in Turkey, 80, 108–109, 133
Modernization processes, 93–95; 102
Monolingualism, 137–138, 146
Mufti marriage: public support, 68–73; reform, 67–73
Muftis, 67
Multilingual municipalism (çok dilli belediye-cilik), 142–153
Multinomial logit models, 62–65
Multivariate regression analyses, 58–73
Municipalities, 51
Muslim minority holidays, 119–121
Muslim-majority countries, 121
Muslim-majority settings, 10

Naming and shaming, 82, 96
National identity, 114–125
Nepotism, 6, 10, 30, 34, 38
Nevşehir Hacı Bektaş Veli University, 124
Non-Muslim minority holidays, 117–118
Nonprobability sampling, 14
Norm-followers, 22
Normative perspective, 22–23

Office of mufti, 67
Official language, 138
Ottoman millet system: definition, 80; Muslim millet, 80; non-Muslim millet, 80
Özal, Turgut, 8

Padovese, Luigi, 114
Participant observation, 12
Pathbreaking changes, 41
Patriarchy, 10
Patronage, 6, 10, 38
Peace Process (2013–2015), 154
Pedestrians: 9; crossings (crosswalks), 9–10

Pilot tests, 49
PKK (Partiya Karkaren Kurdistan), 139
Plausibility probes, 11
Polygyny, 57
Population Exchange Agreement, 110
Power shifts, 44–45
Prayers, 51
Predicted probabilities, 65–66, 71–72
Press Law, The (1931), 136
Pro-Kurdish political parties: 140–142; electoral performance, 141–143; local governments, 142–153; contention, 142–153
Protestant missionaries, 114
Public tender (bid), 9
Purposive sampling, 14

Qualitative data, 12
Quantitative data, 12
Quran, The, 54

Rational choice perspective, 17, 21
Registration Law, The (Nüfus Kanunu) (1972), 136
Religiosity, 59, 63
Religious holidays: 114–117; official regulation, 114–115
Religious legitimacy, 54–55
Religious majority, 108
Religious marriage (dini nikah, imam nikahı, hoca nikahı): 31, 50–67; popularity, 53–54; rationale, 53–54; timing, 52–53
Religious minorities: 108–111; non-Muslims, 109–114; pogroms, 113; securitization, 111–112, 125–126; 134; size, 110; state attitude, 111–114; state discrimination, 112–114
Religious minority holidays: 114–121; state attitude, 121–127
Renaming place names, 136
Renovation of religious sites, 114
Representative case, 10
Research questions, 4
Ronda assemblies, 20
Rondas campesinas, 20
Routinization, 40
Rule-following, 23
Rural communities, 96

Sanctifying formal civil marriage, 54
Santoro, Andrea, 113
Sectarian identity, 59, 63

Secular-religious division (cleavage), 75
Secularization (Kemalist), 50, 91
September 6–7 events, 113
Shadow of the future, 96
Shasta County, 92
Sheikhs, 88
Socioeconomic status, 60
State courts, 82–83
Sub-commission on Minorities, 112
Substitutive informal institutions, 20
Subversion, 13
Subversive informal institutions, 33–34,
    142–158
Sunni Muslim: 91; holidays (Eid al-Fitr, Eid al-
    Adha), 115; majority, 91–92; identity, 80
Superseding informal institutions, 31–32,
    78–107
Superseding, 13
Sur district, 145
Sur municipality, 145, 154
Surname Law (Soyadı Kanunu) (1934), 136
Survey research, 12, 49–50, 152
Survey results, 54–55
Symbiosis, 13, 55
Symbiotic: informal institutions, 30–31, 46–78;
    relationship, 55–58
Syriac Orthodox Church, 118

TEKA (Türkiye'de Enformel Kurumlar Anketi),
    9, 49, 68
Thrace, The, 113

Treaty of Lausanne, 80, 109, 112
TÜBİTAK (Türkiye Bilimsel ve Teknolojik
    Araştırma Kurumu), 46
TÜİK (Türkiye İstatistik Kurumu), 53
Turkey's Constitutional Court, 140
Turkish case, 8
Turkish Civil Code (Law), 30, 46, 50, 165
Turkish nationalism, 137, 144,
Turkish state: minority languages, 133–138;
    language policy, 135–138; Turkification pol-
    icies, 112, 133–138
Turkish War of Independence (1919–1922),
    110
Typical case, 10
Typologies: definition, 18; typological theoriz-
    ing; 18

Underage marriages, 57
Unintended consequences of formal institu-
    tional change, 40–41
Urbanization, 93–95

Vote buying, 10

Widow's pension, 57
Within-case analysis, 11
World War I, 110
World War II, 112

Yazılı olmayan kurallar, 10